Business Process Mapping

Business Process Mapping

Improving Customer Satisfaction

J. Mike Jacka
Paulette J. Keller

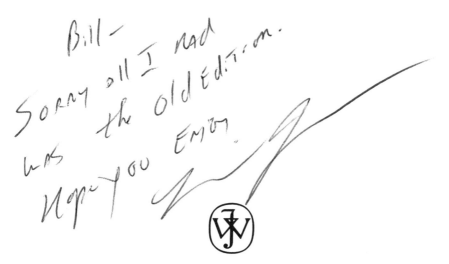

Bill—
Sorry all I had
was the old Edition.
Hope you Enjoy.

JOHN WILEY & SONS, INC.

This publication is designed to provide accurate and authoritative information in regard to the subject matter covered. It is sold with the understanding that the publisher is not engaged in rendering legal, accounting, or other professional services. If legal advice or other expert assistance is required, the services of a competent professional person should be sought.

Library of Congress Cataloging-in-Publication Data:

Jacka, Mike J.
    Business process mapping: improving customer satisfaction / Mike J. Jacka, Paulette J. Keller.
        p. cm
    Includes bibliographical references and index.
    ISBN 0-471-07977-4 (cloth : alk. paper)
    1. Consumer satisfaction.   2. Customer relations.
  3. Reengineering (Management)   I. Keller, Paulette J.
  II. Title

    HF5415.335.J33   2002
    658.8'12—dc21   2001045650

Printed in the United States of America

10 9 8 7 6 5 4

For Kathy, Jessica, and Dakota

ABOUT THE AUTHORS

Mike Jacka, CIA, CPA, and Paulette Keller, CPA, FLMI

Mike and Paulette have both worked for Farmers Insurance for 18 years and have worked together in one capacity or another for 14. Mike spent all but the first 6 months of his career with Farmers in the Auditing Department. Currently, he is the Auditing Manager, responsible for audit activities in seven states from Arizona to North Dakota. Paulette is currently an Audit Consultant in Phoenix, but her career started as an auditor for Farmers' Life Company. She has also worked in Life Special Projects and with the Phoenix Claims Department. Regarding their past prior to Farmers Insurance, it's better not to ask.

During Paulette's time in Claims she was involved in a company-wide quality assurance program. At that time, she and Mike began work on using Process Mapping as an analysis tool. Eventually, they were working together again in the Auditing Department and helped incorporate Process Mapping companywide.

PREFACE

In business, as in life, processes intertwine to provide results, and these processes ultimately lead to the success or failure of an enterprise. The challenge for anyone wanting to ensure that the final result is successful is to find a way to analyze those processes. At the same time, any review must keep the customer as its primary focus.

Process Mapping is a powerful tool that allows the reviewer the opportunity to get a good understanding of the process, effectively find ways for that process to be more successful, and ensure that true value is being provided to customers. We have been involved in a number of successful engagements using Process Mapping, which have ranged from quick one-week reviews of small processes to multimonth projects that analyzed entire operations. It is these successes (as well as mistakes) that we share in showing how to use Process Mapping as an effective analysis tool. The approach is simple yet powerful and can be used by anyone who needs to analyze a process—from management to internal auditor to external consultant.

The action of making process maps in and of itself is nothing more than glorified flowcharting. What we do is show an entire approach that leads to a holistic understanding of the process under review. When all is said and done, Process Mapping results in a product that shows how processes under review work together and provides efficiencies to streamline the successful process, give assurance that operations are under control, and allows all individuals involved in a process to gain a better understanding of that process.

We begin by taking a closer look at processes and what they are. Starting with a concept that is a cornerstone to moviemaking—storyboarding—we show how Process Mapping allows the review to drill down into the area under review. We also become acquainted with some of the terms used in Process Mapping. To help understand the steps in Process Mapping, a detailed example (a fictional Expense Payment Process) is introduced and used throughout the book.

The steps of Process Mapping are fully explained. This includes process identification (working with the client to ensure that everyone has a full understanding of the processes involved), information gathering (learning the underlying concepts behind the process such as objectives, risks, and key controls), interviewing and mapping (building the actual maps that are the cornerstone of this approach), and analysis (using various approaches to help determine how to make the process run more effectively.) A number of tools are also introduced to more effectively complete each of these steps.

Finally, we discuss different applications for Process Mapping and things to avoid during the project. Ultimately, you should wind up with a good understanding of the Process Mapping approach and a series of tools to help facilitate the project. And you should be able to find the same successes we have found.

CONTENTS

Contents

Business Process Mapping

INTRODUCTION

Pinocchio and the World of Business

A film is a petrified fountain of thought.

—Jean Cocteau

In 1938, Walt Disney held a meeting with his animators to discuss an idea he had for the follow-up to his blockbuster *Snow White*. He brought the entire group into one room, sat them down, and proceeded to tell a story. He began by describing a lonely wood-carver. He told of how the man carved a wooden boy and wished he were real. He told of a Blue Fairy who heard the old man and brought the little wooden boy to life but left him made of wood. He then told of their heroic struggles—the boy's capture, being made to perform in a puppet show, being taken to Pleasure Island, and how he eventually saved his father from the whale Monstro. At the end, he told of the boy's transformation into a real boy.

The story he told was *Pinocchio*, and Walt Disney intended it to be his next movie. As he told the story, Disney took on the parts of all the characters. He spoke the words. He acted out the scenes. He led the group on the roller coaster ride that would become his latest triumph. When the entire story had been spread before them, he told the animators, "Make that movie."

The animators were thrown the challenge of taking that series of events—Disney's story of the transformation of Pinocchio into a real boy—and making it a movie. This was a daunting task. Disney had an exact image—from start to finish—of the animated movie he wanted to make. By talking and gesturing and becoming that movie, he had spelled out a story. The animators had the challenge of taking that story and making it a finished product. However, there already existed a tool that was invaluable in developing cartoons—storyboarding.

Storyboards are large areas (at that time, four- by eight-foot boards) on which sketches can be pinned. Key steps of the story are drawn and placed in order. As the story is fleshed out, additional drawings are included. If something is wrong, it is discarded. If the sequence is particularly complicated, more drawings are put in for detail. What results is a pictorial flow of the movie's transformation from beginning to end.

Using Disney's vision and the existing tools of the trade, the animators succeeded, and *Pinocchio* became Disney's second animated feature movie—another smash. The world fell in love with the puppet boy who wanted to become real. They watched as the Blue Fairy brought him to life, as his naïveté caused him to succumb to Foulfellow and Gideon, and as he saved Geppetto from the whale Monstro—a series of actions that led to his final transformation into a real boy.

At its very core, the story of Pinocchio is a process. As all good processes do, it has an input (Geppetto carving a puppet and wishing it were a real boy), it has an output (Pinocchio becoming a real boy), and in between it has a series of events—the actions— that achieve that transformation. Disney's animators documented that process by the use of storyboarding.

Every individual has many stories to tell. Each of these stories is a process—a series of actions that takes input, transforms it, and produces an output. Some are dramatic transformations—life-altering events that shake and move them. For example, a person may tell a story about surviving an earthquake. The story begins with the earth shaking around the person (the input). A number of actions are taken—grabbing the children, running out of the house, falling to the ground—and the final outcome is safe survival. Other stories are less thrilling, but a process nonetheless. Take, for example, waking up in the morning. The alarm goes off (the input), the body goes through a series of movements (the process), and the body eventually is in an upright and (hopefully) alert position (the output). Each story is a process.

In the business world, every company has a story to tell as well. At its most basic level, that story is the transformation of investments into profits. But for that story to reach a positive conclusion, there are a series of more fundamental stories to tell. One story may be the transformation of steel into an automobile, another may be the transformation of a phone call into customer service, and another may be the transformation of computer data into information. But no matter what the process, it is a story told by a group of individuals. Just as each story is a process, each process is a story.

The tool that brings this all together is Process Mapping—storyboarding for the business world. The reviewer sits with the employee who tells the story. As that story unfolds, the reviewer documents the process in a way that will help the worker visualize the transformation that occurs. At the end, the employee can see the finished product and ensure that the story has been told accurately. Each scene can be put together to provide the reviewer with the final movie that is the entire process. Then, much like a director, the reviewer can analyze the finished product to show

how to build a better movie—one that does just what Disney hoped *Pinocchio* would do—result in higher profits.

Process Mapping is a way to graphically represent the transactions and stories that make up a business, but storyboarding in and of itself is not a movie. Instead, it is a tool used to make that final movie. Likewise, Process Mapping by itself is not a complete analysis. Instead, it is a tool that helps complete the final analysis of the process under review.

In this book, we show you not only how the tool of Process Mapping works, but also how it works as part of an overall approach to process analysis. We discuss processes and how to drill down into them. We talk about how processes interrelate with other processes and the information that must be obtained to understand them. Then we discuss the actual mapping of a process—how the tool works and how it can be used to analyze the process.

Before us we have a challenge much like that faced by Disney's animators. Every employee has a story to tell—a scene to share. We, as reviewers, want to learn those stories and understand those scenes to find out what is going on. Our task is to take those scenes and come up with the final movie—the overall epic of how initial input leads through a transformation to final output.

Our review must determine if that movie is the right length. It may take 3 hours to tell the story, but if no one wants to sit through your story for 3 hours, you will sell no tickets. If it takes 4 months for you to deliver your product when no one wants to wait that long, you will sell no product. Does the story require a miniseries or is a one-reeler enough? Are they taking 3 hours to tell a 10-minute story?

Our review must determine if each scene benefits the whole. There is a dictum in moviemaking—if you show a gun on the mantelpiece, it better go off by the end of the movie. What part of the story is truly needed, and what parts are missing? Does every gun go off? Is every process necessary to build the final output?

Finally, our movie has to "play in Peoria" (as they used to say in vaudeville). Even if we have developed the world's greatest widget in the shortest amount of time, it is useless if the world has moved on to sprockets. Do the customers need this? Do they need part of this, but not all of it? If they do not, what should we be doing instead?

Process Mapping will help us achieve that task, just as storyboarding helped Disney's animators. And when we are done, we will have a blockbuster too—an analysis that gives us not only a holistic view of the process, but also the cooperation and buy-in of all levels in the company.

We're ready for our close-up, Mr. DeMille. Lights, camera, action—let the Process Mapping begin.

CHAPTER 1

Defining and Redefining Process

The person who knows "how" will always have a job. The person who knows "why" will always be his boss.

—Diane Ravitch, Professor,
Columbia University Teachers College

WHO CARES ABOUT PROCESSES ANYWAY?

Most companies spend a great deal of time each year developing strategic objectives and goals. High-level objectives are developed that reflect the overall strategy of the company. Business objectives are then generally developed at the department level to support overall company objectives. Goals are developed to measure the progress toward achieving particular business objectives. In a perfect world, there would not be any conflicting goals. All department objectives would actually support the company objectives. Every employee would understand these goals and objectives and how the work performed can contribute to the achievement of those goals and objectives. The company's plans would be executed flawlessly and the story would always have a happy ending—the wooden company would become real.

In the real world, however, strategic objectives may be developed in isolation—from the top and communicated down. Department objectives may be self-serving and may not support strategic objectives. Department objectives may be in conflict with one another. Employees below the management level may not have any idea what the company's goals and objectives are or how the work they do contributes to the achievement of those objectives. People see their story—follow their plot—and have no idea what is going on around them. They do not always understand the company's or department's story and certainly have no idea how they can help give it a happy ending.

The accumulation of activities that takes place in each business process is what ultimately determines whether a business can meet its objectives. Processes must be analyzed to ensure that they support key business objectives. Process analysis is particularly useful in ensuring the accomplishment of business objectives relating to customer service, efficiency, effectiveness, and profitability. In addition, holistic process analysis can help assure controls are in place to minimize risks and exposures.

"TELL ME A STORY"—ANALYZING THE PROCESS

A vital key to transforming business is the complete understanding of the processes involved. This understanding is necessary for any change management approach to be of value, and it is included in total quality management, process reengineering, International Organization for Standardization (ISO) certification, and even in developing a Baldridge Award–winning approach. But getting a handle on the processes is one of the more daunting tasks reviewers must face.

However, this is not unlike the task Disney's animators faced. The animators had to find a way to transform his story into a tangible product. Reviewers must find a way to transform the company's story into a concrete, tangible product that can be viewed, verified, and manipulated. To help understand that story, the reviewer needs a storyteller to bring the stories to life. The animators had Disney; reviewers have the company's employees. Disney knew the story inside and out. He would tell the story to anyone who would listen. The company's employees know their stories just as well, and they are willing to tell the details of those stories to anyone who will listen—where it is going right and where the plot is not quite so good. Each employee knows the job and knows the processes that are completed. These are movies that go on constantly in their minds. Although they often have not thought about it, they know the beginning, the transformation, and the end.

The challenge for any reviewer is to get that information and develop a finished product that anyone can look at and understand, not unlike a finished movie. This requires the reviewer to talk with that employee and learn each of the steps—each of the "scenes"—that make up that process. Process Mapping is the technique that helps the reviewer transform that employee's movie into a finished product that anyone can view and understand.

BENEFITS

There are many obvious benefits to Process Mapping that should already be apparent. These include the ability to visually represent the process, better documentation of the review process, and an overall view of the various aspects of the process. However, this only scratches the surface.

If the only step taken when developing process maps is to graphically document a process, Process Mapping is nothing more than glorified flowcharting. Instead, it must be part of a greater system. When we talk about Process Mapping in this book, we are not talking about the actual map. Instead, we are talking about the system. When all the steps described in this book are used, when the system of process mapping is fully used, there are much greater benefits that may not be as readily apparent.

Holistic

In daily life, processes constantly come in conflict as the objectives of one process directly oppose the objectives of another. For example, every workday millions of individuals climb into their cars. For many, something has gone wrong, and the primary objective of this process is to arrive at work at the proper time. Speed is at a premium and other concerns fall by the wayside. However, each and every one of these individuals runs into two major conflicting processes. The first is the same as everyone else's objective to arrive at work at the proper time. The second is the process cities have developed to ensure achievement of safe travel. Speed limits, stop signs, and traffic lanes all work together to thwart the time-conscious traveler. The driver's objectives (the need for speed) come in direct conflict with the city's objectives (the need for safety.)

In every aspect of our lives, every process is forced to inter-relate with coexisting processes. The same is true in business. To meet the objectives of keeping shareholders, customers, and employees happy, executives and managers must juggle conflicting priorities. The objective of paying expenses comes in conflict with the objective of making a profit; the objective of keeping employees satisfied comes in conflict with reducing expenses; the objective of making a top-quality product comes in conflict with the customer's objective of paying a low price.

Far too often, analysis is done in a vacuum and does not consider how these processes interrelate. Reviewers often talk to one person or one function and find what works best for them. Reviewers may focus on one set of objectives at the expense of another. This analysis in a vacuum far too easily provides benefits to one while taking from another.

Process Mapping provides a method for taking a holistic approach to this analysis. Before sitting and talking with people, the reviewer gains a full understanding of the process's objectives and how they interrelate with the company's overall objectives. The objective of each part of the process is also reviewed to ensure that it benefits some greater objective. And, when identifying and recommending changes, the reviewer will have kept all these objectives in mind to ensure that the effect of the change (on various objectives) is fully understood.

By looking at the whole picture and integrating the various parts, the reviewer sees not only what needs to be changed, but also how this affects everyone. With an overall view, the benefits for one can be weighed against the detriments to another, and the ultimate good can be appropriately considered.

Employees' Buy-In

Too many reviewers come in with a mind-set that management must be pleased. Often, reviewers have preconceived notions of what they will find. And, even if the reviewer is open-minded, the review is often done in isolation from the employees. Discussions may be held with management. There may be reviews of procedure. Files may even be reviewed. But the people actually doing the work are never brought into the picture.

Even if discussions are held with line personnel, the ultimate product is still geared toward management or executives. Many reviewers obtain information on how things are supposed to be done, but they do not use the employee as a resource for understanding how things are *really* done or how they can be improved.

And employees are not stupid. They recognize that reviewers are often there but not listening. And enough people read *Dilbert* to know that every idea may be used to eliminate their jobs.

Process Mapping allows a true buy-in to the completed product. Maps are developed real-time, and the employee can see exactly what is being recorded. They are developed in an interactive atmosphere that allows the employee to physically change what is occurring. Plus, it allows them to provide input on where the system can be improved. In our experience, we have gone back to offices where employees were excited. They told new employees about the review that was going to be completed and looked forward to their turn to talk to us.

Despite the fears previously addressed, employees are still happy to have someone actually listen to them. They have a story to tell. That story can make up eight hours (or more) of their life a day. And when someone actually listens, they are more than willing to share. We have had employees share ideas that changed the way processes worked throughout the company. They were willing to tell anyone who would listen—it is just that no one was listening.

One of the biggest mistakes we made when first implementing Process Mapping was something as simple as not sharing the finished product with all employees. We discussed the results with the branch manager and supervisors, giving them the completed maps. We left assuming that they would share the information. In short order, we heard from the employees that they were very upset. They wanted copies of the completed maps. Even those who had only a small part in the process were interested. It was a product they helped develop. They had ownership, and the owners wanted their product. Ever since, we always make a point of ensuring that all employees are provided the final product.

Sense of Pride

The previous two benefits lead to the third benefit of Process Mapping. Many employees come to work and understand what they do (their story). They take something, transform it, and make it something else. Some are lucky enough to actually interact with customers and see the effect of what they do. But many see only that input and output.

Process Mapping not only provides management with an overall view of operations, but also provides employees with an overall view of how their work adds value and how they are part of a team. The holistic approach allows them to see where their work comes from. They can see the steps that lead to the product they receive and understand the work that has gone before. They also can see why they are doing what they do. Each step in the process should lead to further steps in the map. Eventually, this should lead to a final benefit to the customer. Process Mapping is often the first time employees understand why they are doing the work they do. It helps them understand why a bothersome statistic they have to generate is important to a report that drives future customer transactions. Or it may show why they should not use a certain code they thought would make things run smoother.

In the book *Gung Ho!*,[1] Blanchard and Bowles talk about the "spirit of the squirrel"—the need for people to believe their work is worthwhile. They go on to state that "worthwhile" means that people must understand their work, it must lead to a well-understood and shared goal, and values must guide everything they do in their work. Basic to all of this is that people must understand how their work makes the world a better place.

For some jobs, this is easy. Doctors see immediate results, pilots know they take people safely from one place to another, and politicians . . . well, let's not press it. Other jobs seem so menial or useless that people only think they are part of a cog that makes larger cogs. But looked at as part of a greater process, any job takes on meaning. On one level, the file clerk may only be pushing paper, but on another level, he is ensuring that paperwork is available when decisions must be made. On one level, the janitor handles trash and dirt, but on another level, he is ensuring that the people in the building can achieve their work at its highest level. On one level, the factory worker just puts rivets in metal, but on another level, he ensures that the product meets customer specifications and customer satisfaction. Process Mapping, done correctly, helps provide the information that will show employees the true value of their jobs.

In a recent review, we asked employees what their work accomplished. They were not able to tell us. In fact, they told us that when they asked their supervisor why they did the things they did, they were told, "You don't need to know." We showed them how their work fit in with the overall process. Not only did it provide them with a sense that their work accomplished something, but also it led them to suggest changes and elimination of paperwork that cut days off processing time. Not bad for a bunch of clerks.

Customer-Driven

If a process leads to completion of an output that nobody wants, it is a waste of time—there is no customer. The successful analysis of processes must take customers into account, and that can be any level of customer. Maybe it is the primary customer—the one who buys the product—the one who purchases the car or insurance or legal advice. Or it may be an internal customer—the one who uses that output as their input to their process—the accounting department or the chief executive officer (CEO) or the next step in the production. Bottom line, any analysis must take this into account. It must be driven from the customer's perspective.

Possibly the most important benefit of Process Mapping is that it is customer-driven. To complete a process map, everyone must understand what is being delivered to the customer and why. Initial reviews with employees are established in a way that begins this process—the idea of identifying outputs and how they benefit a customer. Likewise, analysis of the inputs helps the reviewer understand whether the customer is getting a useful product.

And evaluation of the process is meant to help ensure that the operation is as transparent to the customer as possible. Instantaneous response is the hallmark of perfect customer service. However, the fact that operations must occur causes delays in that response time. Customers expect this. However, the longer that delay, the more likely you are to lose customers. Finding ways to make an operation more transparent to the customer (what they cannot see, they do not object to) should be the objective of any review. Process Mapping helps make that step.

PROCESS DEFINED

Life is a complex intertwining of processes. Every action we take is a mixture of inputs, actions, and outputs—the classic definition of "process." Some of these processes are simple. The input is an old piece of paper, the action is wadding and dropping, and the output is trash disposal. Other processes are infinitely complex. The input is raw materials, the action is the combination of those materials into a product, and the output is the space shuttle. Others seem simple, but are infinitely complex. The input is sound, the action is hearing, and the output is enjoyment of a fine piece of music.

It is important to understand that more than an action occurs, however. A better term for what happens is a *transformation.* If the process does not transform the input, nothing has happened. The output is the same as the input, and there is no real need for the process. Sometimes this is the most surprising discovery in evaluating a process—and the most valuable.

To fully analyze and understand processes, there must be a system for classifying and understanding the actions within the overall process. This requires breaking a single process into the various elements that make up that process. The reviewer can then "drill down" as needed, getting into more and more of the detail that makes up a process. Even a simple process like throwing out the trash can be broken down into simpler elements.

Each section of a process is really a smaller process. And when that section is broken down, it too is a process. And, possibly, the sections of that process are another process, and the sections of that process, and the sections of that process, and so on. As this "drill down" takes place, a reassessment of the inputs and outputs should also occur to ensure that true value is being added. In this way, the particular parts of the process can be evaluated, just as the overall process can be.

"DRILLING DOWN" THE MOVIE

Just as each company is made up of an overall process, the story that makes up every movie is a process—an input, a transformation, and an output. Likewise, there is a systematic way of "drilling down" the parts of the movie so the individuals involved in its creation can understand how it is put together.

Each movie is broken down into acts. Each act has an overriding theme or point to it that helps support the overall movie. Each act is then broken into scenes. Again, individual sections that help support the individual acts. Each scene has individual shots. These help support the tone of the scene. Finally, there is the actual script, the specific words and directions that make up the movie.

Let us look at the way it all breaks down (see Exhibit 1.1).

Exhibit 1.1 "Drilling Down" the Movie

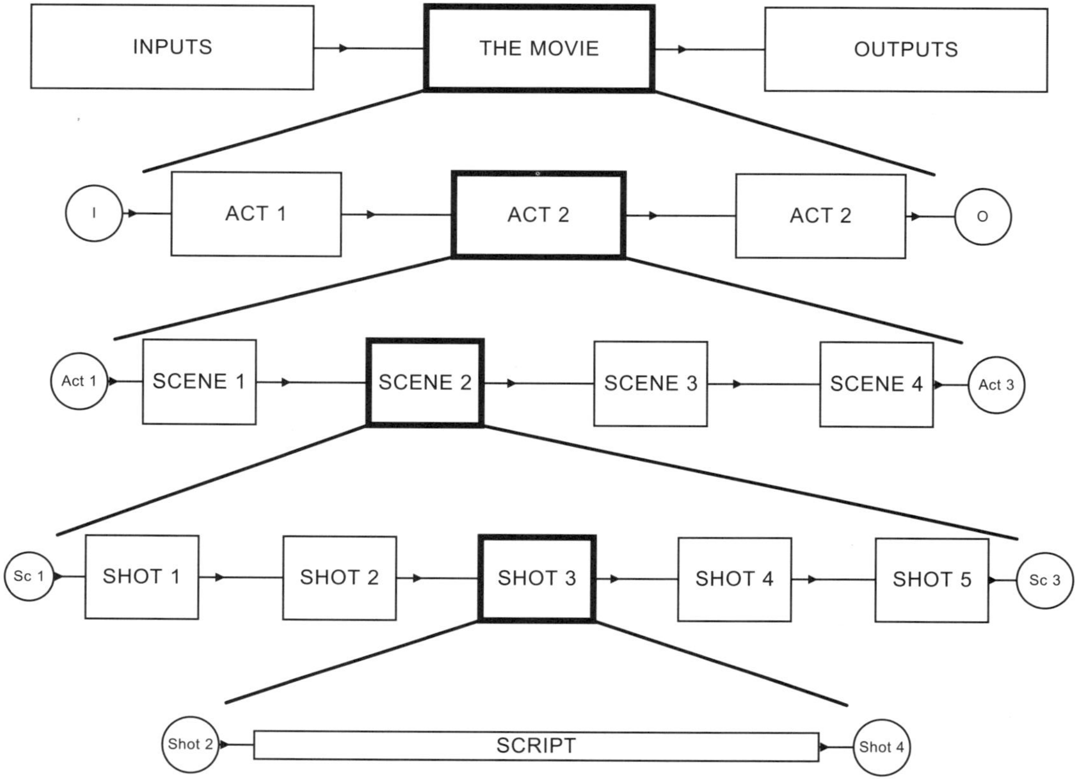

17

The Movie

Think about the classic movie *Psycho*. There is the overall movie about Marion's misappropriation of funds and the events that transpire when she meets Norman Bates. This is actually a process. There is an input—a sum of money and a young girl (Marion) who acts on an opportunity for theft. There is a transformation—people's lives are changed after Marion meets Norman Bates, especially the lives of Norman and Marion. And there is an output—Norman's final run-in with the police and an ending we will not give away (because there is always someone who may not have seen the movie). The movie is the process.

Acts

Each movie or play is broken into various levels to better facilitate an understanding of the action that is to occur. Movies are comprised of a number of acts—usually two to four. These are the major subsections of the movie that represent overall structure. *Psycho* might be broken down into the following acts:

Act I: The opening theft and flight from Phoenix.
Act II: Marion's meeting and interacting with Norman.
Act III: The search for Marion by her sister and the detective.
Act IV: The final confrontation with Norman.

Each of these acts can further be viewed as an individual process (or movie) with an input, a transformation, and an output. The input is from the prior act and the output goes to the next act. Using Marion's initial meeting with Norman as an example, the input is a young girl and her arrival at a strangely empty hotel, the transformation is the subsequent discussions with Norman that begin to reveal his character, and the output is the body left in the trunk of a car that is dumped in a swamp. You also can see that the output of the first act (Marion's flight) leads to this act, as the output from this act (a dead girl) leads to the third act.

Any process must add value, and any section of a movie must add to the final conclusion. In this case, Norman and Marion's meeting brings to conclusion the events in Marion's life and sets the foundation for her sister's search. Accordingly, a true transformation has occurred.

Scenes

The next level is the scene. Each act is comprised of a number of scenes. Just as the acts are subsections of the movie, the scenes are subsections of the act and represent the overall flow of that act. Act II of *Psycho* (Marion's meeting and interacting with Norman) might be broken into the following scenes:

Scene 1: Marion checks into the hotel.
Scene 2: Marion comes over for a snack.
Scene 3: Norman watches her in her room.
Scene 4: The infamous shower scene.
Scene 5: Norman cleans up.

Again, these can be seen as little movies that come together to build the final movie. Just as with each act, these can be seen as little processes. The input for the shower scene is running water and an unsuspecting girl. The transformation is from life to death. And the output is a body. Again, the input comes from the previous scene (Norman and his mother's reaction after talking with the girl), and the output leads to the next scene (a body can raise questions and must be disposed of). The scene adds value by providing the impetus for the search and beginning to show us the twisted minds involved in this movie. The obvious transformation to Marion's death is accompanied by the transformation of the movie into a deeper mystery.

Shots

Each scene is comprised of a number of shots. These are the actual images that make up the movie. As with the previous levels, they are the subsections of each scene, representing the flow of that scene. In the shower scene, Alfred Hitchcock used almost 50 shots from as many as 20 different camera angles. These included shots of Marion's feet, shots of her turning on the shower, shots of a mad person with a knife, and a final shot that pans back from Marion's lifeless eye.

Again, each of these is a small process. While not profound, a well-crafted movie needs every one of them to establish its purpose and mood. At first blush, the number of shots Hitchcock used might seem excessive. But people who watch the film do not notice the number of shots. Instead, they are wrapped up in the action captured in those shots. And each shot has its own input and output. The input for the final shot is the eye of a dead girl. The transformation actually occurs inside the viewer—the realization that we have seen Marion's last breaths. And the output is the dead body. Again, the previous shot's output provides the input for this shot. And the output provides the input for the next shot and, in this case, the next scene.

This shot adds finality to the scene that would not have existed. It provides the transformation described, and, as with the items described previously, moves the movie to the next level. The shot adds many levels of value.

The Script

Finally, there are the actual words that make up the shots, the scenes, the acts, and the movie. These are a written representation of what is supposed to occur. In some scenes, those words are the dialogue. In other scenes, the words are the camera instructions, such phrases as "hard cut to face" or "dissolve to shower" or "fade to black." For the final shot in the shower scene, the script might read:

FADE TO:
MARION'S eye. Camera slowly pulls back as image turns showing face. As full face begins to come into view, stop turn. Continue pull back until full face in view.
HARD CUT TO NEXT SCENE.

Ultimately, words and direction cues build to make the final movie we watch. However, the organization of these words is built around the various subsections of the movie—the acts, scenes, and shots. Likewise, it is these sections that are storyboarded to help the producers, directors, editors, and everyone else involved understand the direction of the movie. The storyboard helps synthesize the script into graphic images.

BUSINESS PROCESSES AS MOVIES

To fully understand processes, they also must be broken down into manageable segments. This allows a more detailed analysis of the parts that make up that process. The subsections used to organize and understand movies work well in a business environment. And, just as with movies, this substructure makes Process Mapping (storyboarding) that much easier.

To help understand these subsections, take a look at the process of making breakfast (see Exhibit 1.2). This might seem to be a trivial process, but keep in mind that this is a process someone evaluating a hotel or restaurant might have to look at. It could be the level needed to properly identify an existing snafu in a food production unit.

Exhibit 1.2 Making Breakfast

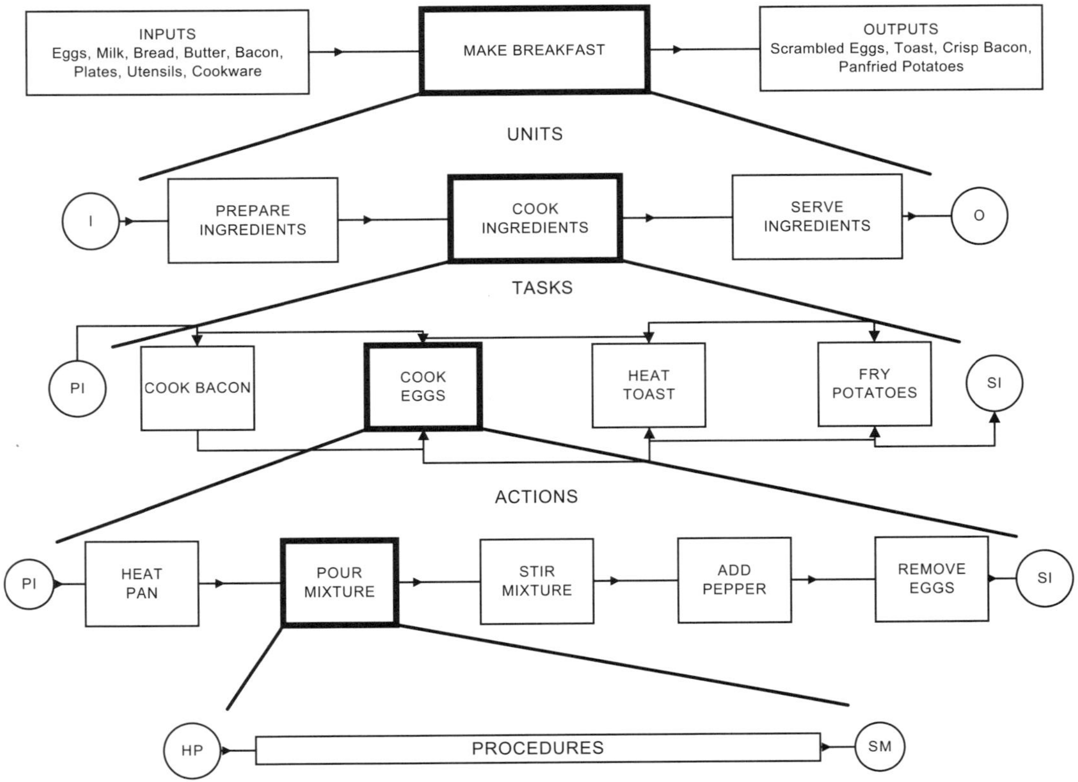

INPUTS
Eggs, Milk, Bread, Butter, Bacon, Plates, Utensils, Cookware
MAKE BREAKFAST
OUTPUTS
Scrambled Eggs, Toast, Crisp Bacon, Panfried Potatoes
UNITS
I
PREPARE INGREDIENTS
COOK INGREDIENTS
SERVE INGREDIENTS
O
TASKS
PI
COOK BACON
COOK EGGS
HEAT TOAST
FRY POTATOES
SI
ACTIONS
PI
HEAT PAN
POUR MIXTURE
STIR MIXTURE
ADD PEPPER
REMOVE EGGS
SI
HP
PROCEDURES
SM

The Process

First, you need to understand making breakfast as a process. The input is the ingredients that go into making a breakfast—for example, eggs, milk, bread, butter, bacon, plates, utensils, and pans. These ingredients go through a transition we call making breakfast. The output is the finished breakfast—scrambled eggs, toast, crisp bacon, and panfried potatoes. (This is not a particularly healthy breakfast.)

Units

The first subsection (equivalent to a movie's acts) is the unit. These are the major subsections that make up the overall process. This breakdown can be made based on location (home office, field office, branch office); type of work (building, testing, installation); stages of work (preparing, cooking, serving); or any logical breakpoint. The intent is to give the best understanding of what makes up the process.

The process of making breakfast is probably best understood based on the stages of the process. These stages might be preparing the ingredients, cooking the ingredients, and serving the final product. As with each act of the movie being seen as a smaller movie, each unit can then be seen as a smaller process. For example, the input for cooking the ingredients is the prepared foods (the output from the prior unit), the transformation is the application of heat and other stimuli to the prepared food, and the output—edible food—becomes the input for the final unit, serving the final product. Any process must add value to be a true transformation. In this instance, value is added by taking raw food and making it edible.

Tasks

Just as each act of a movie is broken down into scenes, each unit can then be broken down into tasks. Determining the tasks that make up a unit is done in much the same way as described for units. However, it is less likely to be dependent on location and more likely to begin focusing on the actual work.

The unit "Cooking the Ingredients" might be broken down into the tasks of cooking the eggs, cooking the bacon, heating the toast, and frying the potatoes. Again, each is a small process that uses output from a prior task or unit and produces output to the next task or unit. It is interesting to note that these tasks are not dependent on any of the other tasks in this unit. Cooking eggs does not require input from cooking bacon and does not provide an output to heating the toast. While a very simplistic example, this is the type of analysis that can take place during Process Mapping.

The input for cooking the eggs would be the mixed eggs. This would come from the first unit, "Preparing the Ingredients." The transformation would be the cooking process. The output would be scrambled eggs and would provide the input for the last unit, "Serving the Final Product." This process adds value by taking raw eggs and transforming them into edible eggs. Therefore, there is a true transformation occurring.

Actions

Each task can then be broken down into various actions. These are the equivalent of the movie's shots that make up each scene. Moving from units to tasks, the definition becomes more and more focused on the individual than on anything else. Actions make this focus even stronger and are more closely related to individuals.

The actions for "Cooking the Eggs" might include heat pan, pour mixture, stir mixture, add pepper, and remove cooked eggs. Note that we have tried to use two-word descriptions for these actions. This is a fundamental approach when developing process maps, so it is a good idea to practice doing so now.

Once again, each of these actions can be considered a very minor process with its own inputs, transformations, and outputs. The input for "pouring the mixture" would be a container holding mixed eggs and other ingredients already added. The transformation is the act of transferring the contents from the container to the pan. The output is the mixture sitting in the pan. Customer value has been added during the process because cooking the eggs cannot be accomplished without this transference. Therefore, there is a true transformation and a true process.

Procedures

The final stage is the actual words. With a movie, this is the script. With a process, it is the procedures. These are written descriptions of how each action is completed. Often, it is the way things are supposed to be done. Pouring the mixture might be composed of the following procedures: "Take the container in your right hand, grasping it between the thumb and fingers. Hold the container above the pan. Slowly tilt the container until the mixture begins pouring into the pan. Continue tilting until all contents are in the pan. Place the container on the counter."

But just like with a movie script, there is room for interpretation or improvisation. Looking at the directions, the following questions might arise. If I am left-handed, do I have to use my right hand? How high above the pan should the container be held? How fast should I pour the contents? Good employees know there is room for interpretation. They may even find better ways to do something than the basic description. Less able employees might see instructions and assume that, despite being left-handed, they must pour with the right hand.

It is also impossible to write down everything that must be done. Accordingly, much of procedure is actually an oral tradition, passed from worker to worker over the years. This lends itself to misunderstanding and the use of procedures that have no basis in need.

During a review, we tried to understand how a certain document was used in the process. We continued to ask for the form by name—the "Journal for Unearned Premiums." Employee after employee gave a dumbfounded stare. Finally, while describing how we thought the form was used, a light went on for the employee who gladly stated, "Oh, you mean the greenies!" Oral tradition describing the green form as "greenies" had long taken over for the procedures, which called them the "Journal for Unearned Premiums."

Employees' interpretations and misapplication of these instructions speak to the root of what is occurring in a process. The good employees are adjusting these procedures to the needs of the situation. The employees ingrained with the "it's a rule, so I'll follow it" mentality are busily using their right hand when they are left-handed or, even worse, sitting waiting for someone to tell them how fast to pour the mixture. And, to make things easier, we will not discuss the companies who insist that better ideas should not be accepted because they are not in procedure or, even worse, think these should go through a committee before being accepted.

That is one of the purposes of the hierarchy of processes. To fully analyze the overall process, the reviewer and the employees must understand the interrelationships of the sections within the process.

As you will see when process maps are developed, they allow you to key on the processes that exist on their own and those that need others. You can see how one unit leads to another, how one task leads to an action, and how they all work together to the final product.

A REAL BUSINESS EXAMPLE

Making breakfast is an interesting example, but it does not lend itself to deep analysis. To get a better feel for the hierarchy of processes and its uses, we use a more realistic business example — Payment by Check Request. This scenario is used throughout the remainder of the book, so this is a good time to get acquainted with it (see Exhibit 1.3).

The first thing to notice based on this description is that the process we are examining is really a unit of another process. Payment by Check Request is a unit of all Expense Payments. The basic units are Payment by Check Request, Travel Expense Report Payment, and Purchase Order Payment. Likewise, Expense Payment is really a unit of General Disbursements that might include Payroll, Expense Payment, and Refunds. Ultimately, every process is a subset of the process that is "the company."

This is a good reminder that the process, units, and associated levels are really defined by the reviewer. The primary process under review provides the base point for further defining the units and lower levels. Keep in mind that the reviewer may have decided to do this review of Expense Payments after identifying it as a unit (or possibly even a task) associated with a broader process within the company. But now it is time to evaluate Check Request Payment by itself, and it becomes the primary process.

The Payment by Check Request process begins with a bill. This is the most usual form of input. The transformation that occurs is the completion of a request leading to a payment. The final output is the check delivered to the payee.

The process might be broken down into the three units based on location: Field Office Prepares Request, Home Office Prepares Check, and Field Office Delivers Check. Each unit is a process in which the output from the prior item provides the input for the next item. Since the first unit is "Field Office Prepares Request,"

Exhibit 1.3   Expense Payment Process

The company has 11 field offices spread countrywide and one home office. Employees of the company incur three basic types of expenses—those incurred during travel, those requiring purchase orders (usually large, tangible products), and all other expenses. The individual incurring the expense initiates the payment process.

Travel expenses are reimbursed through "expense reports." These are prepared by the traveler, approved by the traveler's supervisor, and processed through the disbursements departments—field office and home office.

Purchase orders expenses are all those that require preparation of a "purchase order." These are required for all purchases over $5,000 and all repairs over $2,500. They are prepared by the purchaser, require two to five approvals, and are processed through the purchasing department.

This scenario focuses on "all other" expenses. These are paid through use of a Check Request. Portions of this part of the expense payment process have been centralized in the home office disbursements department to increase efficiency and to reduce costs. Other functions are handled by the field disbursements departments (one in each field office.) The company has committed to having all requests completed within 48 hours.

The purchaser must complete a Check Request form—#1292. The form must be typed, including the payee, address, amount, budget codes, and (if applicable) tax ID information. The support for the payment must be attached to the form. In addition, a properly addressed envelope (stuffed with any necessary documentation) should be included if the payment is to be mailed. If the check is to be returned to the requester, Form #1293 ("Return to Requester") must also be completed. This form is not required to be typed.

The Check Request is signed by the requester and approved by the requester's immediate supervisor. The review is intended to ensure that the request is completed correctly and to verify that supporting documentation matches the request. In addition, if the check is to be returned to the requester, the supervisor must approve an additional section of the check request, as well as the Return Check Request form. If the request is for more than $1,000, a second-level approval (the supervisor's supervisor) is required.

Once the approval is complete, the supervisor submits the form to the disbursements department. This can be either hand-delivered or shipped via interoffice mail.

Exhibit 1.3 *(continued)*

Twice daily (at 9:00 A.M. and 2:00 P.M.) the disbursements clerk processes all requests. The clerk verifies that all required sections are completed, that they are completed correctly, and that all required approvals are present. The verification process includes comparing support to the request, verifying proper coding, and ensuring proper authority. In the event that there is an error, the request is shipped back to the requester via interoffice mail. The clerk initials the form to show the review has been completed. Once approved, photocopies of all requests are made. The original requests along with all support are filed, by date, with a five-day hold-file.

At 3:00 P.M., all request photocopies are shipped overnight to the home office disbursements department. A copy of the shipping receipt is maintained in the hold-file with the original requests.

Home office check requests are handled in much the same manner. However, rather than overnight the payments, the home office disbursement clerk hand-carries the completed requests to the check issuer.

In the home office disbursements department, overnight mail is received at approximately 10:00 A.M. There are three home office disbursement check issuers. One handles home office requests and those for one of the field offices. The other two check issuers handle five field offices each.

At 1:00 P.M., the issuer signs on to the check issuance system and opens the overnight mail. Each request is reviewed to ensure that the disbursement clerk's initial is present. Two of the check issuers complete a log listing those requests without initials. The third check issuer (the one handling home office expenses) photocopies the requests with no initials and maintains them in a file. The check information is then entered in the system and the issuer initials the photocopy. Once all checks are completed, the issuer enters the print command and then signs off the system. At this point, checks are printed from the check printer.

The check printer is maintained in a locking cabinet in a centralized location within view of most employees. The home office disbursement supervisor keeps the key for the cabinet and the key used to enable the printer. At 1:00 P.M., one of the issuers notifies the supervisor that the check issuance is about to start. The supervisor will enable the printer, then relock the cabinet. The treasurer maintains backup copies of the keys.

Once the checks are printed, the issuer gives the photocopies to the check retriever. When all three issuers have turned over the photocopies, the retriever

Exhibit 1.3 *(continued)*

notifies the supervisor, who unlocks the cabinet. After the retriever gets the checks from the check printer, the supervisor disables the printer and relocks the cabinet.

The retriever processes checks in field office code number order. Home office is code 01, the southwest office is 02, the northwest office is 03, and so on. She matches each check to a request. All exceptions (a check with no request or a request with no check) are set aside to be researched later. As each office is completed, the non-exception checks are bundled for overnight delivery. Those offices not completed are given priority handling the following morning. Overnight deliveries are required in the mailroom by 3:00 P.M. The retriever enters the check number on the request and then initials it. Photocopies of check requests are filed by date, in check number order.

Research of missing items is usually completed first thing the following morning. For requests with no checks, the retriever verifies in the system that no payment was made. The request is then returned to the issuer, who processes it in that day's batch. If the review in the system shows that a check was ordered, the request is marked "Stop Pay/Reissue" and returned to the issuer. These are also processed in that day's batch.

For checks with no request, the retriever verifies with the issuer that there is no request. If the request cannot be found, a void is placed on the check in the system, "Void" is written across the payment, and it is stored in a separate file with other voids.

Checks are received in the field office at approximately 10:00 A.M. the day after shipping. The disbursement clerk opens the package and pulls the appropriate day's folder. Each check is matched to a request. The clerk verifies that the amount and payee are correct, enters the check number on the original request, and initials that request to show that the check was received.

If the check is to be mailed directly to the payee, the clerk puts the check in the envelope and routes the payment to the mailroom for delivery. If the check is to be returned to the payee, the clerk completes the delivery log. This log includes the check number, the check amount, the requester's name, and the requester's department.

Once all checks have been recorded, the clerk hand-delivers those checks to be returned to the requester. The clerk takes the check to the requester or an authorized individual in the department. The check is delivered, the clerk signs the log, and the requester (or authorized individual) signs for receipt.

Exhibit 1.3   *(continued)*

If the clerk has a request for that day but no check, the request is returned to the folder. At the hold-file, the clerk prepares the Check Locator Form (#1922) and includes it in the next overnight delivery. This includes all information necessary for home office disbursements to locate the check. The copy of the form is put in the hold-file established for that day.

When a check locator form is received in home office disbursements, it is set aside for the following day. On the next morning, the issuer reviews the system to see if the check was issued. If it has not been issued, a new check is issued using the check locator as support. If it has been issued, the check locator form is returned to the field office with any necessary information.

When the check locator is received by the field office with an indication that the check was already issued, the clerk will verify that the check was not received. If not received, the clerk will complete a stop pay form (that is approved by the disbursements supervisor) and attach this to a new copy of the check request. When the new copy and stop pay are received in home office disbursements, the check issuer will verify that the check has not cleared, process a stop payment in the system, and issue a new check using the stop pay form and photocopy of the check request as support. If the review shows the check has now cleared, the check issuer will obtain documentation from the bank to determine if an Affidavit of Forgery will be required and a potential fraud should be reported (using the Potential Fraud Form—#1099).

If the disbursements clerk receives a check for which there is no request on record, the check is marked "Void," and a Void Check Form (#86) is completed and approved by the disbursements supervisor. The check and the form are returned to the home office in the next overnight shipment. When received in the home office, the check issuer voids the check in the system and stores it in the void check file.

In the event that the check retriever is unavailable after 1 P.M. (absent or detained with other business), the backup is another clerk within the department who is not a check issuer. In the event that a check issuer is out for one day, the work is held until the following day. If the issuer is out for more than one day, the other issuers pick up the additional work. Backup for the disbursement clerk in the field offices depends on the office. Some use the supervisor, some use another clerk in the department, and some do not designate a backup.

the input for this unit is the same as the overall process—the bill. The transformation is the completion of a request that meets home office requirements. The output is the original and photocopy of a properly approved check request.

The "Field Office Prepares Request" unit might be broken down into four tasks: Complete Request, Approve Request, Verify Request, and Mail Request. These subsections are starting to be based more on people than on location. However, the location issue is still important in that there is a task for the employee, one for the supervisor, and two for the disbursements section. The input for the "Approve Request" Task is the check request. However, depending on the disposition of the final check, the input could include a "Return to Requester" form. The transformation is the bestowing of authority on the request form. The output is an approved form.

The "Approve Request" task has a number of actions associated with it, including some decision items. It starts with a decision—"Is check request correct?" If not, "Return Request." If so, "Approve Request." Then another decision—"greater than $1,000?" If not, "Mail Request." If so, "Send to Superior" and the superior will "Approve Request," then "Mail Request." You can see from the description that the breakdown now is totally function-specific, and each still has a basic input and output. The input for the "Approve Request" action is the completed request. The transformation is the review and approval of the request. The output is the approved request.

Take note of the use of a verb–noun approach in the task descriptions. As mentioned before, this is the way maps are eventually generated. Sometimes this can be tough, but it is good to get into the habit as soon as possible.

Finally, there is procedure that underlies every action. In some cases, this may be straightforward, as in "The individual giving final approval to the expense will submit the form to the disbursements clerk." Other procedures may not be as explicit. For example "All amounts over $1,000 must be approved by a second level" does explicitly indicate the approval, but it implicitly indicates that a decision must be made (is the amount greater than $1,000?).

This is the act of "drilling down," finding the processes within the processes. The degree of "drill down" is at the discretion of the reviewer. Likewise, the reviewer determines how broad a process should be at the high level. But, whatever that level, an understanding of the layers of the process is a prerequisite of understanding the full process.

RECAP

The first step in understanding the value of Process Mapping is to understand the reasons for process evaluation in the first place. Ultimately, quality process evaluation is intended to ensure that all processes are in alignment with key business objectives. In particular, these should focus on the customer service, efficiency, effectiveness, and profitability objectives.

The ultimate value of Process Mapping is in getting employees to tell their story—the stories that make up the movie that is the company. Process Mapping is a way of recording these stories in a way that documents the movie.

Aside from the obvious benefits, there are four major benefits from using the entire system of Process Mapping. First, it is a holistic approach that helps explore the interrelationships of processes. Second, it is accomplished in a way that allows all employees—from executives to line personnel—to have buy-in to the finished product. Third, it helps employees understand how their work adds value and instills additional pride in their work. Fourth, it focuses on the customer and how that person sees the company.

To understand process analysis, processes themselves must be understood. A process is an input, a transformation, and an output. The transformation is the important part. Just as a movie can be broken down into acts, a process can be divided into units. Acts can be broken down into scenes, and units can be broken into tasks. Scenes can be broken down into shots, and tasks can be broken down into actions. Finally, the script of a movie provides the actual words that are the movie. Likewise, the procedures of a process are the words that make up that process.

KEY ANALYSIS POINTS

Analysis is the key to success for Process Mapping, so it cannot be isolated to any one stage. Later, there is a discussion of analysis as a final step of the Process Mapping system. However, since analysis is ongoing, each chapter identifies some key analysis points that were brought forward during the chapter.

No Transformation: No Need

For a process to be truly effective, some transformation must occur. Transformation implies a change to an input. If there is no change, why does the process exist? Look for processes in which no real transformation occurs and eliminate them.

Analyze the Written Descriptions

Policies and procedures hold the basic information on how a process should go. Some are too detailed. Others are too vague. Take a close look at these documents, and determine if enough latitude is available to allow people to get their jobs done. Also ask for those handwritten instructions—the ones that the employees used to really learn their jobs.

Keep Alert for Oral Traditions

Listen closely to the stories that are told about how people learned their jobs. There may be an excellent procedure manual, but it is too detailed and boring. Instead, the employees learned their jobs by swapping stories. This oral tradition (sometimes written down in the handwritten instructions described previously) is the actual way the world works. Until you know about the "greenies" (the common reference name of a form or report), you will be the one talking a foreign language.

You Define the Process that Defines the Project

The ultimate process is the company. Within it are numerous processes that support the main process. Defining the level of process helps define the overall review project. By defining that process, the limits of the project are also defined.

NOTE

1. Ken Blanchard and Sheldon Bowles, *Gung Ho!* (New York: William Morrow & Company, Inc., 1998).

CHAPTER 2

What Is This Thing Called Process Mapping?

I may not have gone where I intended to go, but I think I have ended up where I intended to be.

— Douglas Adams

BUT WAIT, THERE'S MORE

We have spent a lot of time talking about what processes are. We have sliced, diced, and spliced processes until we are having trouble telling where procedure starts and processes (units, tasks, or actions) end. So now that we have defined the heck out of the concept of process, when do we get to actually map the process?

All in good time. There are some things that we must learn before we actually prepare what might be called a map. Again, Process Mapping, when applied correctly, is a very holistic system. That means you must understand a few other terms, concepts, and systems before you can dig into the process analysis.

TRIGGERS

The first concept we want to talk about are "triggers." Each process must have input to get started. But input does not, in and of itself, get that process going. Something must occur to trigger the start of the process. This often may be the same as the input, but it is important to determine whether the distinction makes a difference in the process under review.

In the movie *Psycho,* the trigger that starts the movie rolling is the money. The existence of this money tempts Marion to leave her current life and sets the ball in motion for her meeting with Norman. In the act in which Marion meets and interacts with Norman, the trigger is her arrival at the hotel. This allows for the coming interactions. The trigger for the shower scene is Marion's entrance into the shower. This allows her attacker to advance unobserved, a crucial aspect of the scene. Finally, the trigger for the shot of Marion's unblinking eye is her death. At that point, she is known to be truly dead, and that allows the shot to take on its importance.

As you can see from this description, each section helps establish the trigger for the following section. Processes that come before a given unit, task, or action actually help set up the triggers for those events. That is one of the main reasons the full process must be understood—to see how it may cause or delay the application of a trigger.

In the breakfast process, the trigger may be one of two things. The most obvious would be hunger. Less obvious, however, may be the trigger of waking up in the morning. Sometimes we are not hungry, but it is morning and we know we should eat or we will not make it through the day. The Cooking the Ingredients unit is triggered by completing the preparation of ingredients. Likewise, the Cooking the Eggs task is triggered by completing the egg ingredients. Finally, the triggers for the action "Pouring the Mixture" would be having the pan at the right heat and having the ingredients prepared.

In this example of making breakfast, the triggers for the tasks become important because of their unique characteristics. As mentioned when we first discussed these tasks, they are not dependent on the completion of another task. Some ingredients may be ready before others are, resulting in a portion of the unit being completed before others. That means the line between starting one unit and ending another unit becomes more blurred. In a more intricate process, these timing aspects could become critical to the success of the process. By identifying the triggers early in the review, the critical area can be focused on more quickly.

The trigger for Payment by Check Request is the receipt of a bill or other items indicating the amount due. Because the Field Office Prepares Request unit is the first, it has the same trigger as the overall process. The task of Approve Request is triggered by receipt of a completed check request. Likewise, the action of the supervisor Approving Request is triggered by receipt of a properly completed check request.

The trigger is also important because it is often the point at which the customer is first involved. Some action by a customer (internal or external) will be a trigger. If the trigger comes from some other source, it may be an indicator that the process is not customer-driven. This could mean radical change is needed, or it may even mean the process can be eliminated.

TIME ANALYSIS

There are two time factors that should be analyzed as part of process maps. These are cycle times and holding times. Cycle time represents the amount of time it takes to complete a task or action for any one item. Holding time is the amount of time an individual item sits in a hold-file or on a desk. This is nonproductive time.

Any movie must conform to a certain length. In general, movies are under 2 hours long, with most coming closer to 90 minutes. Anything more or less than this can be detrimental. In particular, longer movies have a lot of trouble pleasing the customers. It is possible to come up with exceptions where longer movies were successful, but it is probably easier to remember movies that were too long (even if only 90 minutes long.)

Likewise, the specific timing for each act, scene, and shot is critical for a number of reasons. There is only so long to tell the story. Wasting too much time on an individual section can result in other sections not being properly addressed.

It is the same situation with any process. There is a certain amount of time that is optimal for completion of the process. Longer or shorter periods might be tolerated, but there should be a good reason. Analyzing cycle times and holding times will help get a handle on where timing issues may exist. And remember that cycle times and holding times can be too short as well as too long. Processes that take too long run the hazard of making the process less transparent to the customer, but processes that are too short may be achieving this at the expense of quality. The process losses its transparency again because the customer is affected by it.

In the breakfast example, the timing is very important because the tasks in Cooking the Ingredients are independent of each other. A cycle time analysis might indicate what parts of the tasks are being completed first and why. By analyzing these cycle times, an optimum starting time for each task could be determined that allowed all parts of the breakfast to be completed at the same time. A similar review of the tasks involved in the Preparing the Ingredients unit might show which parts of Cooking the Ingredients could be started while still in the first unit.

In the Payment by Check Request example, both cycle time and holding time work together to hamper timely completion.

There is a promise of payment within 48 hours. However, adding the time involved shows that this is an impossibility. Although this is examined more closely later, there are a few obvious examples from reading the scenario, particularly the cycle times for transfers and the holding times for in-bins.

There are two instances in which paperwork is sent overnight. The first is when the check request photocopies are overnighted to the Home Office. These are sent to the home office at 3:00 P.M. and are received at 10:00 A.M. This is an immediate 19-hour cycle time. Then the overnighted materials are kept in the home office in-bin until 1:00 P.M. This is a 3-hour holding time.

There are various other steps that result in increased cycle times and holding times, but the next major one is when the checks are overnighted back to the field office. Again, mail is delivered at about 3:00 P.M. and is received in the field office by 10:00 A.M., so the cycle time is 19 hours. Luckily, the field office does not hold the checks once received, so there is no holding time.

Without reviewing the process any farther, we have 41 hours of cycle time and holding time. Considering that the expenses for all offices must be handled, it seems a bit of a stretch to expect return within 48 hours. Yet this is not apparent until the process and the associated times are analyzed.

ERROR RATE

There is one other factor that should be considered throughout Process Mapping. This is the error rate. Just as cycle times and holding times cause problems for the timely completion of a process, error rates compound the issue. Anytime processing an item causes an error, people are pulled from production of good units produced right the first time. Evaluation of the error rates may also show where a process is breaking down.

Any decision item in a process is probably the location for an error rate evaluation. In the Payment by Expense Request process, there should be an error rate evaluation at the approval level. The review should ask how many requests are returned to the requester. If a high error rate is found, additional error rate questions should be asked. How many requests are returned for insufficient support? How many are returned for improper coding? How many have incorrect amounts? This can help lead to an understanding of where the problem lies. It may be an education issue with the requesters, or it may mean that someone else should be entering codes.

And, when everything is considered, everyone must understand the true cost of rework. This includes the waste of raw materials as well as people's time. By showing the error rate and the cycle time involved with correction, a true value can be applied.

FOCUSING THE LENS

There is one final concept that must be kept in mind throughout Process Mapping. At the heart of every process is the customer. Any process that does not have an ultimate effect on the customer is useless. So customer service is likewise at the heart. But what is customer service?

If you walk into a store, see what you like, pick it up, take it to the register, have a quick checkout, and leave the store, you have had a good customer service experience. But what if you walked into the store and what you wanted was the first thing you saw, and you then walked straight to the register? Customer service has been improved. Now walk into the store, pick up the item, wave your credit card in front of the object to charge to your account, and walk out. Again service is improved.

Keep thinking about ways to make this go quicker. You do not have to go to the store anymore—you order by phone (or the

Web). Make it better still. You speak out loud and it appears before you. Make it even better. You think about buying it and it appears. Make it better yet. Before you can even think about what you want, it appears before you bought and paid for it.

Now we have reached perfect customer service. Of course, this degree of service will never exist (at least not in this millennium), but everyone is trying to get closer and closer to it.

Think this through again. What we have done is taken a fairly time-consuming task and tried to reduce it until the task itself is nonexistent. The streamlining of operations is an attempt to make processes more *transparent*. This transparency results in the customer's increased satisfaction and delight.

Each process can be thought of as a lens. As each customer's interaction passes through this lens, one of three things can happen. First, the lens can defract that interaction. In other words, the customer's interaction with the company has resulted in additional time and trouble for the customer. The customer has been moved farther away from his ultimate objective. A simple example of this might be a web site that takes too long to pull up. The designers may have built the most beautiful site in the world, but this is not important to the user who just wants to get the information. The customer has been defracted from his objective.

The second thing is that the lens can focus the interaction. This type of interaction is the complete opposite of defraction. The interaction causes the process to speed up or even wows the customer with service never expected. The customer has been helped along toward the ultimate objective. Examples of this constantly change. Years ago, a focusing interaction might be the scanning of goods at a supermarket—it would speed up the process and the customer would get more than was expected. Today scanners are expected, and while they still help focus the customer, they are more likely to defract when not working right.

43

The third thing that can happen is nothing. In other words, the process is totally transparent. When this occurs, the customer never realizes that anything has happened, but the process was necessary to complete the interaction. Ultimately, the objective of all process improvement is to make processes as transparent as possible. One example of a transparent process might be the support systems for the scanner. The customer should never know the computer had to go read the scan, interpret it, and provide the information to the register. Just as with the prior example, the minute transparency reduces, the process tends to defract the interaction. Another example would be any administrative activities. For a company to survive, there are many administrative functions that must be completed: appraisals, purchase requests, vacations. The customer does not care about these and, accordingly, they must be transparent. The minute the tasks become so onerous that they intrude on more important activities, transparency is lost and customer service degrades.

Therefore, process analysis is meant to focus the lenses. Every interaction must be evaluated to determine if it is focusing, is defracting, or is transparent. If any defraction occurs, the lens must be focused. If the lens is focusing, the process should be maintained and nurtured to ensure that customer service continues. Ultimately, process analysis is intended to strive for perfect transparency—the completion of processes without the customer knowing they even exist.

THE PROCESS OF PROCESS MAPPING

It has been mentioned a number of times that Process Mapping as a tool is only part of the picture. Just as a storyboard is not the actual movie, a process map is not the actual analysis. It is time to understand what the Process Mapping system is like.

Somewhere out there, someone has an idea for a great movie. It may be the next *Ben-Hur* or it may be the next *Plan Nine from Outer Space*, but in that person's mind, it is a great movie. Everybody thinks they have an idea for a great movie. Of all those great ideas, a small percentage actually get put on paper. For all the ideas that get put on paper, a small percentage are picked up and read by someone who can do something. For all those that are read, a small percentage are purchased. And, surprisingly, for all the ones that are purchased, only a small percentage are actually shot. By the time the idea goes from the one person's mind to celluloid, the writer probably will not recognize the finished product.

Once a script is accepted, it gets changed. It gets researched and changed. It gets storyboarded and changed. It goes into rewrite and gets changed. It goes into filming and gets changed. It gets edited and gets changed. Sometimes it gets tested by focus groups and gets reedited—and changed. The story that is "the movie" evolves as the many people working on it come to a better understanding of what the story is.

A company's processes go through numerous changes also. Therefore, the understanding of that process gets changed. The CEO and executives have one idea of the process, the managers and supervisors have another, the line personnel have a third, and the person who first imagined the process that would be "the company" probably would not recognize the finished product.

Just as the storyboard is used to anchor a visual understanding of a movie's changes, the process map is a visualization of the changing understanding of the process. When all is said and done, the process map should marry everyone's understanding of the story to mirror the "real" process.

It is the steps that go into changing the map to reflect reality that make the map effective. These steps are process identification, information gathering, interviewing and map generation, map analysis, and presentation.

PROCESS IDENTIFICATION

We know intuitively what a process is. We think we know what the start and end points are. We think we know where the process resides and who the owners are. And we think we know what is important and what is not. However, until we really dig in and find these answers, we are only fooling ourselves.

A scriptwriter sits down thinking the plot will fall into place. However, the characters have their own ideas. Many writers talk about how they knew exactly where the story was going to go, but the characters had a different idea. As the story develops, the good writer allows the characters to determine an outcome that is true to their spirit. That final script looks nothing like the original idea, but it is a better script because it is true to the characters.

Presupposing what the outcome of a process is leads to the same false results that occur from forcing characters to act out of—well, out of character. The reviewer must sit down with the people who know how the processes work and learn the story. But it is more than just getting their story. It is helping them begin to understand that their story is only part of the overall movie. Just as a good writer must think about the audience, a good reviewer must think about the customer. This means taking a trip through the customer's eyes and seeing the triggers that interact with the customer.

DATA GATHERING

Digging deeper into the process, we must understand the information that is available. This may mean statistical information, it may mean who to talk with, and it may simply mean spelling out what the process does. But if we jump into Process Mapping without all information necessary, we can easily miss what is important.

A scriptwriter must have a basic understanding of the subject before writing. The more the writer "guesses" at what the real facts are, the more the viewer's suspension of belief is tested. Think about *2001: A Space Odyssey.* In the entire movie, based on what was known at the time, there was only one scientific error (and it is not the zero-G toilet—that was based on evidence available at the time). As the scientist experiences free fall shuttling from the Earth to the space station for his briefing, he sips on liquid food through a straw. After the liquid is sipped, it falls back into the container. Weightlessness would not allow this to happen.

Now think about *Plan 9 from Outer Space.* People who are dead show up in later scenes (and I do not mean the zombies), scenes that have nothing to do with the movie are included, and headstones in the obviously fake graveyard are knocked over by people brushing into them. Ignoring facts shatters what little credibility the movie might have had.

Okay, it is unfair to compare a megabudget movie against one shot on a shoestring, but you can think of examples of your own— a cola bottle in a scene from *Cleopatra,* a watch on a gladiator in *Ben-Hur,* and the fact that Krakatoa is west of Java (not east as the movie title says.) Factual data are the key to suspension of belief.

For Process Mapping, factual information is the key to sustaining belief. The review must have the facts at hand and be able to use them. This will keep the reviewer from going down roads that are unimportant. It also helps the reviewer understand the information being received through the mapping. Finally, and maybe most importantly, it provides credibility to the reviewer.

INTERVIEWING AND MAP GENERATION

Once the basic information is in hand, the reviewer actually starts making the map, but this is not a process done in isolation. It is a give-and-take interaction that makes the maps living, breathing items. Every interviewee has input and, if desired, a hands-on opportunity to make the map. And every interviewer is one of the artists building the final product.

After a script is done, it is time for the rest of the players to become involved. As we have already discussed, the storyboard provides the medium to begin translating that story. But the director has ideas, the producer has ideas, and the actors and actresses have ideas. The filming of the movie is the time when the words on paper transfer from the storyboard to the film. As each person provides input and change, the storyboard changes. When the film is "in the can," the storyboard may not look at all like the original script.

Each person has an idea of what the process looks like. They know their stories and expect them to match everyone else's stories. The map and interviews help build on those stories until there is a final product that, while it might not match the original map or the original stories, it does represent the final, real process.

ANALYZING THE DATA

This has been happening since the project was first undertaken. Even the first discussions should provide the opportunity for analysis. During one recent review, we began by talking to the head of the department. He told us that, although the processes were the same, the two sections were doing them differently because the heads of those sections each thought that was the better way to do it. Later, while talking to the head of a third department, she stated that she bypassed the mechanical system and used her own spreadsheets. The initial analysis is accomplished. A major problem has been identified. The only question left is why.

Editing the movie starts when the script is being written. No scriptwriter submits a first draft. If so, it will be rejected every time. Changes are made in the writing process, in the negotiation process, in the filming process, and, most important, in the editing process. It is that editing process that really brings it all together. This is where the final storyboard is brought to film. And this is where the final product is really completed, ready for the world to see.

Analysis has been going on throughout development of the maps, but it is at the end that the full effect can be seen. The reviewer can look at the entire picture, seeing the full interactions, identifying the most significant delays, and determining the effectiveness and efficiency of the entire process. This is where the final product and final report come together for all the world to see.

PRESENTATION

Putting all the process definition, data gathering, interviews, map generation, and analysis together should result in a final report. This is the product the reviewer has been working to build, and it is the product that management wants to see.

Eventually, a movie is shown to an audience. That proves its ultimate value. All the writing and research and storyboarding and filming and editing have led to this product. If it is successful, it is used and used again. And the results of that work are successfully apparent to the audience.

Eventually, a report of the process under review is provided. This can be written, oral, or anything that grabs the audience's attention. But all the process identification, data gathering, interviewing, mapping, and analysis have led to this product. A successful map is used many times. And a successful mapping project will lead to more. And the results of that work are successfully apparent to the audience.

RECAP

Beyond an understanding of processes, there are a number of additional concepts that are important for Process Mapping. The first is the concept of triggers. While inputs begin all processes, triggers are the actual actions or items that cause the initiation of the process. Identifying the triggers helps one to better understand why a process occurs and may help focus on the customers involved in that process.

Another important area of analysis is the various time factors involved. The emphasis here is on those that can cause delays to the process. The first is the cycle time, which is the time it takes any one object to complete an action. The second is the holding time and represents the amount of time an object will sit and wait to be processed. By combining these times, the reviewer gains an understanding of how long the full process takes and where the time bottlenecks occur.

The final major analysis measurement is the error rate. This is primarily related to decision points in the map and relates to rework and wasted resources. Low error rates may be ignored, but as the rate increases, the area warrants additional review. The focus should be on determining why errors occur, not in streamlining the correction process.

To get a handle on how processes can be fine-tuned, it is helpful to think of them as lenses through which customer interactions travel. The lenses can defract or focus that interaction. When defraction is found, the process must be viewed closely. Ultimately, all processes are striving to become perfectly transparent. A transparent process is one that the customer cannot detect. If all processes are transparent, the customer receives perfect customer service.

As has been mentioned before, Process Mapping is more than making a map. It is the whole system that results in a successful project. The steps in that system are process identification (learning what makes up the process under review); data gathering (learning what exists within the process and with whom we will be involved); interviewing and map generation (learning and recording the actions within a process); analyzing the data (learning what can be done to make the process better); and presentation (showing others what we have learned).

KEY ANALYSIS POINTS

Trigger = Customer

Triggers start a process in motion. If that trigger does not in some way originate from the customer, there is a good chance the process is unnecessary. Even if the trigger is the boss wanting a report, that report needs to ultimately be useful for the customer (it helps drive pricing decisions, it helps drive budget considerations, etc.) or it should not be done.

Independent Processes Can Start Sooner

Buried within some processes are units or tasks that are independent of the units or tasks surrounding them. It could be that a set of tasks all originate from the same unit and feed to the next unit, but are not reliant on each other for completion. When identified, you can determine if some are being delayed needlessly, waiting for the start or completion of other independent tasks. This can speed up the entire process.

Eliminate Holding Times

Batch filing is the bane of customer service. The longer a document or part or phone call sits waiting, the longer the delay in processing. While this can be allowed in some situations, it generally is better for any process to eliminate these.

Do Not Streamline Error Correction—Eliminate It

In the analysis of error rates, it is more important to look at what caused the errors. Even the most streamlined error correction procedure adds no original value to a process. If something is done right the first time, everyone saves time and money. Look first at why errors are occurring. High error rates come from within the process and usually mean that the process must change. Only when this is completed should analysis of the error correction process be evaluated.

Focus Defraction or Turn It Transparent

Any process that affects a customer can cause one of two things:

1. Customer satisfaction or
2. Customer dissatisfaction.

Look closely at processes that are hindering the customer's opportunity to be satisfied. In addition, look for those processes that should be transparent to the customer. If anything in that process affects customer satisfaction, a better way must be found.

CHAPTER 3

Process Identification

*As for the outside world, you will be confronted by what you see.
And what you see is primarily what you look at.*

—Zen saying

WHAT DO YOU SEE?

As we look at a business from the inside, the movie we see may not be anything like the one our customers see. Operating within the business structure, we see only what we do. We see our individual jobs, the tasks within those jobs, and not much else. We often see the purpose of our work as just getting the tasks done. We do not think about the impact of our work on our customers or on the company as a whole. We do not often take the time to look at what we do in a different way, to see it as a novice, the way our customers may see it when they first come into contact with the business. We see the organization as it has been defined from within.

Our customers, however, define our business by the experience they have when they touch the organization. They do not know about our internal structure, and, frankly, they do not care. It is, or should be, invisible to them. We must start looking

53

beyond what we normally see and look at what our customer is seeing. What are our visible processes?

Imagine that you were in a car accident. This is a traumatic event in most people's lives. It may be the first time they have really experienced dealing with an insurance company. The experience begins when trying to report the claim. Who do you call? Trying the claims office would seem reasonable. However, when you call the claims office, the receptionist tells you that no one in the office can take the report of your claim and that you will have to call your agent. You call the agent's office, but he and his secretary are out for the day. You spend a worrisome night wondering what to do with your car, how you will get to work the next day, and what to do about the pain you are starting to get in your neck.

Day 2: You reach your agent. He takes down the information about your claim and tells you that someone from the claims office will be contacting you soon. You wait for the phone call all day. Nothing.

Day 3: You phone the claims office. The receptionist tells you that your claim must be assigned to a claims representative. However, assignments for claims reported yesterday have not yet been made. You should be hearing from a claims representative soon. You ask what to do about getting transportation and about the pain in your neck. She says you will have to talk to your claims representative. You remind her that you have not yet been assigned one. She repeats that yesterday's assignments have not yet been made. You hang up and wait by the phone all day again. Nothing.

Day 4: You get a ride from a friend to the store to get more aspirin for the pain in your neck. You return home and the claims representative has left a message. You call back and get his voice mail saying he will be out of the office for the rest of the day.

Day 5: You finally speak to the claims representative. He explains what you need to do to get your car repaired and arranges for a rental vehicle. You tell him you are experiencing some headaches and pain. He explains that he only handles the portion of your claim regarding your car. He will report that you are injured, and another claims representative will be assigned to handle that portion of your claim. It takes two more days for the medical claims representative to call you.

It has now taken one week for you to complete the process of reporting your entire claim to the company. At this point, you probably are not very impressed with the service delivered by the insurance company. Surprisingly, the insurance company's measurements indicate that this claim was handled successfully. The company requires claims to be reported through the agent— Success #1. The company requires claims to be assigned within 24 hours after being reported—Success #2. The company requires claims representatives to contact customers within 24 hours of receiving the assignment—Success #3. The company requires claims to be assigned to claims representatives based on specialty— Success #4. By every company measurement, the process was a resounding success. From the customer's point of view, this was a service failure.

You see what you look at.

Now imagine a different scenario. When you purchased your insurance, you were given a sticker for your glove compartment and an ID card with a number for reporting a claim. You are in the same accident. This time you call the number from the accident site using your cell phone. The person on the phone says the company will have a claims representative to you in 10 minutes. He will have a rental vehicle delivered, find a repair facility for your vehicle, have your vehicle transported, and assist you in obtaining prompt and immediate treatment if you are injured. The claims representative arrives in 5 minutes and first asks about your injuries. He gives you a list of physicians you can see at no cost to you. He arranges to have a rental car delivered to the scene in the next 15 minutes, again at no cost to you. It is 1 hour after the accident, all your questions have been answered, your vehicle has been delivered to a repair facility, you have arranged to see a doctor tomorrow morning, and you are driving away in a rental vehicle. Which company would you rather deal with?

The first company defined the claims reporting process from the company's point of view, setting measurements of success from an internal rather than an external (customer-oriented) perspective. They did not consider the customer's experience but only internal process constraints when developing measurements of success. The second company structured the reporting process around the customer's experience. The measure of success is significantly different. This company built processes to support a rapid resolution of the problems facing customers when they are involved in an accident. Success to this company was having a person on-site to deal with the customer within 30 minutes of the time the company is notified of the claim. This representative was empowered to resolve all immediate customer problems such as removal of the vehicle, obtaining a replacement vehicle, and even authorizing medical treatment for injured parties. The actual reporting, processing, and authorization for both companies may take a week. But while the first company is a slave to the processes at the expense of the customer, the second company has allowed these processes to take a backseat to customer service.

Examining business processes gives the company an opportunity to look at the business differently, outside its normal organizational structure. The process of reporting the claim from the customer's point of view begins when they have an accident and ends when they have voice-to-voice, face-to-face contact with someone who can answer their questions or concerns. Identifying all the pieces that make up the claims reporting process for the company, and then looking at the total potential cycle time for the entire process could reveal the source of some service failures for the insurance company.

FINDING THE STORY

Some businesses are organized geographically, some functionally, and some as a mixture of both. Organizational structures generally are not process-oriented. One department may be responsible for a certain piece of a process and another department for another piece. The reviewer's first job then is to identify just what processes take place in the company or segment of the company being reviewed.

A company that is not organized around processes may never have identified the broad processes that help it achieve its objectives. If this is the first attempt by the company to classify operations as processes, this exercise will take some time and discussion. It is not always easy, and the classification process can be somewhat arbitrary. For example, if the business is organized around functional areas such as accounting, marketing, and support services, it will be necessary to define the particular processes taking place in each of these functions. Job titles rather than actual processes are often used to classify the work being done by an employee. Titles such as Accountant I or Accountant II do not offer much information about the actual processes involved in these particular jobs. The reviewer must look beyond the department name, beyond the traditional job title, and systematically determine what work is being accomplished. The goal is to make sure that all critical processes have been identified and defined.

Using accounting as an example, some companies may have this department handling all monetary transactions. That means it accepts payments for sales, makes disbursements for expenses, and receipts petty cash. It is necessary to separate these into the correct processes.

To ensure a customer-focused approach to analysis, begin by telling the story of the business from the customer's perspective. What is the first scene in which the customer is involved? What is the next scene, and the next, and the next? . . . all the way to the final scene. What triggers the movement from one scene to the next? And, eventually, what is that process called?

TRIGGER EVENTS

When looking at the business through the eyes of the customer, look for the series of trigger events that indicate contact with the customer. Trigger events are actions or items that cause the process to begin. Customer trigger events are those events started by the customer or initiated to react with the customer. Using the Expense Payment Process as an example, the trigger is the bill. In this instance, the customer is the payee, although that is not someone normally considered a customer.

Every business has a unique series of these events. Even in industries where the companies are almost identical, there are quirks that differentiate them, and these unique triggers will generate unique processes.

Identifying the customer triggers really requires putting yourself in the customer's shoes. What you are really looking for is all the interaction points your company has with its customers. In *At America's Service,* Karl Albrecht calls each of these interaction points a "moment of truth" for the company. He gives credit to Jan Carlzon, president of Scandinavian Airlines System, for adapting this metaphor from bullfighting. He defines moment of truth as:

> . . . any episode in which the customer comes into contact with any aspect of the organization and gets an impression of the quality of its service.[1]

Albrecht goes on to state that these moments of truth are the "basic building blocks of the service product . . . the basic atom of service, the smallest indivisible unit of value delivered to the customer." The moments of truth are the real products the company delivers to its customers. These are what customers judge the company by, so it makes sense to focus on moments of truth when analyzing business processes.

> The moment of truth is typically neither positive nor negative in and of itself. It is the outcome of the moment of truth that counts. The sum total of all the possible moments of truth your customers experience, both human and nonhuman, becomes your service image.[2]

We want to make sure we look at all the critical trigger events in any process being reviewed and for the business as a whole. We want to see the complete movie, not just clips from the movie. Just as the audience in the theater is in the best position to understand the final movie, the customer is often the only one who sees the big picture. The complete movie will cross many organizational and departmental lines, but the customer perceives it as one experience with the company. Failure at any point along the way can mean failure for the entire company. It is easy to get caught up in the tasks of our jobs. Every business is the sum of its processes. We must identify just what the processes are so we can step back and take a look at how they affect business outcomes.

Consider the scenes involved in a customer's interaction with a cellular phone company. Start the camera rolling and record all the actions and trigger events chronologically as they occur.

Scene 1: Customer reads ad in the paper regarding "free long distance." A potential customer is born with a need or desire. This need or desire is one of the two triggers for the first scene. A potential customer's first interaction with the company is usually a response to these needs. A second trigger for this scene is the advertisement that catches the customer's attention. For this potential customer, the advertisement has focused on his need for free long distance. The company advertisement specifically addresses the potential customer's need or desire, setting off the trigger. This first scene is really the initiation of the overall cellular phone customer interaction.

Scene 2: Customer responds to ad by calling the company's 800 number. The next interaction with the company comes when the potential customer pursues his need and makes contact to obtain further information about the product. The contact is the trigger that starts this process. The first moment of truth has gone well, and the customer responds by using the phone number. Note that the company has helped focus the interaction by providing the 800 number.

Scene 3: Customer asks about costs, coverage, and features. This is the first voice-to-voice interaction with a company representative. It is the first moment of truth that depends on instantaneous interaction with the company. The potential customer solicits information about the particular product or service needed. The customer's questions are the trigger for the scene. The quality of this interaction will help determine if the potential customer will become an actual customer. The success or failure of the customer relationship will depend on how the customer's expectation matches what the company delivers—both in the way of customer service and in the quality of the product.

Scene 4: Customer purchases phone and service plan. While it is true that each scene relies on the success of the prior scene, this seems no more evident than now. Unless the potential customer's needs have been met in the prior three scenes, the potential customer will not become an actual customer. The acceptance of the terms and conditions by the potential customer is the trigger that elevates him or her to an actual customer. Upon purchase of the phone and service plan, the processes under review step up a notch. Studies show that the cost of getting new customers can be anywhere from 3 to 10 times more expensive than the cost of keeping them. Therefore, the efforts spent on enhancing processes from here on out are far more effective than those spent on getting to this point.

Scene 5: Customer's phone is connected. A lot has happened between scene four and scene five. But none of the processes affect the customer. At least, they should not affect the customer. The processes that occur between scene four and scene five are an excellent example of transparent processes. Notification may need to go to billing and connection. The customer database probably needs to be updated. Connection may need to wait until billing verifies credit card authorization. All computerized systems may go down. However, if any of these causes a delay from the customer's expected connection start date, the moment of truth is not faring well. In spite of the transparent processes, the trigger for this event is the customer's acceptance of the offer. At this point, service initiation can begin.

Scene 6: Customer uses phone. There are actually two triggers to this scene. The first is the customer receiving the phone. The second is the customer using the phone. And it all leads to the ultimate moment of truth. After all is said and done, if the phone does not work (or, even worse, if the phone is not received), the customer has not received what was promised. There are a number of issues involved in this also. It is not only a matter of the phone working, but also how well it works, whether the reception is good, whether the caller gets cut off, and any of the various service issues that arise with cell phones.

Scene 7: Customer receives bill. This event is triggered by a date — the date the billing period ends. The resulting process is another test of the customer's satisfaction. This is the moment the customer decides if the service received warrants the associated expenses. Once again, there are a number of processes behind receiving the bill, processes that should be transparent to the customer. And these processes should ensure that the bill arrives on time, includes only the services requested, and is billed at the agreed upon rate.

Scene 8: Customer pays bill. This is the final scene in our movie. The happy ending in which the company receives compensation toward making a profit and the customer rides into the sunset, receiving excellent service for as long as the two do business. The trigger is the payment actually arriving (by check, credit card, Internet, etc.) at the billing center. Once received, the cycle starts over with the customer using the phone again.

Experiencing the business from the customer's prospective can help identify obvious processes. Each of the scenes represents processes necessary for the successful completion of the overall process, but it has also helped us identify processes that should be invisible to the customer. Even if the customer does not know these processes exist, they will directly or indirectly affect the customer's experience with the company.

In the preceding example, we identified billing, connection, and database management as transparent processes, but there are many more support processes. The first direct contact with the company is through customer service, so the recruiting and training of customer service representatives is an extremely important process for this company, but one that should be transparent to the customer. Another example might be supply management. Without a solid process here, phones might not be available to potential customers. Again, although we have identified eight "moments of truth," there are a number of transparent processes that must exist to make the moments of truth go right.

NAMING THE MAJOR PROCESSES

After listing the key trigger events from the customer's perspective, take a look at these events from the company's perspective. A process name may already exist and be obvious for the event. If so, you are in luck. If not, you must put on your creative hat on and come up with a descriptive name for the overall process. Keep in mind that there may be several units making up the process, but you are trying to first identify the overall major business processes.

From the customer's perspective, one process generally will lead directly to another, although there may be some gaps. Behind the scenes, the gaps should be filled with internal processes. In addition, there may be processes that exist in isolation. Business support processes such as training and quality control are examples of such processes. They should be transparent to external customers, but they still exist to help support the company's objectives. Eventually all processes should be identified, but it is better to begin by concentrating on the obvious processes that are visible to customers.

A Process Identification Work Sheet can be used to facilitate documentation (see Exhibit 3.1). Included in the header of the form is the business being reviewed. The first column is a list of all the trigger events corresponding to the scenes encountered by the customer. The example shows this completed using the cellular phone purchase and subsequent billing as an example. It is a good idea to start with the overall process and the broad trigger that begins the process. This will help you focus on the work to be completed. Also notice that we have added one more set of triggers to the worksheet—Payment Not Received and Customer Cancels. This is the unhappy ending to the story. For whatever reason, the processes have failed to fill the customer's needs, and the Termination of Service process must begin. Notice that, while these two triggers are different, either can set the process in motion.

The second column lists the process name. This is the name you or the client have agreed upon to describe the overall process. Again, the names are somewhat arbitrary. Two people may look at the same triggers and see different groupings or come up with different names, but there should be agreement from all working on the project about what processes they represent.

Exhibit 3.1   Process Identification Work Sheet

Area of business being reviewed: Cellular phone customer interactions	
Trigger Events	**Process Name**
Potential customer has need or desire for mobile phone. Potential customer reads advertisement.	Solicitation
Potential customer contacts company.	Customer inquiries
Customer accepts offer and places order.	Order completion
Request for service Initialize service Ship phone	Service initiation
Customer receives phone.	Phone delivered
Customer begins using service.	Phone support services
Billing period ends.	Customer billing
Customers make payment to the company via check, credit card—by mail, by phone, or on the Internet.	Customer payment process
Customer does not make payment by specified date. Customer cancels service.	Termination of service

Look at the example and see how the triggers described in the previous scenes lead to the associated processes. The overall business under review—cellular phone customer interaction—is initiated by the needs and desires of the potential customer for a cellular phone. When the customer reads an advertisement that plays on his needs and desires in such a way that he takes action, the overall process has begun. The process of Customer Inquiries starts with the potential customer making contact with the call center and includes the call center providing appropriate product and pricing information to customer. The Order Completion process begins when a customer places an order and ends when information is forwarded to the service department so service can be initiated. Service initiation begins when the request to set up a phone is received and ends when the service is established and the phone is shipped to the customer. The Phone Delivered process is the single act of delivering the phone to the customer. This could be done by mail, or the customer may pick up the phone at a retail outlet.

The Phone Support Services process involves the ongoing use of an existing phone and, while in most instances there is only one type of trigger (the customer uses the phone), the various circumstances that result may be reflected in many different units within the process. The Customer Billing process begins at the end of the billing period and involves the actual generation and circulation of the bill to the customer. The Customer Payment Process begins after the bill is received and involves the method of payment and determination of whether a payment has been received. Depending on the circumstances, this process can trigger the next process. Termination of Service begins when one of two triggers exists—a payment is not received or the customer requests cancellation. The process ends when the service is actually disconnected.

You may have noticed that we did not use the Expense Payment Process of this example. As mentioned before, this process is actually a unit of bigger processes that may be units of a bigger one. From a broad perspective, the area of business being reviewed could have been disbursements. The customer in this case is actually an employee of the company. From that customer's perspective, the trigger event to the overall process is receiving a bill. Note that when we talk about the Expense Payment Process as outlined in the scenario, we are talking about a small part of this grand process of disbursements. In fact, the Payment by Check Request is only part of one of the processes that makes up Disbursements. However, this fine-tuning of the process—finding the level of best analysis—is often what is necessary to get to the root of a problem.

PROCESS TIME LINES

Development of the initial storyboard for the business can now begin as the major processes or acts have been identified. These should be relatively high-level processes—the major acts—and may include many scenes within each process. Visually depicting the chronology of the processes under review in a rough time line is the first step. This can be accomplished with a Business Process Time Line Work Sheet (see Exhibit 3.2). This work sheet is designed to show how the customer experience processes lead from the first trigger event to the last. It also is used to show how transparent processes support the customer experience. Accordingly, the first processes recorded should be the customer experience processes.

What is the first event in which the customer is involved? What is the last event? These visible events make excellent bookends for the time line. In our example, customer inquiry is the starting point and termination of service is the ending point. Between these you can list the processes included in the Process Identification Work Sheet (see Exhibit 3.3).

Now ask, are there other invisible events that the customer does not see that really start the process? One example might be the hiring of employees. If we do not have employees, the solicitation process cannot begin. So before the business can begin, it

Exhibit 3.2 Business Process Time Line Work Sheet

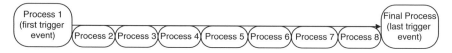

66

Exhibit 3.3 Visible Process Time Line
(Customer Perspective)

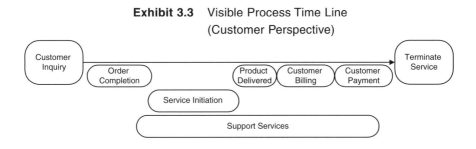

must hire employees. This business also uses call centers for customer inquiries. Therefore, there must be a process for purchasing or renting office space and for maintaining that space. Before there can be a response to an advertisement, that advertisement must be designed and distributed. There must be a sales and solicitation process in place to accomplish these objectives. Finally, some processes may be administrative and have their own unique time lines. For example, financial reporting may be done on a fiscal year basis. The gathering of and reporting on financial data is another process.

Another good way to identify transparent processes is to look for gaps in the customer experience processes. As discussed before, there is a gap in the process between purchasing the phone and receiving the phone. This is the result of transparent processes that must be completed before the next customer experience process. These may be shown on the time line by leaving gaps in the initial customer experience time line. Below that time line, the transparent processes that fill the void can be shown.

Those processes that are not specifically part of the overall customer experience should begin on separate lines. If possible, they should be placed to show how they relate to the customer experience. For example, advertising and sales actually occur before the customer makes first contact and should be placed accordingly. Employee hiring occurs throughout the experience, providing support at every stage. This should also be shown graphically.

Within these supporting processes, identify those that are dependent on the completion of another process for a beginning and show these linked together next to each other in the time line.

An attempt should be made to capture all the major processes relating to the particular business or segment of the business being reviewed. This should include visible processes and transparent processes. Exhibit 3.4 shows an example of a Business Process Time Line Work Sheet that includes all processes that are required to support potential customer solicitation, to obtain and support actual customers, and finally to terminate the customer relationship.

Exhibit 3.4 Comprehensive Business Process Time Line Work Sheet

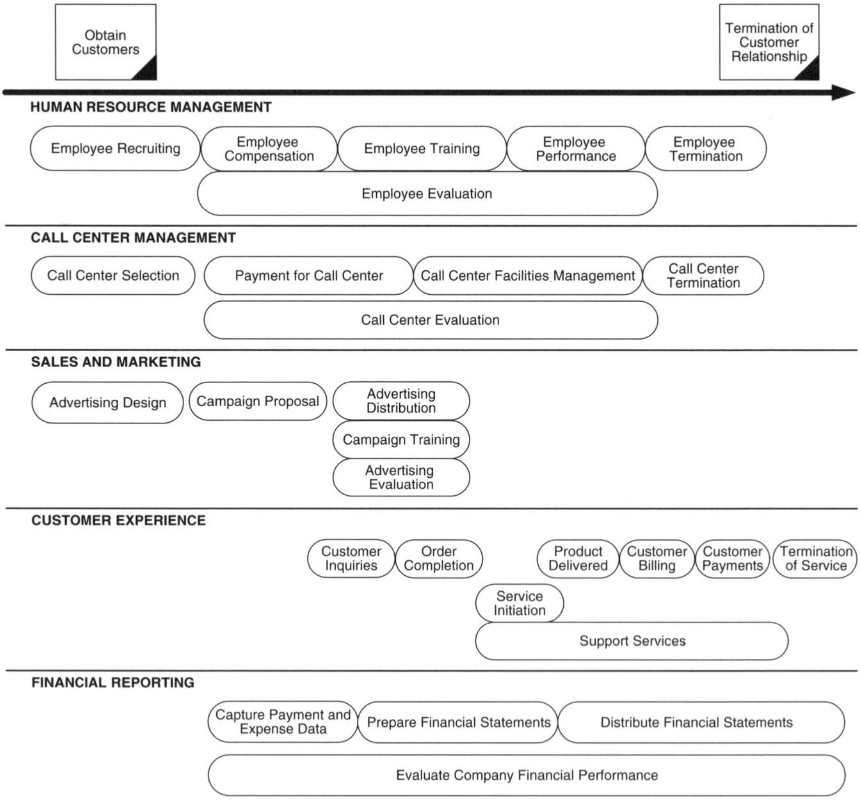
Obtain Customers
Termination of Customer Relationship
HUMAN RESOURCE MANAGEMENT
Employee Recruiting
Employee Compensation
Employee Training
Employee Performance
Employee Termination
Employee Evaluation
CALL CENTER MANAGEMENT
Call Center Selection
Payment for Call Center
Call Center Facilities Management
Call Center Termination
Call Center Evaluation
SALES AND MARKETING
Advertising Design
Campaign Proposal
Advertising Distribution
Campaign Training
Advertising Evaluation
CUSTOMER EXPERIENCE
Customer Inquiries
Order Completion
Product Delivered
Customer Billing
Customer Payments
Termination of Service
Service Initiation
Support Services
FINANCIAL REPORTING
Capture Payment and Expense Data
Prepare Financial Statements
Distribute Financial Statements
Evaluate Company Financial Performance

By defining the beginning and ending events and the inter-relationship of processes, we have set the overall boundary or frame for each process. You can see at a glance how one process may depend on another.

CUSTOMER EXPERIENCE ANALYSIS

A customer-focused business wants to make sure that the customer has a starring role in each and every part of the story. For generic business processes such as marketing, sales, customer service inquiries, or customer billing, it is easy to understand that relationship.

Other processes, however, have a direct impact on a customer's satisfaction, albeit in less obvious ways. While there is no direct interaction with the customer, areas such as quality of products or services delivered are affected by these processes. These critical supporting roles can determine if your customer is really a star or a mere extra on the set. Areas such as asset management, distribution management, facilities management, supplier management, employee management, and training all indirectly affect the relationship with the customer.

Let us take a look at how understanding the overall customer experience processes, along with the supporting processes, can give us a better understanding of the customer's role in our movie. Billing is always a critical interaction point with customers. As mentioned before, it is the point at which the customer makes a real decision about the value of services versus the expense. If the billing process itself goes wrong, businesses run the risk of losing customers immediately. Consider purchasing a cellular phone:

Scene 1: The sale. A customer phones an 800 number to purchase a cellular phone. After discussions with the customer representative, she decides to purchase a phone with free long distance—250 minutes a month free—for $49.95 a month. The order is reviewed with the representative. The customer representative activates the phone and inputs the details of the sales transaction into the computer.

Scene 2: Preparation of the customer bill. A computer-generated bill is prepared once a month. The date is based on the original sales transaction. The amount is based on the initial agreement plus the actual minutes used.

Scene 3: Delivery of the customer bill. Bills are mailed 20 days before the due date to the address on the original sales transaction.

Scene 4: Accepting customer payments. Customers can make payments at the retail outlet, by mail using the return envelope provided in the bill, by phone using a credit card, or on the Internet using a credit card.

Scene 5: Recording customer payments. Payments received at the retail outlet are posted at the close of the business day. Payments received by mail are posted the day after they are received. Payments accepted over the phone are posted two days after they are received. Internet payments are posted two days after they are verified.

Now we will look at a comedy of errors that we want to edit from our movie:

Outtake 1: The customer traveled frequently and relied heavily on the cell phone for contact with the office. At a critical time, she went to make a call and could not get out. When she phoned the customer service department, she was told that the phone was disconnected because of nonpayment of her bill. She stated that she had not yet received her initial bill. On further review, it was discovered that her billing address had been incorrectly input and she had never received her initial bill.

Outtake 2: When the customer received the bill, it was for $250 for two months. She was expecting to pay $49.95 and again phoned the customer service department for an explanation. They informed her that "free long distance" was not available from her calling area. While her base fee was still $49.95 a month, she would be charged a roaming fee unless she was calling from a specified city. She also learned that she was being charged for call-waiting, which she had not ordered. Customer service informed her that she must pay the full amount by the 15th of the month to keep her service.

Outtake 3: The customer decided to use the Internet to pay her bill. She logged onto the site on the 15th, made her payment by credit card, and logged off. She went to use her phone the next day and again it was not working. The customer service representative informed her that her payment would not be posted until the next day.

Exit—stage right!

While the customer was ultimately lost as the result of problems with the billing process, the real problems initiated with what should be a transparent process—order completion. The company's failure to ensure the accuracy of transaction inputs caused two potentially lethal problems: (1) failure to receive an initial bill and (2) inaccuracies in the bill. From the customer's standpoint, she only knows that she provided someone in the company with all the information necessary. This included the required service and the information about who she is and where she wanted the bill sent. The incorrect input from the order fed directly to the preparation of the customer bill and directly impacted the delivery of the customer bill. These processes should be invisible or transparent to the customer. However, the process became visible to the customer because of a failure in performance.

In analyzing this situation, it may be that sales representatives are measured by the number of calls they process and not on the accuracy of information recorded. On the one hand, the company is trying to measure customer success—the ability to get to customers' calls quickly. On the other hand, it has not looked at the entire customer service picture. In this case, the measure of success is contributing to the flow of inaccurate information. If the customer service representatives were measured on the number of correct transactions or were penalized for errors made in the original order entry process, a different outcome may have been realized.

Rather than being a billing problem, the final outtake occurred because of an informational issue. The customer was not informed when payments were actually recorded. Perhaps warning language could have been provided on the Internet site, explaining when payments would be posted. Perhaps the customer service representative needed additional training to recognize that the method of payment might increase the danger of service interruption. But each of these issues places the responsibility on the customer. And no matter how much the company would like to blame the customer, it all finally results in customer dissatisfaction and the potential loss of that customer. The customer's role in each and every scene, each point of interaction, must be critically analyzed to ensure that the company is accomplishing its objectives.

Let us look at the claims reporting process in the same way. The customer will be lost because of this process, but it is really the supporting processes that cause the problem. In an effort to ensure that claims representatives are fully trained, the company has made the decision to have them specialize. However, the result is that the customer has to turn in the claim to an agent, the customer cannot talk to anyone but a claims representative once it has been turned in, and as soon as the claim becomes complicated, another expert comes in to slow down the process more. This focus on the supporting process of training has caused the company to lose sight of what the training is meant to achieve—better claims service. In the example, there are additional support processes that need improvement—the customer service training of the receptionist, the availability of employees empowered to handle the steps of the process (the agent and the claims representative), and the use of the dreaded answering machine. In such situations, it is not uncommon to see a company blame the customer for not understanding its procedures. But customers do not pay for procedures, they pay for results. Transparent processes that become visible only inhibit customer satisfaction.

In the expense payment scenario, we see some of the same things. To the customer (in this case, the company's employees), the visible aspects of the process are submitting the request and receiving the check. In an effort to make a better controlled or more streamlined operation, the company has lost sight of who the customer is. Again, the focus is on measurements that are important to the processors but not to the customer. It is often a problem in companies that internal customers are ignored. It is true that the internal customer is less important than the external customer, but there should be ample reason to put the needs of one internal customer below that of another. In this instance, it is true that the customer is not likely to take his business elsewhere. It is likely, though, that a more expensive option may occur — employees may go to a company where they can get their expenses reimbursed more easily.

RECAP

The first step in identifying processes involves identification of trigger events. However, identifying these critical triggers and the associated processes requires viewing them from an external perspective, not an internal perspective. This means walking in the shoes of your customers and understanding your business processes from their perspective. Look for those events that lead to interaction with the process.

Trigger events may be thought of as "moments of truth." These are the episodes in which the customer comes into contact with any aspect of the company and forms impressions of the company's quality of service. While these moments of truth are not in and of themselves positive or negative, the customer's experience with the company—the sum of all customer interactions—makes the experience positive or negative. One negative event can outweigh all other positive moments. Identifying these trigger events will lead to the most critical processes. The Process Identification Work Sheet can be used to capture this information.

The next step is to identify the supporting processes. When customers perceive the company, they do not see all the processes. In fact, they do not see most of them. Underlying the customer experience processes are a multitude of transparent processes. These transparent processes are necessary for the customer process but must not interfere with them. When a transparent process becomes exposed, it may result in a negative event— the type of negative event that makes the overall experience negative.

Once all processes are identified, they must be named. While this may seem a trivial task, it is often the first time anyone in a company has been required to think of what the actual processes are. Some names will be obvious, whereas others will take creativity and a lot of negotiation.

The next step is to prepare a Business Process Time Line Work Sheet. This is a graphic representation of the major processes, including how they interrelate and support each other. It can be thought of as a broad overview process map. It should include the starting and ending events for the process, visible and invisible processes, and dependent and independent processes. These will help focus the review on the areas most sensitive to customer needs.

The basic steps in process identification are:

1. Identify the trigger events.
2. Identify the customer critical processes.
3. Identify the supporting processes.
4. Name the processes.
5. Prepare the broad overview process map.

Once processes have been identified, it is time to start summarizing the information that has been gathered about the process so far and to start developing plans for gathering additional detailed information about each process.

KEY ANALYSIS POINTS

Keep an External Perspective

Throughout the analysis process, from the moment you take on the engagement to the moment you leave, you must think like the customer, not like the company. The failure of many reviews occurs because the reviewer approaches the problem just as the company did, and that usually means ignoring the customer's perspective. "If you are not serving the customer, you had better be serving someone who is" is as true for the reviewer as it is for the employees.

"Moments of Truth"

Identify each and every time the customer comes into contact with the company. Every one of these is a moment of truth, the chance for the company to make a lifelong ally or enemy. If these are not adequately identified, the real value of underlying processes may never be known.

Measure the Right Things

Make sure that measurements are focused on the customer, not on the company. For a company to be successful, its measures of success must relate to customer satisfaction. Do not be fooled by measurements that claim to support customers but still look only at internal processes. You get what you measure. If that measure is focused internally rather than externally, you measure only internal success. Ultimately, the measures of success must be geared to reach the overall objectives.

Supporting Processes Must Be Transparent

Look for supporting processes that are inhibiting the success of critical customer processes. There are a large number of internal processes that are necessary for a company's success, but they can never be more important than the key customer processes. As soon as these processes begin to intrude, they become visible. If it is not important to the customer, it need not (and should not) be seen. When you find a transparent process that has become visible, you have found one of the focal points of your review.

NOTES

1. Karl Albrecht, *At America's Service* (New York: Warner Books, 1992), p.26.
2. *Ibid.,* p.27.

CHAPTER 4

Information
Gathering

The fog of information can drive out knowledge.

—Daniel J. Boorstine, Librarian of Congress

WHAT YOU NEED TO KNOW
AND WHERE YOU GO TO LEARN IT

Before performing any detailed review of the process, the reviewer must gather as much background information as possible. If we were Walt Disney's animators trying to put together that first storyboard, we would need to reaffirm and establish our understanding of each scene. Disney knew what actions should take place in every section of the movie. He knew which characters were playing in each scene, what each character should do, and what he wanted to accomplish with each action. Those attributes are what he showed his animators while acting out the movie, but one exhibition was not enough (just as one discussion will not tell you everything that is happening in a process). Before the animators could start the storyboard, they talked with each other and went back to Disney to better understand what made up the movie.

Process reviewers must also have a complete understanding of the business movie they are reviewing before they try to put together a process map. Just like Disney's animators, they have heard the story, but now they must go back and piece together information to capture the essence of the process.

Information gathering occurs from the first moment you consider analyzing any process and continues throughout the completion of the mapping process. A thorough understanding of the process under review is critical to the success of any Process Mapping project. However, it is almost like coming in as the movie is being filmed—without the benefit of understanding how it was developed. And to make things worse, there usually is no one "director" in charge of the process, someone you can approach to understand the master plan. The result is that people involved in one action may not have any idea what is going on in the entire scene. The answers lie in bits and pieces of each act and scene and in the actions taken in those scenes. The reviewer must start assembling the story as information unfolds one piece at a time, much like putting together a jigsaw puzzle.

The challenge for the reviewer is to determine where the resources are that will provide the entire picture. To do this, someone with a good overview of the entire process must be found. It may be difficult, especially if functional or departmental lines are crossed as the process occurs, but it must happen to get an effective start on Process Mapping. Therefore, managing the information gathering process begins by identifying the individuals who own the whole process. These process owners have both the responsibility and the authority to affect the processes under review. They will be your key resource and are most likely your key customers in the Process Mapping engagement.

If the company is not organized around processes, you may find it a bit difficult to determine who actually owns an individual process. There may be a multitude of owners and little or no accountability for the entire operation. Process owners may be somewhat elusive. A collaborative effort on the part of the reviewer and company management personnel is necessary to develop an accurate picture of the processes under review.

PRELIMINARY INFORMATION

Any analysis of processes requires a systematic methodology for gathering and documenting information. There are many possible approaches, but this is the approach that has worked best for us:

- Identify the process (see Chapter 3)
- Describe the process
- Identify the process owners or unit owners
- Interview the process owners or unit owners:
  —Verify your understanding of the process
  —Determine the business objectives
  —Determine the business risks
  —Determine the key controls
  —Determine the measures of success

While each step is somewhat dependent on information from a previous step, it is not always possible or practical to gather this information in a linear fashion. Information about process measurements, for example, may become available before process owners are identified. The reviewer must be aware of the information requirements in each step and be alert for information sources.

The goal is to use your information sources in the most efficient manner. As you gather information, you will need buckets to put it in. The work sheets described in this chapter are your sorting buckets for the different bits of information you will be getting. At the beginning of the project, the reviewer should establish a set of blank and partially completed work sheets to store key information as it is received.

You will be putting together this puzzle one piece at a time, sorting out the straight-edged pieces to get some framework around your story; sorting out the colors to identify the pieces of each part of each scene; and sorting out the shapes to find the pieces that interlock. Unfortunately, you do not yet have the box top that shows the puzzle picture. Rather, the picture is emerging before your eyes as the pieces come together.

PROCESS IDENTIFICATION

The first bit of information gathered is at the macro level. As described in Chapter 3, the reviewer is trying to identify what processes are involved in a given business or function. Individuals with a good understanding of the overall business operation — executives and managers — are the best sources for this type of information. It may be beneficial to have joint meetings with people who represent a good cross section of the business when attempting to identify key processes. Face-to-face meetings are preferable. Maybe most important, sufficient time should be set aside. This meeting can easily take half a day.

The reviewer should definitely facilitate this session, helping to identify triggers and categorize processes as discussed in Chapter 3. While the owners of the process have the best understanding of what is occurring, they probably do not have an understanding of the framework the reviewer is trying to establish. By facilitating the session, the reviewer can ensure that the outcome matches the needs of the review without forcing a particular result.

PROCESS DESCRIPTION OVERVIEW

After major processes are identified, a complete description of each process should be prepared. The Process Description Overview summarizes all business processes by name and basic definition. The simple two-column form consists of the Process Name and the Process Definition.

These processes are the major acts in the business movie. The process names should have been determined during the process identification phase, and now descriptions should be developed. Each description should include enough information to determine where the process begins, where the process ends, and what major actions occur in the process. A partially completed work sheet based on the cell phone example from Chapter 3 is shown as Exhibit 4.1.

There are some interesting things to note from this example. In general, the beginning and end of each process are evident from the description. However, Service Initiation presents a different case. Because this process is significantly broader than its description might imply, the end is specifically identified in the description. Without the extra information stating that the process ends upon delivery, it would be easy to assume that the process includes only actual initiation of the service.

The Phone Support Services process is unique in that it is really an amalgam of many processes. Rather than try to identify all the processes that might be included in Phone Support Services, the reviewer has chosen this broad definition. This could imply that the various services will not be reviewed in depth, or it may be intended to allow additional flexibility in the review of the area. This process is also unique in that its start and end points are defined with the phrase "monthly usage." The same type of situation is reinforced by the use of the phrase "appropriate day of the month" in Customer Billing. Finally, the Customer Payment

Exhibit 4.1   Process Description Overview

Area being reviewed:	
Process Name	**Description**
Customer Inquiries	Call center employees receive inquiries from potential customers, providing requested information.
Order Completion	Upon the customer's acceptance of the company's terms, call center employees record sales transactions into the company order receipt system.
Service Initiation	The service department receives the customer order from the call center to initialize service based on product and features ordered by the customer. This process ends with the delivery of the product and service to the customer.
Phone Support Services	The unique usage of the product and services by the customer on a monthly basis.
Customer Billing	On the appropriate day of the month, the system mechanically issues a bill to the customer.
Customer Payment Process	The customer makes payment to the company by mail, phone, or Internet.
Termination of Services	If payment is not received by a predetermined date, or at the customer's request, service is terminated.

Process uses a definition that helps point out the various modes of payment available—mail, phone, or Internet.

All these nuances are intended to enhance the reviewer's understanding of the process and help others who may look at the supporting work to better understand what has been accomplished.

These descriptions may be revised as additional information on each process is gathered.

IDENTIFYING THE PROCESS OWNERS

During the initial meetings, you should have been able to identify the major processes. At the same time, you also should have obtained a good understanding of who the process owners are. In fact, you probably have been speaking with some of them. Creating a visual image of the key processes and associated owners helps the reviewer better understand how the people who own those processes relate to overall operations. A Process Owner Chart is the perfect vehicle to accomplish this.

The Process Owner Chart may pertain to the entire business or to only a specific area of operation. The reviewer should begin only with process owners and then create additional charts "drilling down" to the unit owners. If the operation is relatively simple, the reviewer may develop one chart that includes both process owners and unit owners.

You probably will be unable to name all the processes when you begin the project, and, accordingly, you will not know all the owners. But as you gather information, the picture will become clearer as more and more owners become apparent. The people identified in the Process Owner Chart should be process owners — the individuals ultimately responsible for the overall process. Depending on the circumstances, this can be a one-to-one, a one-to-many, or a many-to-one relationship.

In Exhibit 4.2, the first node identifies the operation under review (XYZ Operations in the example). Separate nodes are then created for each process (Processes A through D). Again, at the beginning you may not have these all identified, but start with what you know and add information as you gain it. The major

Exhibit 4.2   Process Owner Chart

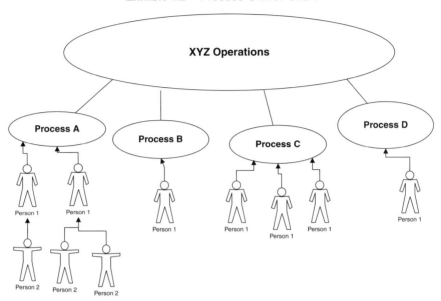

process owners are listed next (Person 1 in the examples). You also may need to identify subordinate owners if appropriate. These should not be unit owners (these will be identified as part of the individual process data-gathering effort) but should be individuals involved in complicated processes who work as "deputies" to the process owners.

The exhibit shows the situation that might occur when processes cross functional lines. Processes B and D are all contained within one function and have only one owner (a one-to-one relationship). These also could be within the same function, and the owner could be the same person (a many-to-one relationship.) Process A covers two areas and Process C covers three areas, resulting in two and three separate owners, respectively (a one-to-many relationship).

The Process Owner Chart can be completed using any basic flowcharting or drawing software. A traditional organization chart structured by process can also be used as a Process Owner Chart, but it is important to remember that the identity of true owners may not be obvious. The goal of the chart is to be able to see at a glance what processes are involved and who owns them.

To make best use of an individual's time, as thorough an identification as possible should be completed before any detailed data gathering. This way, if an individual is responsible for more than one process, appropriate questions can be addressed on each process at the time of the data-gathering interview.

MEETING WITH THE PROCESS OWNERS

Meetings should now be held with the highest-level individual involved in the process or processes under review. It may be a good idea (depending on the politics of the situation) to have all the reviewers who will be involved included in the initial meeting. In fact, it is important to have all reviewers involved in all aspects of the project. This helps ensure a team approach, makes sure all clients know everyone involved, and helps build trust with all participants. Most important, however, it allows the reviewers to better understand the broad perspective, which results in a better evaluation.

Some of the objectives of this meeting may have already been accomplished during the process identification phase. If they have not, however, the meetings must be established. Discussions should include the objectives of the mapping project, the approximate time frame in which the project will be completed, and the names of individuals who will be included in the project. This also is the point at which the reviewer can begin to obtain information on the process owners and subordinate process owners, business objectives, business risks, measures of success, and key controls (these last concepts are discussed in more depth later.) The reviewer also should request that process owners be notified about the details of the project, including when they should expect to be contacted by the reviewer.

Interviews should now be conducted with process owners, subordinates, and eventually unit owners. Discussions should again include the objectives of the mapping project, the approximate time frame in which the project will be completed, and the names of individuals who will be included in the project. In addition, the process owner should be informed which units will be the focus of the review and approximately how much time the reviewer will be spending in each unit. An indication of the amount of time expected to be spent with each employee should also be given.

The reviewer now starts obtaining contact information and specific information about the process from the process owner and subordinate process owners, including business objectives as perceived by the process owner, business risks, measures of success, and key controls. At this point, the reviewer also starts obtaining information about specific steps in the processes. While it is not time to start the actual map, the reviewer should be aware of this and record the information to be used in the map generation phase.

Some of these meetings may be held with groups of clients. For example, the highest-level owner may be included with the process owners. This will make for a longer single meeting, but it should be quicker than a group of individual meetings. It is also a good time to hammer out differences the owners may have in their understanding of what makes up the process.

During one initial meeting, we began discussing our understanding of the primary processes in an operation. The department head was new and was looking for us to help him gain an understanding of the entire operation. We had the department head and his four managers in the meeting. We explained what we saw as the first major process, and everyone agreed. We explained what we saw as the second major process, and there was general agreement, although one manager looked uncomfortable. We explained what we saw as the third major process, and a riot ensued. What we had found was that, although three of the managers had identical operations, the processes were being done three different ways. When we left that meeting, we had identified the differences and reached an agreement on how each was running. We also received the thanks of the department head, who was finally beginning to understand why there was no consistency in his department.

Ultimately, the information obtained from process owners may or may not agree with the information provided by the high-level process owner, but it is important to resolve these differences immediately. If conflicting information is obtained, identify the sources and document all the issues. All individuals involved in the review (the client and the reviewer) must approach the project using the same metrics. If there is already disagreement on something as basic as, for example, objectives, the project may be doomed to failure. The discrepancy probably will be a significant portion of a final report, but the reviewer cannot wait for that report before discussing the information. Only with agreement by all major parties can the reviewer have a basis for the review that will be accomplished.

If process definitions have been developed, review these with the process owners and the subordinate process owners. If they have not yet been developed, a portion of these meetings should be used to identify and define the processes.

Units and unit owners will generally be identified during your discussions with the process owners. Once their identity has been revealed, the Process Owner Chart can be revised to include the individual unit owners. If there are too many owners to make this practical, a separate chart for each individual unit may be necessary. As stated before, the goal of the Process Owner Chart is to visually depict each process owner, the units in each process, and the unit owners of each unit. Including all unit owners will only make this understanding more complete. When completing the chart, remember that one process owner may head a few units or all of them.

By now you should have created a visual diagram of the ownership relationships. This will help you determine who you need to talk to about different issues. Exhibit 4.3 shows a combined Process

Exhibit 4.3   Combined Process Owner/Unit Owner Chart
EXPENSE PAYMENT PROCESS

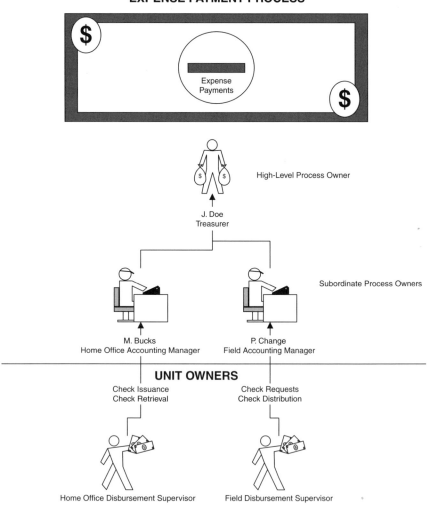

88

Owner/Unit Owner Chart for the Expense Payment Process introduced in Chapter 1.

In this exhibit, the Treasurer is the owner of the expense payment process. Within that process are two subordinate process owners, the Home Office Accounting Manager and the Field Accounting Manager. In this instance, the subordinate owners reflect different aspects of the payment process—home office and field. Within this process are the units that make up payment of "All Other" expenses. For the home office, there is one unit owner—the Home Office Disbursement Supervisor. For the field office there are 11 unit owners—one Field Disbursement Supervisor for each office.

WHAT TO TALK ABOUT

Some of the points to be covered in the owner interviews have been mentioned and discussed in depth already. These include the process name, process description, triggers, and process or unit owners. However, there are some additional areas that must be included in the interview that are a core consideration when analyzing the process. These are the areas that everyone must understand and have a basic agreement on.

Business Objectives

In talking with owners, one of the primary questions the reviewer should ask is "What is the process trying to accomplish and how does that tie to the theme of the business?" As discussed earlier, every movie has an underlying plot or theme. Each act within the movie and every scene within the act has a purpose or objective that supports the overall theme. In the same way, every business has key strategic objectives that it is trying to accomplish. Every business process should support one or more of those key strategic objectives. If any one process does not, it may not be warranted and may need to be eliminated. Even if it does support a strategic objective, a complicated process may be supporting one of the less important objectives and may represent a waste of resources. The true success or failure of a process can be determined only if specific, measurable objectives are identified that tie in with the company's strategic objectives.

If management does not specifically identify objectives, processes may be completed based on employees' perceptions of what the right thing to do is. The reviewer must understand what the process owners expect from that process and what they expect the process to achieve. Then the reviewer must determine if the process owner's goals and objectives conflict with the company's strategic goals and objectives. More often than not, the goals for a process (or unit) may have been developed at a high level and then passed down. However, when passed down, the intent of those goals (how they tied in with the company's strategic objectives) usually is not included.

Without a firm understanding of the true objectives, these differing perceptions result in inconsistent low-level objectives. The high-level owner may have an objective of making a certain profit while delivering a certain level of customer service (a very common objective). However, if the subordinate owner has heard only the need for profit and interpreted this to mean that costs should be cut, there is a miscommunication. Thinking that the primary objective is reduced costs, the subordinate owner may be eliminating costs that turn out to be essential to the performance of the process. By putting policies in place that fly in the face of a true profit objective (it takes money to make money), the subordinate owner has undercut the success of the process.

In one of our first attempts to apply objectives to processes, we learned how seldom numerical objectives are actually given in strategic terms. Before reviewing a claims office, we spoke with senior executives about the claims department's objectives. They were very simple and straightforward—objectives such as ensuring that our claimants' lives were restored to order and maintaining the highest quality staff. We had no problem assigning these objectives to the major processes we had identified. We then began working with the manager. Again, we started with a discussion of his objectives. He provided his objectives for the year, and we went on our merry way. Once we looked at what was provided, we were very disappointed. What we received were the statistical numbers for which he would be held responsible. Examples included return all phone calls within 4 hours, set up all files within 24 hours, and use computer-generated letters for all correspondence. There were also some very esoteric goals such as placing an emphasis on outside education, increasing teamwork between claims offices, and improving communication with the sales force. Immediately, you can see that there are either no measures of success for these goals or that the measurements may not be available. We discuss measures of success later in this chapter, but it was painfully apparent as we reviewed these measures that there was no context for the goals. Each had the same weight and each stood alone. Even when we talked with the manager, he had no understanding of how these supported the strategic objectives of the company. He only saw that he had to meet all these goals.

This shows that it can sometimes be a bit difficult to match goals and objectives at the process level to the overall objectives. For advertising, a business strategic goal may be to maximize sales. It is very easy to see how a process-specific objective of increasing sales in a certain target market by 20 percent in six months helps support this. However, the process of customer inquiries would have the identical business strategic goal of maximizing sales—in this case through superior customer service.

The process objective could be answering calls in 2 rings; answering 45 calls per hour; or a goal established based on the number of sales per hour or day. The tie-in to the strategic goal is less obvious and shows how important it is to make sure that the people responsible for the goals understand why that goal exists. In particular, the first two measures can be reached without affecting sales at all. Only when customer service understands how those goals impact the overall strategic goal will their efforts be effective.

Again, we are starting to discuss measures of success a little prematurely, but to determine if people understand the reasons for objectives, it is important to see how measurements affect their perception. Different service results will be received, depending on the actual or perceived objective of the process. If customer service employees are measured on sales alone, simple customer inquiries may not receive the appropriate attention. If customer service employees are measured on number of calls per hour, each customer may not receive the attention he or she deserves. If customer service employees are measured on the quality of results, including required rework or complaints; representatives will take more care with each call. Unless given evidence to the contrary, people determine important objectives by how they are measured. The old saying "you get what you measure" (or what people perceive you are measuring) is very true. Conflicting goals and objectives can often be the root cause of a service breakdown.

Looking at the cell phone example, if maximizing sales is the main objective, customer service employees may have an incentive to add additional features that the customer did not order to boost the employee's sales numbers. They may also have an incentive to hurry through the process to get to the next order if accuracy is not part of the measure. In the customer billing process, a business strategic goal may be to maximize revenue with a billing objective of providing accurate bills to all customers by the 10th of each month. In this situation, a conflicting objective may be occurring in the Prospect Inquiry or Recording Sales Transaction process. If reps are paid by the numbers, not by accuracy or quality, billing errors may occur and go undetected. The billing process in isolation may be working perfectly; however, inputs to the process may be corrupted.

Taking business objectives down to the process level is not intuitive. We write business objectives and set budgets on a departmental basis, not normally at the process level. One department may be involved in phases of many different processes. Process objectives may be dictated by procedure or policy, or they may be set by management as a performance standard. Many people involved in the process do not have the slightest idea what the process is trying to accomplish or how their particular piece contributes to the overall picture.

Actors in the movie that is the business have been exposed only to their individual frames. They may play bit parts, walk-ons, one frame out of hundreds or thousands. They have never seen the entire scene or act, let alone the whole movie. They may have an idea what the movie is about, but they cannot provide you with many details. If these actors at least know about the scene, its purpose, and their motivation, they can help make sure that their performance is consistent with the whole movie. By providing clear process objectives, employees can know their motivation and provide performances consistent with the strategic needs of the company.

Likewise, the reviewer must understand these objectives and motivations to determine how each part of the process fits the big picture. Process Mapping facilitates the accomplishment of goals and objectives by providing a holistic, visual view of how the business processes individually and collectively fit together to achieve the desired results. By defining the business processes and associated objectives, the reviewer has an increased awareness of the different points of impact with the customer. The reviewer can more clearly see how action taken in one area may influence another—the plot of the movie is known, the scenes that are a part of the movie, and how those scenes support the plot. Even if you as a reviewer go no farther than this point—never creating a single process map—you would be ready to help your clients handle their business in the future by having identified clearly each process and associated objective.

Business Risk

Once an understanding of the objectives has been accomplished, the next question to be asked is "What would prevent the accomplishment of the key business objectives?" Many processes are developed with the purpose of achieving some objective—making things go right. Often, however, very little thought is put into determining how the process should be developed to ensure that the objective is completed—making sure things do not go wrong. Process owners should be aware of the key business risks and have plans in place to address these risks. One value of working with the client to identify the key business risks is to ensure that they have thought about these risk issues.

The other purpose of this discussion is to help the reviewer spot issues related to the key business risks as maps are created. The goal is to have a process that eliminates or at least mitigates the business risks. For many Process Mapping projects, the reviewer will focus on efficiencies. Usually there is an implied understanding here that the key objective is reducing costs, and the risk is that processes will not run efficiently. Therefore, the reviewer is trying to address those aspects of the business. But looking only at efficiency is much like trying to watch a movie without sound and color—you get only part of the story, and the part you get is out of context.

While it is true that efficiency detection is a large benefit of Process Mapping, focusing on one risk hobbles the reviewer. Getting the full range of objectives is the first step, but getting the broad view of risks is the next step. Basic risks could include poor detection of fraud, customer dissatisfaction, low morale, and increased fines and penalties. These seem obvious and most reviewers would keep them in mind, but it is easy to get caught up in the "efficiency" paradigm.

One of the most obvious objectives is fraud prevention. In every company there are a number of processes in place that are intended to prevent or reduce fraud. Two-party controls are one of the most common. By the same token, any review will show that having two people involved in a process is less efficient than having one person involved. A pure efficiency review will suggest reducing the workforce. A review that encompasses all risks will recognize that the need to reduce fraud in this situation far outweighs the need for efficiency.

A mapping project's effectiveness is increased by including as many of the key objectives as possible, and the company's exposure to these risks is decreased if the mapping project has a broader focus than just efficiency. Working with the client to determine these risks helps everyone understand the exposures.

Key Controls

For each objective we have found the associated business risk. The next question is "What controls have been established within the process to ensure that these risks are eliminated or mitigated?" Process owners often understand their objectives and may even have an understanding of the risks to those objectives. They probably also have a thorough understanding of procedures in place within the process, but they have seldom made the connection between risks and procedures put in place to control those risks.

Unit owners are more likely to know what controls are in place because they will have a much more detailed knowledge about the process, but they may still not have made a connection with the risks involved. And individuals actually performing the process often do not have a clue about controls—they are just doing their job. This often means that the reviewer is the one who has to identify the existence, or lack of existence, of key controls. This represents a good opportunity to educate process owners about controls and how they help achieve objectives.

During discussions about key controls, reviewers may find that people have a misunderstanding of which controls are important. During a review of an accounting process, every person we spoke with could outline procedures on how the office made sure the check printer key was secure. There were procedures for when the manager was there, there were procedures for when the manager was not there, there were procedures for when the manager should use the key, and there were procedures for what type of lock should be used on the desk where the key was kept. This one aspect of the risk of loss from fraudulently issued checks was mitigated—and then some.

There also was a procedure requiring each supervisor to review a certain number of files for every employee on a monthly basis. Because these employees were given a great deal of autonomy, it was the only real review of supporting documentation. Much like the prior control, this review helped prevent fraudulently issued checks. However, it was also a key control to ensure that files contained all regulatory required documentation. Furthermore, since this provided the supervisors an opportunity to review the employee's work, it was an important control to ensure that all employees were receiving proper training. However, every single supervisor told us the same thing—there was not enough time to do the reviews.

The good news was that the check printer key was secure; the bad news was that it was being used to turn on a check printer that could be printing improper or unsupported payments. Because of the emphasis on the key as an important control, everyone in the office had lost sight of the importance of the file review as a control. This "key" control for three different areas had lost out to a control over a key.

It may be that the process owners or unit owners do not have a good feel for the key controls. The discussion should try to determine them as best as possible, but they may not have the detailed knowledge necessary. This question may go unanswered until mapping of the process begins. Once these key controls are determined, the reviewer can also use the mapping to determine if the key controls really are the important ones and to help determine if control breakdowns are occurring.

Measure of Success

Once we know the objectives, there is another important question to be asked, "How does the process owner measure the success of this process?" As was mentioned when discussing objectives, the process owner probably is measuring a number of areas, but there is not always a direct connection to strategic or even process objectives.

First, come to agreement on the existence of specific measures. If there are none, you will need to work with the client to determine what they think those measures should be. It is a better idea to try to develop some as the project goes on rather than complete it without any measures. This provides clients a new way to measure their own success, and provides a benchmark to eventually show the Process Mapping project's success.

This is the point at which you should start taking a hard look at these measurements. Again, misplaced measurements can be as detrimental as a lack of measurements. Make sure that the measurement in place matches the identified objectives, risks, and controls. As an example, we performed a review of an area that wanted to increase the number of independents marketing a product. The overall objective was an increase in sales, and there was a determination that more salespeople meant more sales. One of the business risks identified by the client was that the objective could not be reached with a stable or declining sales force. In discussions, they were unable to identify a true key control, although they cited numerous criteria that had been established to ensure that only quality candidates were accepted.

The measure of success was an annual net increase in the number of marketers. The measurement had been met for the past two years. We discussed the key controls with them in more depth, and they began to recognize that the controls they brought up dealt more with a customer service objective—providing customer service by ensuring contact with skilled individuals. Discussing this more, everyone realized that there was no measure for the existing sales force. In addition, while gathering statistics before developing the maps, we noticed that the number of independents removed from the marketing plan over the last two months of the year was almost zero. The department was successful in getting what it measured—a net increase in the number of bodies. However, this measure did not address the real key controls or the full business

The reviewer also should determine if information on the measures of success for the process is readily available. If reports are not readily available, determine if they can be extracted from other data. Remember that if you cannot readily obtain statistics that are required for measures of success, the process owner probably cannot determine if success has been met. In one process, a measure of success was maintaining or reducing the balance for outstanding receivables. However, discussions showed that the report containing this information had not been received for over six months. This raised two questions: (1) how was success actually being measured? and (2) if the information was not received for six months and no one noticed, was this a truly important measure?

Obtain the measure of success information as early in the review as possible. It will be helpful in discussions with process owners and unit owners. Also pay particular attention to cycle times that are measurements. As the map is developed, these cycle times will be identified and will become an integral part of the analysis.

Maybe most important, if measures of success have not been specifically defined, how do the process owners know when the process has failed? Sometimes success can be measured only by the absence of failure. Ultimately, it is imperative that the process owners and the reviewer know the measurements of success to know whether the process is working.

Which Came First, the Objective or the Risk?

It should be apparent from the previous discussions that these four areas do not exist in isolation. Discussion with the process owners, unit owners, and even line personnel will all touch on various aspects objectives, risks, controls, and measures. And these discussions will not flow directly from one to the next. It is the reviewer's job to ensure that the discussions stay somewhat on track while still getting as much information as possible. It is also necessary to ensure that all four questions are answered in as much detail as possible.

After the discussions are complete, the participants may not realize how much information they have given. The reviewer may also have a hodgepodge of information—a situation in which everything necessary was recorded; it is just a question of finding it. Therefore, it usually is a good idea to have another meeting with the entire group. The reviewer should sort through the information and provide a summary (as discussed in the next section) that shows everything that was agreed upon regarding these areas. It is one more chance to ensure that everyone is on the same page.

PROCESS PROFILE WORK SHEET

One of the most important work sheets you will put together is the Process Profile Work Sheet. This form will be created for each process under review. The work sheet is intended to be a centralized repository for the critical information obtained about the process. It will be completed in phases, as information is gathered from various process owners. This same form can be used to develop a profile of individual units in the process (a Unit Profile Work Sheet). Process-level work sheets should always be created (see Exhibit 4.4). In addition, unit-level work sheets should be done whenever mapping will be completed at the unit level.

This work sheet will help anchor the mapping process. A well-developed profile can also help focus the review on the most critical areas. One of the most difficult aspects of Process Mapping is determining how the details fit the whole picture. In Process Mapping it is easy for the reviewer to see only the individual shots in the movie, often out of context. The process profile helps the reviewer identify the context of that shot in the overall scene and act.

The following sections provide a description of each section of the work sheet.

Process Name and Number

The form provides a space for Process Name and Number. The Process Name developed in the process identification exercise should be used. It can also be useful to assign each process a number. This can facilitate the numbering of units, tasks, or actions

Exhibit 4.4   Process Profile Work Sheet

Process Name and Number	Process Owner

Description

Triggers
Event beginning:
Event ending process:
Additional events:

Input—Items and Sources

Output—Items and Customers

Process Units	Process Unit Owners

Business Objective(s)	Business Risks

Key Controls	Measure of Success

in documents to ensure that the reviewer understands what portion of the process is under review. They can also allow for easier cross-referencing of charts and work sheets maintained in the work papers. For example, the main process of paying other expenses may be process 1. Units of the process might include Field Office Prepares Request (1.1), Home Office Prepare Check (1.2), and Field Office Receives Check (1.3). The tasks for Unit 1.1 might be Complete Request (1.1a), Approve Request (1.1b), and so on. The numbering method should reflect the process–unit–task hierarchy.

Process Owner

The Process Owner field provides a space for listing the individual process owners by name and title. These should mirror the information recorded on the process owner chart. Reference information (e.g., phone numbers or a secretary's name) can also be included. If the work sheet is completed at the unit level, the unit owners should be listed.

Process Description

The process description should reflect the overview descriptions developed after the processes were named. These should be taken from the Process Description Overview developed during the first phase of the review, as discussed earlier in this chapter.

Triggers

Key triggers were noted in the Process Identification Work Sheet (see Exhibit 3.1). A process may include a number of trigger events. All of these events help explain what goes on in the process, but the most critical triggers are the events that begin the process and the events that end the process. Clearly outlining these triggers helps ensure that processes do not overlap and that a clear beginning and ending have been identified for each one. Very often, the trigger for one process is the final task or action from the prior process. Any additional trigger events should also be included. Additional triggers are significant actions that are required to keep the process going. They also may eventually be recognized as triggers for individual units and tasks.

As an example, the event beginning for Service Initiation (as defined in the Process Description Overview) would be the customer order being received by the service department from the call center. The event ending would be delivery of the product to the customer. Additional triggers might include contacting the client to set an appointment for delivery or, in a just-in-time environment, receiving the product for delivery.

Inputs and Outputs

At the very beginning we discussed the importance of inputs and outputs to the definition of a process. Identification of the key inputs in the process at this point—including the item and source of the item—helps clarify exactly what piece of information starts the process rolling. Both the item and the source of the input should be identified. In the Service Initiation example, the item that starts the process is the customer order form. The source of this form is the call center. Likewise, the key output from the process should also be identified, along with the main customer for the output. The customer for the output could be an external customer or an internal customer. This identifies what the process is supposed to produce. For Service Initiation, the output item is the cell phone ordered by the customer, and the customer is the service purchaser.

Looking at the definitions for the prior two sections, you can begin to see the difference between triggers and inputs. In general, triggers represent a process or event, whereas the input is an actual thing. For Service Initiation, the trigger for the beginning of the process is receiving the customer order. The input is the order itself. The trigger is an event that is the culmination of a prior process (as shown in the Process Description Overview). The input is an item that is the result (output) of the prior process. Understanding both is necessary to get the full effect of how a process begins and ends.

Process Units and Process Unit Owners

By this point there should be a good idea of the key units within the process. These can be recorded here. Take a look at the critical trigger events included as "additional events" in the Triggers section. These triggers are causing transformations during the process and can represent units within the process. Make sure that each unit represents a trigger and every trigger represents another unit. Also include the Process Unit Owners. If you are taking the Process Profile Work Sheet to a unit level (the Unit Profile Work Sheet), information will probably need to be gathered from unit owners to determine the tasks within the unit. The task information can then be recorded in this section.

Business Objectives

The business objectives determined in the meetings with process owners should be included here. There should be no more than two or three major objectives for the process being reviewed, and they should be stated in a fairly concise manner.

Business Risks

The risks recorded here should also be fairly high level. These may not have a one-to-one relationship to the previously listed objectives. However, if this correlation can be made, the information should be entered to reflect this. Completing this section will help the reviewer focus on all risks involved.

Key Controls

This section should include the key controls as agreed upon in meetings. There should be a much clearer correlation between objectives and controls or risks and controls. This should be made clear by the way the information is entered in the work sheet. Again, these should be fairly concise descriptions intended to give the reader a feel for the control, not the exact process steps.

Measure of Success

Finally, enter the agreed upon measures of success. These should be concise and specific. Maybe most important, they must be measurable. Do not fall into the trap of repeating objectives here. This is where the exact numbers that represent success or failure should be recorded.

Process Profile Work Sheet Summary

The Process Profile Work Sheet should be used as a work in progress. The reviewer should start with any initial assumptions and modify it as discussions occur. As each discussion takes place, the reviewer can go over the work sheet with the interviewee and make any necessary changes or additions. Bear in mind that the farther you go in the project, the less likely you should be to make those changes. You do not want the work sheet to strictly reflect what the last person you talked to said. Instead, it should reflect the consensus of discussions. Intermittently throughout the project you should go over the process-level sheets with the process owner and the unit-level sheets with the unit owners. This will accomplish two things. First, getting their agreement will validate your understanding. Second, it will help the owners begin to understand where misunderstandings are occurring.

Exhibit 4.5 is an example of a completed Process Profile Work Sheet for the Expense Payment Process.

This process would have been identified in an overall process identification exercise with Treasurer, J. Doe. At that meeting, basic units of the general disbursement process were identified and included payroll, expense payment, and refunds. If we were examining all of these processes, a separate Process Profile Work Sheet would be developed for each one. However, in our example the project is focusing on expense payment.

After identifying each of the disbursement units, the reviewer asks Mr. Doe to identify the owners of the various disbursement units. Mr. Doe identifies M. Bucks of Home Office Disbursements as the owner of the expense payment process. Mr. Doe has a general understanding of how the process works, but he defers the discussion regarding the description, triggers, and other process details to Mr. Bucks. Mr. Doe says his objectives for this process are to ensure that no one steals any money; that no inappropriate expenses are generated; and that all of the bills are paid promptly, accurately, and within the discount period. This information is entered in the Process Profile Work Sheet. From this, the reviewer is able to determine both the objectives and the initial business risks.

The reviewer then meets with M. Bucks, who is able to provide descriptions of the units involved in the process. These are added to the work sheet. She also points out that she is responsible only for check issuance and check retrieval. The check request and check distribution processes are the responsibility of P. Change, the Manager of Field Accounting. This owner is added to the process owner portion of the work sheet. At this point, M. Bucks

Exhibit 4.5 Process Profile Work Sheet

Process Name and Number	Process Owner
Expense Payment Process—EP	J. Doe—Treasurer M. Bucks—Mgr HO Disbursements P. Change—Mgr Field Accounting

Description

The process of paying for incurred business expenses other than travel and purchase order.

Triggers

Event beginning: Receive bill
Other events: Complete check request, obtain approval, submit request, issue check
Event ending process: Distribute check to employee or mail to payee

Input—Items and Sources

Bill/Invoice, or other support—employee

Output—Items and Customers

Reimbursement check—vendor

Process Units	Process Unit Owners
Check request	Field Disbursement Supervisor
Check issuance	Home Office Disbursement Supervisor
Check retrieval	Home Office Disbursement Supervisor
Check distribution	Field Disbursement Supervisor

Business Objective(s)	Business Risks
Prompt and accurate payment of valid, properly approved business expenses.	Fraudulent payments Delayed payments—missed discounts Customer dissatisfaction

Key Controls	Measure of Success
Segregation of duties—requester and approver—requester, issuer—issuer, retriever	All checks issued within 48 hours Utilization of early pay discounts Complaints about delays Absence of duplicate payments

and P. Change might be considered subordinate process owners or co-owners of the process.

M. Bucks used to be a field accounting manager and is very familiar with the field process. The reviewer obtains an overview of the process from M. Buck and is able to complete the Description, Triggers, Input, Output, and Process Units portions. Additional refinements to the work sheet are made after discussions with P. Change. This includes determining that one measure of success is that the home office will issue all checks within 48 hours.

Once these discussions are complete, a brief meeting is held with J. Doe, M. Bucks, and P. Change to discuss the work sheet and fill in additional details. In particular, the key control of segregation of duties is identified, along with the additional measures of success—use of early pay discounts, complaints, and identifying duplicate payments. There is some discussion about measurements to identify fraudulent payments (e.g., terminal digit analysis, data mining, or address analysis), but the owners think the controls are sufficient to limit the need for this measurement. With complete agreement on the work sheet at this stage, the reviewer can go on.

MEETING WITH THE UNIT OWNERS

Meetings should now be held with the individual unit owners. If a unit-level Process Profile Work Sheet is being completed, the same information discussed previously should be obtained from the unit owner. Even if a work sheet is not being completed, much of the same information should be obtained. At the very least, discussions should again include the objectives of the mapping project, reviewing the detailed information-gathering plan, the approximate time frame in which the project will be completed, determining the individuals who will be included in the project, and making final arrangements for the actual mapping inter-views. In addition, you will want to let the unit owner know which tasks will be the focus of the review and approximately how much time the reviewer will spend with each employee.

If work surveys are used, let the unit owner know when the surveys will be sent and what the expected turnaround time is for the surveys. (Work Surveys are explained in the next section.) Establish a plan for conducting the interviews, for example, one every two hours. Determine who will control the flow of inter-viewees.

Measures of success should be specifically discussed. The unit owner is more likely to have the actual data than the process owners, so determine if the information on the measures of success for the unit is readily available. If reports are not readily available, find out how the owner obtains data. Get the actual measurement data as early in the process as possible. It will be helpful in discussions with the owners and line personnel. If it is not readily available, determine if there are tests that can be per-formed at the time of mapping to verify the success or failure of the process.

WORK FLOW SURVEYS

The next step is to start determining the actual tasks and actions within the process. Unit owners and employees working for unit owners are the best source for this information, and that means the reviewer is beginning to enter the interviewing and mapping section of the project.

However, before actual interviews are started, the reviewer must get a feel for what each employee does. To facilitate this under-standing, a Work Flow Survey should be sent to all employees involved in the process under review (see Exhibit 4.6).

Exhibit 4.6   Work Flow Survey

We need the following information in order to complete a work flow study of your department. We are asking you to provide us with a summary of your job duties, as well as information on how you complete the individual tasks involved in your job. Please feel free to use additional copies of this form if one page is not sufficient. Thank you for your assistance.

Name:	Summary of Job Duties: (list general job duties here)	
Department:		
Title:		
Length of time in present position:		

Please provide information concerning specific tasks you perform.

Task	Work received from? (Dept., mail, phone?)	What specifically do you do? (How do you process your work?)	How long does the process take? (estimate)	Where does your work go when you are finished? (to another dept., customer, agent?)

The form is relatively simple, but it can reveal a wealth of information. The top section asks for basic information—the employee's name, job title, length of time in present position, and a quick summary of job duties. Then it gets into a little more detail. Employees are asked for information regarding the individual tasks they perform. This includes a basic name for the task, how they receive the work (from whom), what they do with it when they get it, the approximate cycle time, and to whom it goes when they are done.

This is an incredibly useful tool in the interviewing process. From the reviewer's perspective, it helps identify individuals who are involved in the process being reviewed and gives the reviewer an overview of what actions are being taken to perform the process. By including cycle times, the reviewer is already becoming aware of bottlenecks and other efficiency issues.

However, there also is great benefit to the employees. Initially, it helps take some of the mystery out of the process for employees. You also can see that the information is laid out in a way that gets everyone started thinking of their individual duties as processes. If employees have begun thinking in terms of processes, it makes the subsequent discussions and mapping go easier. The survey also shows employees that someone is actually interested in the work they do. This may be the first time anyone has asked them to outline exactly what they do for a living. Although the survey is meant to be an overview, some people react by becoming very detailed in the completion of the form. We often have people attach several extra pages to provide us with the best picture possible of their job.

Surveys should be sent out one to two weeks before they are needed. This will allow employees the time necessary to give the survey some thought and complete it fully. Also allow enough time for the reviewer to go over the surveys before conducting interviews. When surveys are returned, the reviewer should begin getting an understanding of the tasks and actions within the process, determine who actually performs those tasks (this could be different from the owners' understanding), and highlight any issues that must be pursued during the actual interviews.

Surveys can be customized to better reflect actions in a particular job. One survey may work well for clerical employees and another survey may work better for supervisory employees. For clerical employees, the reviewer is probably interested in the actual flow of work and the individual tasks. For supervisor, the emphasis is generally on known job duties, for example, approvals, training, supervision, budgeting, span of control, and other management functions. Rather than cycle times, a reviewer may be interested in the percentage of time management employees are spending on certain duties.

If an area has been reviewed before, the survey may emphasize known duties. As an example, we have used this approach to our claims office reviews for the past two years. A number of these reviews are conducted annually, so many of the basic processes are well known. In spite of what we think we know, a work flow survey is still important. In response to this, the survey sent to our claims representatives focuses on areas from which we know we need specific information. In general, tailor the survey to the individual and to your specific information needs. Examples of two surveys specifically tailored to claims processes are provided in Exhibit 4.7 and 4.8. Exhibit 4.7 shows a sample claims representative survey, and Exhibit 4.8 shows a sample for management employees. You can see how the same types of information are solicited, just in different formats.

DATA GATHERING

You may have noticed an interesting thing about our discussion. The title of this chapter is "Information Gathering," yet we have talked very little about getting any hard data. Obviously, the focus of information gathering is learning about the process. It is about sitting and talking with people. However, some basic data should be obtained before beginning the real interviewing process.

The first data to accumulate are any that match the measures of success. These should include not only the final statistics, but

Information Gathering

Exhibit 4.7 Claims Work Flow Survey—Claims Representative

We need the following information so we can complete a work flow study of your claims office. Please complete the information requested. If necessary, attach an additional sheet of paper.

Name:	Claim Type	Authority Levels by Type of Claim		
ID number:	APD	Reserve	Settlement	Negotiation
Title:	Liability			
Length of time in position:	Property			

Task	Action Taken
	Please provide the following information concerning how claims are processed
Assignment	When received? (times per day, week) How received? (fax, jacket file, paper file)
Investigation	Where is your investigative work documented? (field file, master file) If you use a field file, when is documentation transferred to the master?
Reserving	When are reserves established? How do you document your reserve request? (by memo, in the log) Who is your file routed to when you request a reserve? (Supervisor, secretary, input clerk?)
Additional Units	How do you request additional units on a claim? (by memo, in log, special form) Who approves the request? Who inputs the additional unit?
Subrogation	How is subrogation potential documented in your file? (Special form, log notes, stamp) What information do you gather for subrogation input?
Claim Settlement	Who is involved in the negotiation process for claims within your authority? (Explain when your supervisor would be involved and how.) How is the settlement amount approved? (on check request, in log, on settlement advise) Are checks returned to you for delivery? What happens after final payment is processed? (return the file to you, file to closed file area, file to supervisor)
File	How often are case reviews scheduled? What files are reviewed at case review? How often do you submit a status report on a file?

Exhibit 4.8   Claims Work Flow Survey—Management Personnel

We need the following information so we can complete a work flow study of your claims office. Please complete the information requested. If necessary, attach an additional sheet of paper.

Name:	Summary of Job Duties:			
ID:				
Title:				
Length of time in present position:				
Task	Work received from? (BCO personnel, mail, phone)	What specifically do you do? (How do you process your work?)	How long does the process take? (estimate)	Where does your work go when you are finished? (To someone in the office, to the customer?)
Assignments				
Reserving				
Claim Settlement				
Subrogation				
File Review				
Closings				
Quality Assurance				
Other (explain)				

also the data used to drive the results. Obtain historical information to get a sense for the trends. Also look for data that might be useful for additional measures of success—areas the reviewer thinks might be important but have not been identified by the client. In the expense payment example, the reviewer has some concerns about fraudulent checks that are not shared by the client. The reviewer may look for data that would be used as fraud identifiers (e.g., numerous checks to one address or a large number of checks in round dollar amounts).

It is always wise to obtain personnel statistics if they are available. Turnover ratios and employee tenure information can help show which processes may have the most problem, either because a large number of new employees work on the process or because problems in the process are resulting in job dissatisfaction. Newer employees can often be a great source of innovative ideas. They often are unafraid to ask the questions everyone else thinks have been answered. However, longtime employees have a broader view and may be able to help identify longtime systemic problems.

Also gather any information about accounts involved in the process. Take a look at current information as well as trends over time. Wildly fluctuating balances or accounts that suddenly grow may be representative of a process problem. Additionally, aging account balances will help show where processes may have gone wrong.

In general, any data should be gathered that would help provide a snapshot of the current processes. Gathering the information will also help the reviewer obtain a fuller understanding of the process.

RECAP

Information about a process will unfold a piece at a time. It is important to know what information you are going to need and identify who can provide you with the required information. Data must be gathered to:

- Identify and describe processes
- Identify process owners
- Identify units and unit owners
- Complete process and/or unit profiles

Data gathering plans should be developed for all phases of the process review.

To obtain the necessary information, meetings must be held with the process owners and unit owners. It usually is best to start with the highest-level owners and work down. Joint meetings—one at which a number of owners at various levels are present—can be very beneficial in ironing out differences in everyone's understanding of the process basics.

A large amount of information is required, but once the basic processes and their owners are established, some of the most important are:

- Business objectives (What is being accomplished?)
- Business risks (What can stop this from being accomplished?)
- Key controls (How are these risks mitigated?)
- Measure of success (How do they know they are successful?)

The reviewer must get agreement on these basic areas before proceeding.

Because there is so much information to be gathered, the following data-gathering tools should be used to document background information about the processes, units, tasks, and actions.

- Process Description Overview: An overview of all processes identified along with a brief description.
- Process Owner/Unit Owner Chart: A visual representation of all processes along with their owners and unit owners.
- Process Profile Work Sheet: A single repository of critical information regarding processes and units.
- Work Flow Surveys: An employee's synopsis of the work accomplished and tasks completed.

KEY ANALYSIS POINTS

Conflicting Business Objectives

If you are analyzing multiple processes, you may immediately see that the objectives of one process are in direct conflict with the objectives of another process. Even more critical, you may see that the objectives of one process are in conflict with the overall objectives of the company. Your maps then can help show how conflicting objectives are affecting the overall company performance.

Unknown Business Objectives

Another important aspect of business objectives is that they may not have been communicated clearly. Individual process or unit goals are often passed on to employees without the benefit of knowing how they fit to strategic objectives. In those instances, goals are often followed too literally. This can result in processes that focus on the wrong area or less important areas. Determine whether people understand why their goals exist and, make sure actions match the company's strategic direction.

Absence of Process Measures

The reviewer may find an absence of success measures. Maybe the process has always existed in isolation, without any real measure of success. If there is no success measure, maybe this process is not even necessary. The reviewer will need to spend some additional time understanding what value is being added by the process. The success measure for one process may also be defined by the input and output of the process or by the gap it fills between processes. Process owners may not recognize this dependency relationship.

As the pieces of the whole puzzle come together, the reviewer may begin to see clear measures of success that were not obvious to any of the owners.

Existence of Key Controls

Once risks are identified, it is a great time to go through the exercise of identifying key controls that help mitigate or eliminate the risk. This is a time to establish the process owners' ownership of controls. The reviewer can show them how the control may specifically address a risk. If no controls exist, the reviewer can begin looking for where controls are needed and determine how best to add them with the least effect on efficiency.

Clear Start and End Points

Try to identify very distinct start and end points and agree upon these with the process owners and unit owners before proceeding. If you do not, you may end up with overlapping processes that are hard to isolate. Furthermore, if the client has not made that distinction, there may be duplication at the process transfer points.

CHAPTER 5

Interviewing and Map Generation

Map defined: A conventionalized representation of spatial phenomena on a plane surface. Unlike photographs, maps are selective and may be prepared to show various quantitative and qualitative facts, including boundaries, physical features, patterns, and distributions.

—*The Columbia Encyclopedia*, Sixth Edition, 2001

CREATING THE STORYBOARD (FINALLY)

Let the fun begin! This is truly the most exciting, rewarding part of any Process Mapping engagement. This is the point at which all the information really begins to come together. While working with employees, you will see their excitement as a picture of the process evolves around them, their ideas are taken seriously, and they learn that someone cares about what they do for a living. In addition, you will find yourself inundated with ideas and solutions. Working on the first project, you will feel swamped and a little intimidated—it is tough trying to sort through all that information.

But you also will be amazed by how much you learn. And when all is said and done, you will feel exhilarated but wrung out—it is tough learning and synthesizing the tons of information you are about to receive.

The key to successful Process Mapping is the interview, and the key to a successful interview is creating an environment in which information can be openly shared. This type of environment comes from being prepared, being willing to spend some time talking to people in a nonthreatening environment, and being ready to listen.

Interviews for Process Mapping are not particularly different from any information-gathering interview. It is all a matter of planning, talking, and, above all, listening. But many Process Mapping projects fail for lack of these very things. It is important to revisit some of the basic rules of interviewing and see how they relate to Process Mapping.

GROUND RULES

Buy-In

The mapping project must have buy-in from the very top to be successful. Upper management must understand why the project is being completed and agree that the benefits outweigh the cost that results from employees spending "unproductive" time on the project. During the preliminary information-gathering phase of the review, the project should be explained to everyone you contact. Process owners and unit owners must understand who supports the project, why it is being done, what it is expected to accomplish, and how the project will be conducted. If any of the interviews must be handled at a site away from where the process owner resides, always have an individual meeting with site management before conducting any of the interviews. Treat that individual as you would any other process owner.

If possible, it is an excellent idea to have a floor meeting with the entire office before the project begins. This provides the opportunity to explain exactly what the project is about, why it is being done, and what it intends to accomplish. We also like to use the time to explain exactly what employees should expect when we interview them. This helps alleviate some of the fears that are inherent when an outsider comes in.

Setting Aside Adequate Time

The detailed map interview can take anywhere from 15 minutes for an individual involved in limited processes to three or four hours for key individuals involved in multiple processes. Be perfectly honest with people about the amount of time the interview could take. Longer interviews can be broken up, but be sure you set the two meetings relatively close together. If there is too large a gap between the meetings, there may be a lot of time wasted while you catch up to where you were.

There is a tricky balance here between the time to spend on each interview and the time available for the entire project. If you learn that interviews are taking longer than you first thought, you may find yourself having to make a choice between less information and more interviews and fewer interviews with more information. In a recent review, we had no more than two hours with each person. There was one section in which each employee handled a large number of different types of transactions—the interview easily could have taken five hours. The decision was made to ask each person what he or she thought the highest risk transactions were. The maps then focused on those transactions. It was interesting to note that most of the employees identified the same area, resulting in our completing maps of what were obviously the highest risk areas.

However, the interviews were still not long enough to get to some important aspects. In particular, we were unable to ask the employees what they specifically thought should be changed. This is a crucial question because employees can usually tell you exactly what is wrong with a process and how it can be improved. A number of significant opportunities were probably lost, but we accomplished what we could within the time available.

What this ultimately means is that the time availability will dictate the interview process. Remember that, as a reviewer, you are trying to fit into the employee's schedule—not he or she into yours. It is usually best to try to get one contact person in the department to act as a coordinator. This will usually be a manager or supervisor, but there may an informal leader to whom management will direct you. We will give them the list of people to be interviewed and ask them to bring them in as they are available.

Secure a Private Interview Area

If you want people to be candid, provide them with the privacy to speak without someone looking over their shoulder or listening to every word they say. Some people like to perform interviews at people's desk. They believe this is an area where the interviewee feels comfortable and can get to any information they may need as the interview progresses. However, this is usually counterproductive. First, working on the floor lends itself to far too many interruptions. We already talked about how scarce a resource time is, and setting yourself up for more interruptions will only make it worse. People also have a tendency to show you every piece of paper they touch as they perform their work. Part of the job of the interviewer is to sift through all the details the interviewee will provide and determine what is really important. Therefore, the interviewer must control the information that is received.

However, the most important reason for setting an interview session away from the floor is the feeling of privacy and intimacy. It is important that the interviewees feel they can tell you almost anything. They will know that the information is being used as part of a project that goes to management, but a private setting for interviews will help them feel that what they are saying is being held in some confidence.

Set a Friendly Tone

Set a friendly tone when conducting the interview. This should go without saying, but we have seen many people go into these interviews as though they had something to prove or had a big secret to discover. The participants should not be adversaries—they are working together to make the process better.

Start with some small talk—how long they have been with the company; anything personal you may know about them; or even chat about sports, the weather, or something that will put the interviewee at ease and let him or her know you are human. Spending five minutes talking about someone's children or grandchildren may return a wealth of information in the future.

Give them an overview of what the interview will be about. If process maps are already on the walls, use them as an example of what the project is about. Let the interviewees know that they are the experts and you are here to learn from them.

Once the interview gets into the actual processes, maintain an objective demeanor. When someone reveals an issue that may be a major problem, sometimes it is very difficult not to react to the information instantly. Just take the information in stride and move on with the discussions. Later you can verify what you have just learned.

We have been involved with individuals who literally told the interviewee, "Well, that is totally wrong," or "You're *not* doing that, are you?" Instantly, the interview becomes useless. Any additional information that might have been obtained during the interview is lost. Ultimately, maintain a professional but friendly atmosphere and you will be amazed at what people will reveal.

Actively Listen

This may sound very basic, but we cannot tell you how many people we have seen conduct interviews as if they had a preset script—never listening to what the interviewee is really telling them. If that approach is used, they might as well have sent out a survey and tallied the results. Many people go into these interviews with a long list of questions to be asked. They do not think their work is done until every question has been answered. We find that the best approach is to have a very limited list or no list at all. The list should include some of the key points we want to include, but never include more than four or five. This is a conversation with people about what they do for a living. Quite simply asking, "What do you do next?" is often the best approach and will keep most people talking for hours.

The people you are interviewing are the experts. If you listen, they will tell you about the issues they are facing. As a result, they will tell you about the control issues, efficiency issues, and management issues that are keeping the process from accomplishing its objective. They probably even know how to fix the problems— all you have to do is sit back and listen. You still need to control the conversation because it will often go places you definitely do not want to go, but you also have to let people say what is on their minds. Active listening involves spontaneous questioning based on responses you are hearing. You must have a good feel for the "right questions" to ask in order to get complete information.

You must also maintain an objective viewpoint. This means never arguing with the interviewee. You are gathering facts—hold the opinions for later. You, as a reviewer, should have a good idea of how the process works, but it is not up to you to give the answers. Interviewing is not reading a list of questions and recording the answers. It is maintaining an active conversation with people—an exchange of ideas. It is taking a true interest in what they are saying.

Select the Right People to Perform Interviews

A Process Mapping project may involve a team of several people, but each interview should have two people involved—one to act as the primary interviewer and one to act as the primary information recorder. Selection of the members for this team is critical to the success of the project. The primary interviewer should be someone who has a good knowledge of the processes under review and an ability to actively listen and set an appropriate tone. A significant amount of detailed information must be obtained in a short period from a wide variety of people. The interviewer should be someone who can think on his or her feet and has a friendly, professional demeanor. The interviewer must also be capable of directing the information-gathering process.

The second person is assigned the job of recording the information obtained during the interview process. This person is responsible for identifying the significant portions of the conversation between the interviewer and interviewee and recording the information in a document for future reference. Accordingly, this person must be able to process information quickly, but also must have sufficient technical skill to input data directly into a document while the interview is progressing. The information recorder can still participate in the interview process (neither one of us can help ourselves—we always have to participate in the interview), but he or she acts mostly as a recorder of information.

The review team is trying to capture the major actions; the major shots in the movie. The interviewee will want to tell you about each action they take and each paper they touch. The team must be able to process the detailed information that is received and determine how it fits into those major actions. The recorder should capture the details. The interviewer, as the map producer, must synthesize the information as the interview is going on, classifying the details into major actions. If there are problems with a particular part of a process, the interviewer must be ready to "drill down" into specific areas of the process and create a more detailed chart on a targeted area. It is the right combination of skills and people that makes a successful interview team.

STICKY-NOTE REVOLUTION

When we attempted our first real process analysis project, we went to a smog-filled valley in southern California (you literally could not see across the parking lot to the mountains a few miles away). We spent a week talking to people about their processes. We sent out preliminary surveys, recorded the information in detailed notes, and learned about major issues. We had private interview areas, learned (more than we wanted to) about what was and was not working at the site, and got plenty of suggestions on how to improve the processes. We left the office after one week with reams and reams of information and began the daunting task of creating maps based on the interviews. At this point, we realized that the project could last another couple of months before we finished maps of everything. We had only two weeks.

We had a lot of information, but no way to quickly organize it. Plus, as we constructed the maps, we realized that we had all our notes but, since we had no further access to the employees, there was no way to get additional questions answered. We had some successes—when people tell you how to fix things, it is easy to have successes—and we did produce some maps, but we were not happy with the time it was taking after the field interviews were done to produce a final product.

Six months later we were both at a seminar where the presenter was creating process maps in real time using yellow stickynotes. That idea revolutionized our approach to Process Mapping. It was the solution to the problem of creating maps after fieldwork. Instead, we could create maps in the field while we were doing the interviews. Using sticky-notes to document actions and poster-sized sticky-notes to record the various tasks, we set out on our first sticky-note adventure.

We arrived at an Arizona claims office with sticky-notes in hand. We even bought some special colored ones so we could color-code areas of the maps. As the interviews began, giant Post-it® notes with yellow badges of courage (yellow sticky-notes) were hanging from every possible wall surface in a small, closet-sized interview room. People were thrilled as they saw the processes unfold before their eyes. The only negative comment we got was that we did not get to everyone and some individuals felt left out because they did not get to be interviewed. This simple process of visually displaying the process as we conducted the interview created a curiosity that helped promote a positive atmosphere. It also allowed us to change maps as information changed and provided for a fast, easy method to input results into a flowcharting software package for more detailed analysis.

We have often been asked if the same effect would be achieved by inputting information directly into a flowcharting package. The answer is that you probably could do it, but you would not get the same collaborative effect, and, as a result, employees would not feel as free to share information about the process. That is one of the greatest benefits of this approach. It is totally interactive, involving key members of the process. It enhances their understanding of the whole process by showing them how their various activities relate to the big picture—how their actions relate to the tasks or scenes in the company's movie. And by showing them something where their work fits in, they are seeing something they may never have seen before.

BASIC RULES

Before sitting down and beginning the Process Mapping interviews, there are some supplies you need to have on hand and a few basics you must know.

Supplies

Have a lot of poster board–size paper on hand. (At a minimum you will probably need one for every task you will review.) Flip charts are fine, but we have found that among the most useful products are 2′ by 3′ sticky-notes (yes, they really do make them that big.) As you begin each process or task, you will need another sheet. You will find yourself working on a lot of the sheets at the same time. Even when you think one is finished, you will need to keep it handy in case someone else you interview wants to add something about the process. If you use a flip chart, you will constantly find yourself going back and forth, losing track of where you want to be. To make every chart easily accessible, we stick them right to the walls of the room in which we interview people. If you tape up your charts, you never know what effect the tape is going to have on the walls. You will also find yourself retaping the sheets as you constantly move them around the room. The poster-size sticky-notes solve these problems.

Have a lot of smaller sticky-notes (3″ by 3″). Every action will need a sticky-note. Every task will have a number of actions. And you will find a need to rewrite a number of these as you misunderstand and reunderstand the process. So let us repeat that point—have *a lot* of these sticky-notes on hand. Feel free to explore the various color selections available. These can be used to identify certain phases of the process or different individuals. One individual we worked with started by outlining each sticky-note to make it look more like a flowchart symbol and then tried to find a way to have them preprinted with flowcharting symbols.

Use bold, felt-tipped pens. The darker they are, the easier they are to read. And you cannot write upside down with a ballpoint pen (there will be times you need to write upside down while constructing a map.) It is usually good to have a combination of colors available also. Much like the different colors of sticky-notes, this allows you another opportunity to color-code different aspects of the processes (e.g., blue for controls, red for risks, and black for basic processes). Do not use the very smelly kind of markers. This is something you really want to check out before you begin the interviews. You do not want to be in that first interview, open the pen, and smell an odor you know will make you light-headed by the end of the day.

The Process

As mentioned before, use a separate sheet for each major task. It is not necessary to have every sheet prepared before the first interview. In fact, it is probably a better idea not to do so. You want people to understand that you have no preconceived ideas, that you only know what people tell you, and that they are the experts. Prepare each sheet as you go along. When interviewing people, prepare another sheet if a new task emerges. Sometimes you may find that you prepare a sheet and the task only has two steps. That is not a problem. Paper is inexpensive, and it is better to err on the side of being prepared for that simple task that turns into your worst nightmare.

For each new sheet, note the task name as a title in red across the top of the page. The individuals involved in the process are then listed horizontally below the title. These become the columns that will show the action completed by that individual. It is usually best to list these in chronological order of involvement from left to right. However, you may not learn who that first person is right away, so there are three options. The first is to recreate maps later in the interviews. With the use of sticky-notes, this is a fairly simple process, involving only the moving of the notes to a sheet updated with the individuals in the correct order. The second approach is to list individuals as you hear about them. This may result in a more complicated initial map, but it often provides the same information and helps the interviewer quickly see where the information was obtained. The final approach works if you have a basic understanding of the process before you start out. The principal person in the task is listed in the center. Others involved in the task are listed to either side, but the action always comes back to the center character.

Maps are constructed so that time runs down the page from top to bottom. While it is a simple concept to understand, it is often hard for people to put into practice. But it is a key concept in creating the maps. The first action in the task should be the first sticky-note on the chart. If employees are being listed chronologically, the task starts in the upper left-hand corner with employee A. If employee A handles the next action, it is listed below the first action. As employee A handles each action, they are listed going down the chart. If employee B handles an action, it is listed horizontally (under employee B's title) next to the prior action. If B handles the next action, it is listed below the prior task. If an employee besides B handles the next action, it is listed horizontally from B unless there is already a task in that location. Then the action should be listed below the last task handled by that other employee. All the actions in the task are to be documented this way—process boxes under the appropriate employee, moving down the page as the events occur over time. If you get to the end of the poster sheet, either stick another one below it or use a connector to a new sheet. You may also find that subsequent discussions reveal an earlier starting point to the task than originally thought. If it is one action, just squeeze it in. If it is more than one action, add a sheet or make a connector.

Use the small yellow sticky-notes to denote actions taken by employees. Each sticky-note should include a symbol denoting the type of action and a description of that action. This should be stated in its simplest terms. Try to stick with a verb–noun format to help limit your description of the action. For example, if an employee says, "I look at the form and check to see if the person who signed the form is on my authorization list," the yellow sticky would say "Verify authorizations." In this example, the interviewer might have a tendency to want to add information about the authorization list. However, that should be done some other way besides including it in the action description. For example, the interviewer can make a separate note on the process map or the recorder can put it in the notes. Ultimately, the more you can stick with the verb–noun format, the more succinct your process maps will be. If you find yourself straying from this format, you probably are trying to put too much information in that particular action.

The symbols you use on the sticky-notes should be fairly straightforward. Process Mapping is not a document flowchart, so we use only a few basic symbols to keep the maps simple and readable. Sticky-notes already make a good representation of a box, so we use them for most actions. The diamond shape is used for decisions, and this is easily accomplished by turning a sticky-note on its corner. If we see an action that is causing a delay in the process, we use a big D.

When a task goes straight from one action to another, there usually is little problem in keeping it straight. However, decisions and the resulting loops make it harder to construct a process map that is truly chronological. If the decision leads to two completely different sets of tasks, connectors to the new sheets are the best solution (see Example 1 in Exhibit 5.1). In many situations, one choice in a decision will lead to a series of actions that eventually lead to the action that followed the other choice (e.g., does the work sheet include the code? Yes—send to employee B. No—enter code and send to employee B.) To keep the tasks in chronological order, the extra tasks should follow the decision and the second choice item should follow next (see Example 2 in Exhibit 5.1). If a hold-file is used more than once for the same documents, there may be a resulting series of decision trees. In that situation, either the number of times checked or the time in the hold-file should be used as a decision. Each referral back to the hold-file should (if possible) return to that part of the map, and a subsequent action should exist after the first decision (see Example 3 in Exhibit 5.1).

Remember that time flows down the page. Therefore, there should be connecting lines and arrows all flowing down the page with only an occasional instance in which an arrow goes uphill. In general, process map actions should not refer back to actions above them. This is very common in flowcharts—document flowcharts in particular—but a process map serves a different purpose. It is a visual representation and, as such, it must be as uncomplicated as possible. Maintaining the linear flow of actions helps keep it simple. Connectors can be used if you need to continue to another page.

As the map is developed, additional measures should be included to keep track of various aspects of the process. The first is the cycle time. For each action within the map, try to get an estimate from the employee of how long it takes to accomplish the action. If you get this information for every action, you will eventually have a feel for how long the entire process takes. It will also

Exhibit 5.1   Examples of Decision Trees

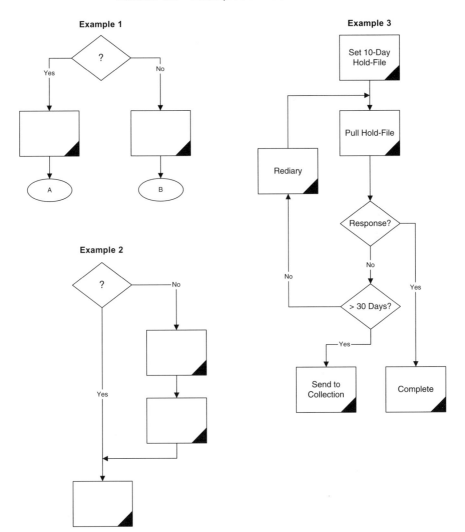

show the actions that take up the most time. These are the ones that are ripe for change.

The next measure to record is holding time. Any time an item is batch processed or any time it sits in a bin, there is a resulting delay in the handling of the item. Intuitively, this means that someone took a look at the process and determined that, overall, time was saved in processing all items at one time at the expense of delaying the single items a short time. This may be the assumption, but it is seldom correct. Even if someone made this conscious decision, it was probably made a long time ago and things have changed since. Every time an item sits being held for any reason, the "D" symbol should be used. Any time the "D" is used, get an approximation from employees of how long the item will sit. When this is added to the cycle times already recorded, there is a more true approximation of how long a process takes.

For any decision symbol, try to get an idea of the percentage of items going down each path. For example, the decision may be "Is there an attorney involved?" (Using the verb–noun format, the action should read "Attorney Involved?") The interviewer should try to get an approximation from the employee of how many items have attorney involvement and how many do not. From this it can be determined how often processes related to attorney involvement are used and how often non–attorney involvement processes come into play. This percentage should be entered directly on the map.

These percentages are especially important when dealing with rejected or error items. Any time an error that requires rework is identified, there is a resulting loss of efficiency. In some instances, you will find whole departments whose sole purpose is to correct the errors of another department. Any rework means there is a process that should be reviewed to determine whether the errors could be reduced or eliminated. Enter the error percentage directly on the map also. Those areas with the highest error rates are the ones where the reviewer may want to spend additional time. Another flag that can be used by the reviewer to help identify these areas on process maps is an "R" symbol (for rework).

CONDUCTING THE INTERVIEWS

The beauty of this methodology lies in the fact that you can interview people in any order, even if they are involved in multiple processes, and still document their piece of the puzzle accurately. As mentioned before, we generally have someone at the site refer interviewees to the interview area.

It may be helpful to start with a supervisor or manager who oversees several major aspects of the process. There is a chance you already spoke to this individual as a process owner, unit owner, or subordinate owner. In fact, you may have already begun to obtain some information about the tasks and actions during those meetings. But now it is time to start the documentation in earnest.

Use the information you gain from these individuals to start creating shells of maps for the major tasks. They should be able to provide not only the tasks, but also the names of the individuals involved in the tasks, and where those tasks start and end. Interviews with these individuals may take a while, so we try to conduct them first. This helps prepare them for how long other interviews may take. Also, by getting the managers' and supervisors' perceptions first, we can see how well reality matches their understanding.

From this point on, you will probably interview employees haphazardly throughout the processes. That may mean key person #3 is interviewed before #1 or #2. And key person #3 may not have any idea what #1 and #2 do. Just record the actions for each person as you interview them. Connections can then be made after you get the entire picture. One individual will probably be involved in multiple processes. Just keep adding them to the appropriate maps as your discussion proceeds.

If you circulated preliminary surveys, they will give you an idea of which processes people participate in and what type of actions they generate in each process. If you have not done a preliminary survey, you will need to spend a little time in the interview going over the interviewee's basic job duties.

When you begin discussing a particular process, try to get the interviewee to go through the basic sequence of events—from start to finish—of his or her particular aspect of the process. The interviewer should be controlling the dialogue without stifling the flow of information. If an employee can only describe a task by including actions in other tasks, you will have to work with that. You will probably find yourself having to create new maps as the discussion progresses, and find yourself working back and forth between a couple of maps during the interview. If either the interviewer or the recorder needs clarification about the discussion, clear it up immediately.

You need to know who the interviewee receives work from, what he does with it when he receives it, and where it goes when it leaves him. If things are sitting for some time before processing, use the "D" symbol to indicate a delay. Be sure to note the cycle times, error rates when applicable, and the percentages with decisions. One question to always fall back on is "What is the next action you take?"

At the end of each interview, walk the person through the maps you have created. Repeat each action, where it comes from, and where it goes. Get his agreement that this is the process as he understands it. There should then be three final questions you ask. First, "What would you change about this process/your job if you could?" There are times you will get nonsense answers such as "Get a raise," or "Work fewer hours," but more often than not you get a thought-out answer. Again, these are the people who know their jobs, and they know what needs to be done to make them better. And this is often the first time anyone has really asked them for their opinion. Some of the best solutions we have provided our customers came directly from the suggestions of their employees.

The second question—"What do you wish I had asked you?" This is a little like the first question, but with a different slant. You are less likely to get an answer to this question, but when you do it may be more valuable. By asking this question, we have learned about morale problems in departments, supervision issues, and even ethical issues leading to fraud investigations. People in these situations are looking for someone to talk to. If you have built the right kind of rapport during the interview, they will want to talk to you.

The final question—"Is there anything you would like to add?" Again, this is really a different way of asking the preceding two questions, but it is one more opportunity to solicit additional information. The best use of this question we ever saw was actually as part of a statement between a claimant and a claims adjuster. The typed statement had taken up 20 to 30 pages before the adjuster thought he was done. He asked if there was anything the claimant wanted to add. The claimant said he just wanted to mention that he had not been driving the car. The adjuster asked, "You weren't driving?" The claimant replied, "No, I was too drunk to drive. My friend was driving." Although this question led to another 30 pages of statement, asking it helped ensure that the interviewer had all the necessary information.

CREATING A FINAL MAP

You should try to finalize your maps only after all interviews are completed. Each conversation has the chance of adding another action. Sticky-notes are easy to change; finished maps are a little tougher to amend. This is the point where you can straighten out any portions of the map that may not be constructed correctly. When we create maps, we have a tendency to stick things wherever they fit (sometimes sticky-notes go off the charts and onto the walls.) But you will find that in your haste to create maps on the fly, the rules discussed previously get bent. Putting the final map together is like the final proofreading of a report—it is the opportunity to make everything right. It is also a chance to see what may have been missed or what questions did not get asked. Take this opportunity to ask them.

Once the maps are finalized, have some of the key employees review them. It is one last chance to make sure everyone agrees that the content is correct. It also is one more opportunity to show these employees that they are an important part of the process. If anything is wrong, correct it immediately and let them see the revised product.

EXAMPLE

To get an idea how a process map is developed, we take a closer look at the claims settlement process described in Chapter 3. Imagine you are at the company's claims office interviewing people and creating maps. Could Process Mapping have helped identify why the service they were delivering was less than satisfactory for the customer? Could it help the company pinpoint the "moments of truth" gone wrong? Let us work it through and see.

We want to look in depth at the claim reporting process and the claim assignment process. Work-flow surveys were received from the following: an agent, the receptionist at the claims office, the claims loss assignment clerk, the auto claims adjuster, the medical claims adjuster, and the claims supervisor. Interviews were held with all six individuals.

Surveys and Discussions

The survey and discussions with the agent show that the agent is primarily involved in one task—receiving the claim. When the

138

phone call comes in, the agent completes a "report of claim." This form contains all information necessary to report the claim in the company's system. After getting the information, the agent inputs this information into the company claim system. This is done on the day the claim is reported or, if it is late in the day, it is input the following business day. When the office is closed (from noon to 1 P.M. on weekdays, all day Saturday and Sunday), the answering machine is used. The message states that the caller should leave a number and that the agent will get back to the caller as soon as possible. The message has no additional information about what to do if the client has had an accident. The agent also indicated that one of her staff might handle the entire process.

Reading the receptionist's work-flow survey and talking with her indicate that her main contact with clients is by phone. When she gets a call from a claimant, she looks on the computer to see if that claimant has a claim number. If he does not have a claim number, she tells him to call his agent to report the claim. She knows that the claims supervisor assigns claims to adjusters every afternoon at 3:00 P.M. If someone calls and says he reported the claim in the morning, she tells him that he will be assigned to an adjuster in the afternoon and the adjuster will call him back the next day. Occasionally, the computer system will be down and assignments cannot be made. The office staff lets the receptionist know when this has occurred. If the system is down, she advises clients about the cause for the delay and explains that they may not receive a call from the adjuster for two or three days.

Discussions with the supervisor and the work-flow survey show that the supervisor is responsible for reviewing the loss reports input by the agents and assigning them to a claims adjuster. For claims involving only auto damage, the assignment is made to an auto claims adjuster. If injuries are indicated on the loss report, an assignment is also made to an injury claims adjuster. This process is done from 1:30 P.M. to 3:00 P.M. daily.

139

The loss assignment clerk's discussion and survey match much of what was indicated by other employees. After assignments are made (normally from 3:00 P.M. to 4:00 P.M. daily), the loss assignment clerk prepares for the claims adjusters. The files are placed in the adjuster's in-bin. Adjusters usually pick up their files after 4:00 P.M. every day. If there is a particularly heavy volume of claims into the claims office on a specific day, the clerk may not complete all the assignment files until the next morning.

The auto claims adjuster states he goes into the office every day at 4:00 P.M. to pick up his assignments. He contacts all customers the next morning and goes out in the field on inspections after making all customer contacts. If he learns about injuries in his initial contact with the customer, he writes up an injury referral and drops it off at the office when he picks up his assignments.

The injury claims adjuster's story is much like that of the auto claims adjuster. The adjuster picks up assignments daily at 4:00 P.M. He contacts customers the following day. Many times these assignments are generated by the auto claims adjusters initial contact with the claimant.

Overview and "Drill Down" Maps

An overview map is a high-level map that summarizes the major tasks in the process and those individuals or departments involved in those processes. "Drill down" maps are completed to dig into each task as needed. When we first started Process Mapping, we assumed that it would be easy to create the overview maps at the beginning of the project and then go on to the "drill down" maps. In practice, we learned that it is usually easier to create an overview map after you have created detailed process maps. In addition, creating detailed maps helps you learn about processes that were not visible to you before you began your review. However, to help get a handle on this process, we start with a high-level look at the process.

Overview maps should be created for every project. They are like a table of contents for the process maps. A systematic numbering process is used to tie the overview maps into the detail maps. If we use the previous example, an overview map might only have three entities—the customer, the agent, and the claims office. Then there would be five major tasks. Each would receive a unique number: Report Claim 1, Input Loss 2, Assign Claim 3, Investigate Claim 4, and Settle Claim 5. This representation is shown in Exhibit 5.2

The map for a process then includes the number, for example "1.0 Claim Reporting." Each box on the map is labeled with sequential numbers—1.1, 1.2, 1.3, and so on—throughout the chart. This is an example of drilling down from the overview map.

As is discussed in one situation that follows, you may also find it necessary to "drill down" into just one area of concern in a particular process. If you maintain the numbering sequence on the maps, creating a new detailed map is the same process outlined

Exhibit 5.2   Claim Process Overview

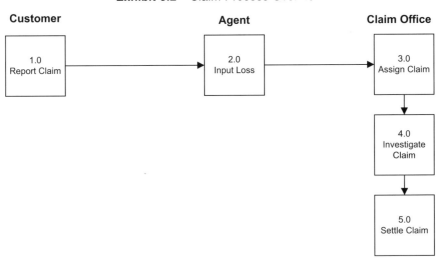

previously. Use the number of the box in which the detail is being exploded for the title of the new detailed chart. For example, if you need more detail on how auto claims are assigned by the supervisor, you may explode out box 3.3 on the claims assignment process map (see Exhibit 5.3).

This technique is very useful. It helps you avoid too much detail on one map, but it allows you the freedom to explore any area in as much depth as is necessary. This technique can also be useful for assembling training materials, as you can really "drill down" into a step-by-step process, even to a narrative if necessary.

Claim Reporting Process

Turning to the processes, the key individuals in the claim reporting process are the customer, the agent or agent's staff, and the claims office receptionist. Three columns are used to represent the process, one for each key individual. The customer actions start with a box to represent reporting the accident. After this there is a decision—does the claimant call the claims office or the agent? If the answer is the claims office, the next actions lead to the receptionist. If the response is the agent, the actions relate to calling the agent.

Because all subsequent actions relating to this process will eventually lead to calling the agent, the receptionist's actions are shown next. The first action is to get the claim number from the claimant. Then there is a decision for the next action—is there a claim number in the system (Number Exists?) The next decisions do not relate to the claims settlement process, so a terminal symbol is used.

Up to this point, elapsed time has not been an issue. However, any action that leads to the report being made to the agent can result in a delay if the customer cannot reach the agent. Since time is beginning to elapse, it becomes important to start noting minimum and maximum elapsed times. As stated before, use the

Exhibit 5.3 "Drill Down" Example
Claim Office XYZ
3.3 Assign Auto Damage Claim

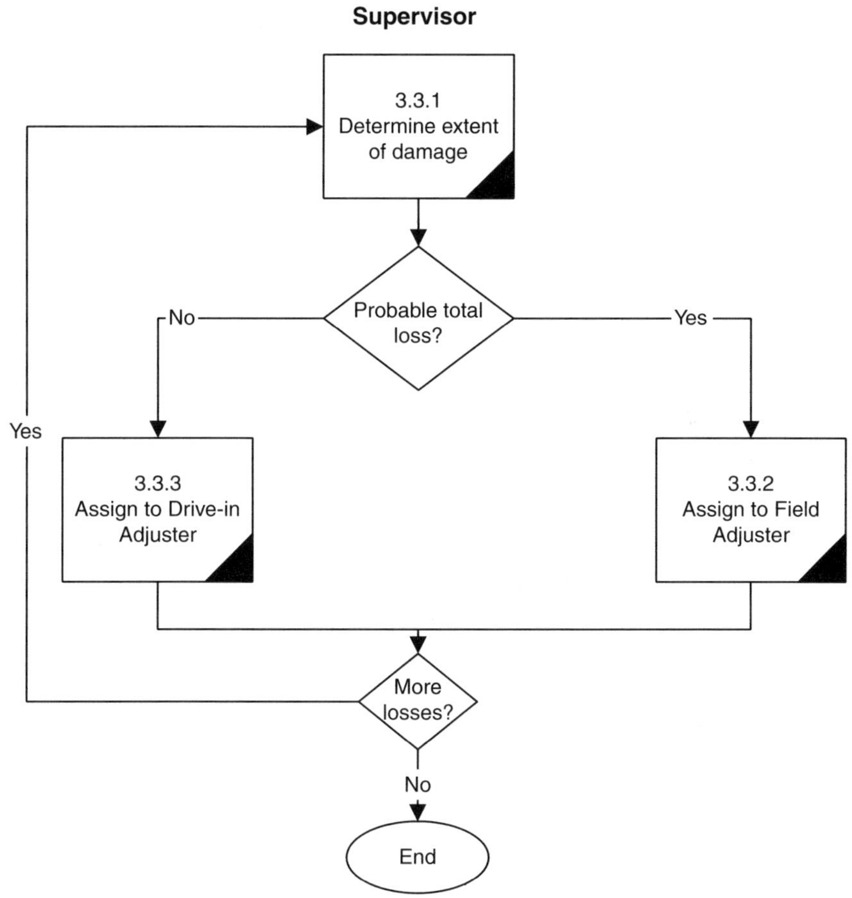

Supervisor

```
┌──────────────────────┐
│        3.3.1         │
│  Determine extent    │◀──────┐
│     of damage        │       │
└──────────────────────┘       │
           │                   │
           ▼                   │
    ◇ Probable total ◇         │
 ┌─No─     loss?     ─Yes─┐    │
 │                        │    │
 ▼                        ▼    │ Yes
┌──────────┐       ┌──────────┐│
│  3.3.3   │       │  3.3.2   ││
│Assign to │       │Assign to ││
│ Drive-in │       │  Field   ││
│ Adjuster │       │ Adjuster ││
└──────────┘       └──────────┘│
     │                  │      │
     └────────┬─────────┘      │
              ▼                │
         ◇ More ◇──────────────┘
          losses?
              │
              No
              ▼
          ( End )
```

"D" symbol if you immediately recognize that a delay may occur in a particular area. The action of inputting the report of claim has the potential of resulting in a delay because this is also a place where action may not occur immediately. Work could stack up here and delay the entire process. You should note the minimum and maximum elapsed times in the box or on the chart. In this case, it may be anywhere from five minutes to one day.

See Exhibit 5.4 for the final map of the claim reporting process. There are a number of important aspects to consider in this map. First, we started with the first event—reporting the claim. Because the customer generates the process, he is listed first. The action is put in the upper left-hand corner. This first action leads to the first decision. The results of this decision lead to one response that results in the claimant continuing to work with the agent, or another response that results in the claimant working with the claims receptionist.

Second, notice how time is moving down the page. To help facilitate this time flow, the two decisions the receptionist makes are placed in the order in which she would normally ask them.

Finally, notice that there is a handoff from the receptionist back to the customer if a claim number has not yet been assigned. If we want to make our moment of truth more positive, the company may want to consider having some means for the customer to report the claim to the first party he contacts—either the agent or the claim office. When you visually review a process map, you should look for these handoffs back and forth between key individuals. These handoffs can often point to inefficiencies in the process.

At the bottom of the chart, we summarize the minimum and maximum elapsed times for this particular process. As processes are added, you can add together the minimum and maximum elapsed times to determine what range of time can be expected for the entire process.

Also note the use of the numbering hierarchy. This is particularly important because, although we have given the map one name, it includes information about a second process—the Loss Input Process. Realizing that you have two processes in one map is the type of discovery you may make after having already gone

Exhibit 5.4 Claim Office XYZ
1.0 Claim Reporting and
2.0 Loss Input Process

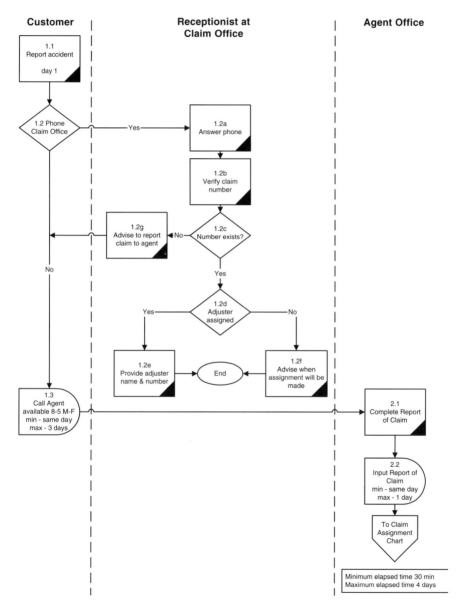

deep into the mapping process. Accordingly, just adapt the map and move on. For numbering purposes, 1.0 has been assigned to the first overall process—Claim Reporting—and 2.0 to the second process. The receptionist who answers the phone has been identified as a task and been given the number 1.2. The "drill down" is accomplished on the same map, so actions related to answering the phone have numbers 1.2a to 1.2g. For this last "drill down," we could have also used 1.2.1 to 1.2.7, much like in the previous discussion about "drilling down."

Claim Assignment Process

The claim assignment process begins when the loss has been input and ends when the adjuster picks up the assignment. There are three key individuals in the process—the supervisor, the loss assignment clerk, and the adjuster. The first step in the process is the supervisor's review of the loss. This is entered in the upper left-hand corner of the report and is followed by a decision regarding the type of claim.

The next actions are placed under the Loss Assignment Clerk column. A box is completed for obtaining the loss reports. A diamond is used next to reflect the different actions for losses with and without an injury. It is important to record minimum and maximum elapsed times for both the supervisor and the loss assignment clerk processes because potential delays could occur here. The adjuster has only one action at this point, but it is important to note the time the assignments are picked up because this will also help identify minimum and maximum elapsed times. All elapsed times should be added together to determine the maximum elapsed time.

See Exhibit 5.5 for a completed map. You will notice that the "D" symbol has been used twice. These actually come one after the other. The first relates to the loss assignment clerk batching files

Exhibit 5.5   Claim Office XYZ
3.0 Claim Assignment Process

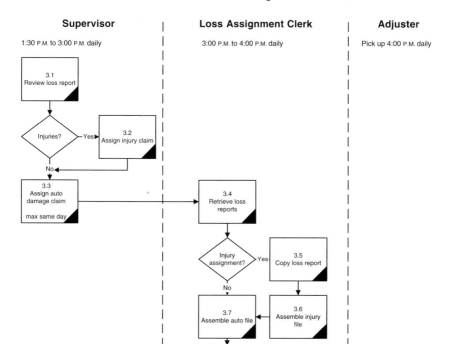

Supervisor	Loss Assignment Clerk	Adjuster
1:30 P.M. to 3:00 P.M. daily	3:00 P.M. to 4:00 P.M. daily	Pick up 4:00 P.M. daily

3.1 Review loss report

Injuries? —Yes▸ 3.2 Assign injury claim

No

3.3 Assign auto damage claim — max same day

3.4 Retrieve loss reports

Injury assignment? —Yes▸ 3.5 Copy loss report

No

3.7 Assemble auto file

3.6 Assemble injury file

3.8 Pitch assignments to bins min same day max 1 day

3.9 Pick up assignments min same day max 1 day

To Claim Investigation map

Minimum elapsed time 3 hours
Maximum elapsed time 2 days

before taking them to the adjusters. Since assignments are made at the end of the day, this delay may mean that the adjusters hold claims an additional 24 hours before making contact. The second delay relates to assignments sitting in the adjuster's in-box before being handled. Because adjusters are coming in or out of the office, this delay can be anywhere from zero to one full day.

Notice that we have made a decision to keep this map at a high level. There could be numerous steps involved in "review loss report" or "assign claim." For example, review loss report might include the supervisor's looking to see if injuries are reported or looking at the loss report to see the potential extent of damage before making a determination of potential injury. Assigning the claim could involve reviewing available personnel or accessing the computer to complete the assignment. If needed, the detailed information can be charted in "drill down" maps. But you should only map the level of detail you need, even if the people you are interviewing give you "drilled down" details. If, for example, significant delays were occurring in this portion of the process you may want to do a "drill down" map on the supervisor's assignment process to determine exactly where the delays are occurring.

As the reviewer prepares the chart, it becomes obvious that if the assignments are not completed by 4:00 P.M., the customer may experience a delay of another 24 hours in the process. Issues that are readily apparent, either control issues or efficiency issues, should be noted directly on the chart. You may use a special color, an open-ended box, or just a text box.

Map Implications

Looking at the maximum elapsed time on the two charts, a total of six days could go by before the adjuster receives the assignment. (This is all assuming that the agent actually responds to claimants' voice mails.) The adjuster always phones the customer the day after the assignment is received, so it could take up to a week for the client to receive a call from the adjuster. The best-case scenario would be receipt of the loss by the adjuster on the same day it was reported, and then the client would be contacted the next day (24 hours). However, if an injury claim was not originally identified as an injury, it could take up to 10 days from the date the customer reported the accident for the customer to be contacted by the injury adjuster. The original assignment could take up to a maximum of 6 days to be completed; there is an additional day for the auto adjuster to contact the customer and forward information on the injury assignment; another 2 days (maximum) could be used before the injury adjuster receives the assignment, and then contact with the customer would occur 24 hours later.

By viewing the process through the eyes of the customer, you can see where service improvements can be made. In this example, what if the customer could call into one central number to report the claim and the claim was electronically assigned and received immediately by the claims adjuster? The company could go from a maximum of 6 days to receive an assignment to a maximum of receiving the assignment the same day the claim is reported. Looking back at the questions we asked at the beginning of this example, it is easy to say that we would quickly identify why services are creating customer dissatisfaction and help the company pinpoint the "moments of truth" gone wrong.

RECAP

The interviewing and actual mapping of processes can be the most fun and rewarding part of the Process Mapping project. It is the opportunity for you to see the fruits of your work and the opportunity for the interviewees to learn the value of theirs. But it can only succeed with the right preparation and the right approach.

The basic ground rules should be followed to ensure this success:

- *Get the buy-in of all senior clients.* Without their approval and support, very few people will be interested in helping to make the project succeed.
- *Set aside enough time.* To get all the information you need, you will need all the time you can get.
- *Set aside a private area for the interview.* This will ensure fewer interruptions and help build a feeling of privacy with the interviewee.
- *Set a friendly tone.* This establishes the rapport needed for a full exchange of information.
- *Actively listen.* The interviewee needs to believe that you are genuinely interested in what is being said. Sit back and let him give you his ideas.
- *Select the right review team.* Special skills are needed to conduct an effective interview. Make sure that the people on the team have those skills.

Once everything is in place, you can begin building maps. These should be built in real time using the sticky-note technique. This allows for a very interactive session that results in more information and further ensures its accuracy. The top of the page should show the individuals involved. Time should progress as you move down the map.

Keep the maps and the symbols simple. You are not trying to impress anyone with how much information you can get on a page. Instead, you are trying to make an easily understood visual of the process. Use "drill down" maps when you need to explore more detail, and create overview maps to summarize the processes under review.

KEY ANALYSIS POINTS

Follow the Ground Rules

If you obey the basic ground rules, suggestions will come pouring in. In particular, providing people with a situation in which they feel comfortable talking will result in more openness. While this is not really an analysis tool, you will receive enough information to make it look like you spent forever in analysis.

Maps Flow in Chronological Order

By creating maps that flow chronologically, disruptive actions will show more easily. Look for obvious "blips" in the process. These are the tasks or actions that should be "drilled down" into. This may also be an indicator of actions that can be eliminated.

Pay Attention to the Symbols

Look for the two symbols that show there is a problem—"D" (delay) and "R" (rework). These are indicators of significant problems. Batch processing slows down every process. When real-time processing can be accomplished, the process will run smoother. Rework means something has gone wrong. Look for what is causing the rework and see if the process can be improved to eliminate it.

Ask the Right Questions

You are talking to the people who know how things are done and know how to correct the problems. Ask them how to make things better. Give them every opportunity to tell you the solutions. Take these ideas and compare them to the entire process to determine if they are feasible. Ultimately, the answers will come from every discussion.

CHAPTER 6

Map Generation: An Example

A picture is worth a thousand words.

—Napoleon

TRY IT—YOU'LL LIKE IT

It is time to take a very close look at our check request process. By taking a step-by-step approach to determining the units, tasks, and actions, you should get a good idea how a map is developed. Before we jump into this, however, take a look at the example and obtain a full understanding of what is going on. Next try your own hand at building some of the maps. In the previous chapter, we walked you through part of an example. Now it is your turn.

Before you go on, let us repeat—try your own hand at building some maps. It is only through practice that you will get better, and only through practice that you will gain an understanding of the some of the points that we have been and will be discussing. Take a look at the expense process and start thinking through the various levels. Then build your own maps. We will go on now and assume that you took our advice.

UNIT LEVEL

The first step is to "drill down" to the first level and determine the units. In Chapter 1, we discussed the appropriate units for this process. The easiest way to break this process down is by using the geographic locations of the field office and the home office. Each has a specifically identifiable purpose and the process flows well between them. The first unit (1.0) is Prepare Request, the second unit (2.0) is Prepare Check, and the third unit (3.0) is Deliver Check.

A simple unit-level map can be drawn with units 1.0 and 3.0 under the Field Office and unit 2.0 under the Home Office. While this is very rudimentary, it serves as the basis for the work to follow. Notice that we are already using the basic traits of a process map: only simple process diagrams are used, the function involved is the header for each column, and time runs down the map. In addition, the beginning is shown with the input item (Receive Bill), and termination of the process is also identified. Finally, note that we have begun our numbering system and have documented it on this high-level map.

TASK LEVEL

Prepare Request Unit

Exhibit 6.1 broke the process into various units. The first is the Prepare Request unit. Now, Exhibit 6.2 shows the "drill down" from the unit level for unit 1.0, Prepare Request, to the various tasks involved in this process. As mentioned, the units were defined

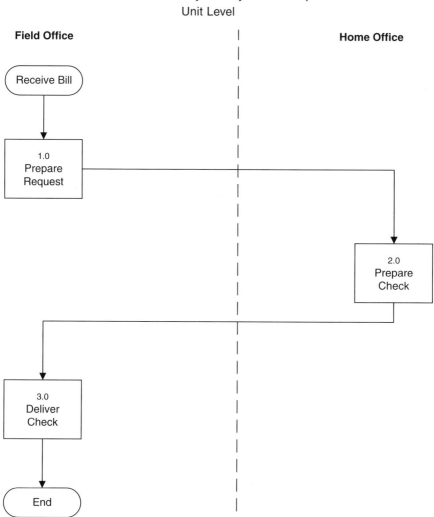

Exhibit 6.1 Payment by Check Request
Unit Level

Field Office   **Home Office**

based on their geographic areas. This also corresponds to different high-level departments. These were also chosen to show significant changes between sets of activities.

This approach should be used for the task level also. For the Prepare Request unit, all actions occur within the field office.

Exhibit 6.2 Payment by Check Request
Prepare Request (1.0)—Task Level

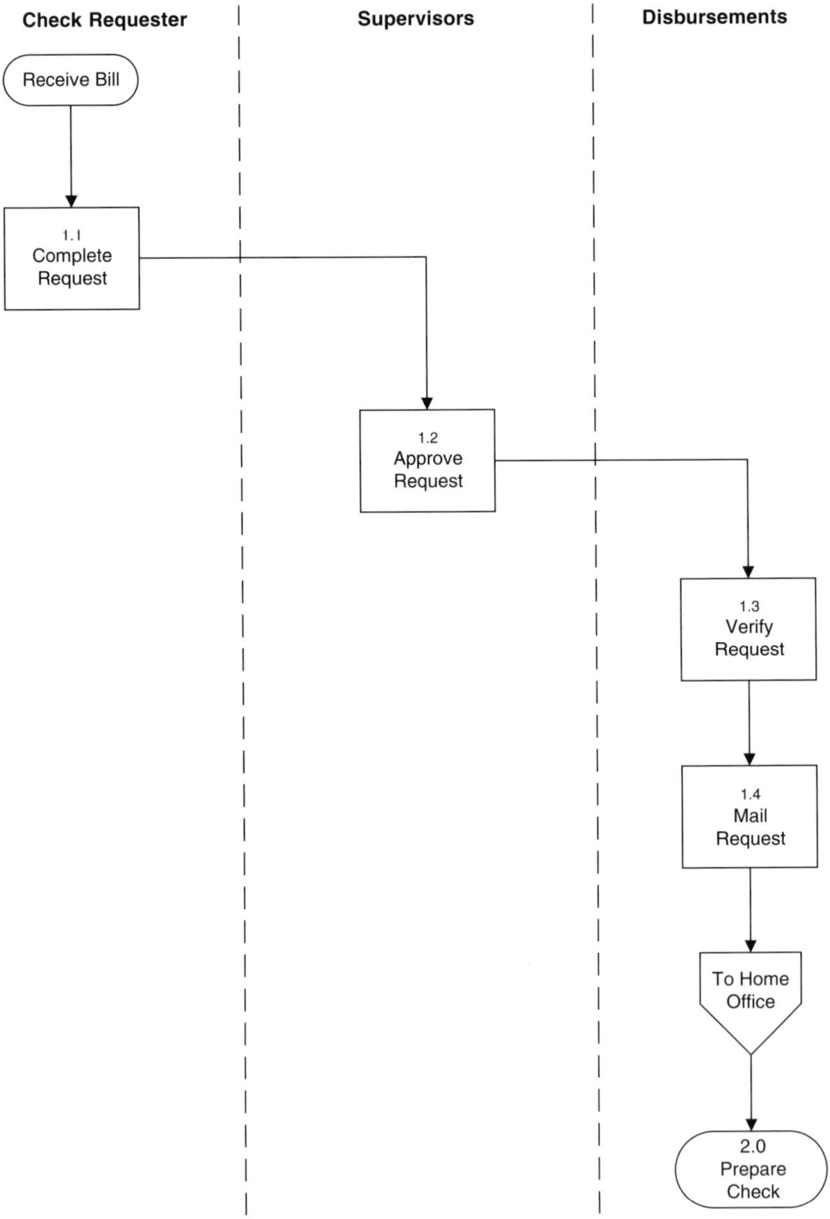

Check Requester	Supervisors	Disbursements

- Receive Bill

1.1
Complete
Request

1.2
Approve
Request

1.3
Verify
Request

1.4
Mail
Request

To Home
Office

2.0
Prepare
Check

However, it is still easiest to break the tasks down based on departments. There are three involved in this unit—the requester, the supervisors, and field office disbursements. Therefore, "drilling down" into the unit reveals four tasks.

The first department is the one that actually receives and pays the bill—the requester. (Note that we are already moving away from department names in the headers and using titles that refer to a single person.) The next department is the employee's supervisor or, depending on the size of the request, supervisors. The final stop is in field office disbursements.

The first task is Complete Request as done by the requester. The second task is Approve Request as done by one or more supervisors. The next task, as performed by field office disbursement, is Verify Request. The final task is Mail Request. This is a relatively simple task and, when we go to the action level, you will see that there are few associated actions. However, because this shows the transfer of information from one unit to the next, it is an important step and should be emphasized at this point. Also note that the map ends by showing the connection to the next unit.

Prepare Check Unit

In Exhibit 6.1, the next unit is Prepare Check (2.0). Exhibit 6.3 shows the task level activity in this unit. Exhibit 6.1 shows that there is only one department involved in this unit—home office disbursements. However, there are two primary functions that occur: (1) check issuance and (2) check retrieval. Because these are distinct sets of individuals in the department and to help show the separation of duties controls established by the department, the two functions are listed as part of the task-level map in Exhibit 6.3.

In Exhibit 6.3, the map begins by showing the unit providing the input as well as an indication of the source of the input (From

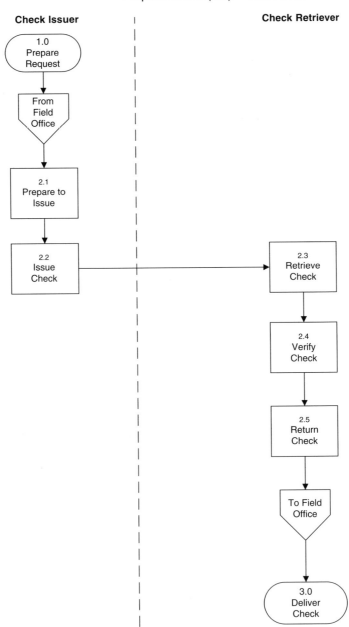

Exhibit 6.3 Payment by Check Request
Prepare Check (2.0)—Task Level

Field Office). For the check issuer, the first task involves a number of operations, including initiating the printer, getting the requests, and reviewing the requests. We do not want to "drill down" to that level yet, so a more general task must be developed. In this case, Prepare to Issue was chosen. This encompasses the many actions the issuer must complete before the check can actually be issued. The next task is to actually Issue Check.

The next tasks relate to the check retriever. The first task is the most obvious—Retrieve Check. Next is the review process—Verify Check. Finally, just as we did with the prior unit, we want to emphasize the transfer of information. Therefore, the relatively simple task Return Check is included.

You may have noticed that the process description includes a lot of detail about what is done when things are not exactly correct. Some of these review and hold-file systems may even be tasks. However, even at the task level we are trying to be fairly simple. The intent is for these maps to provide an overview, and complicating them now will only make the final mapping more complicated.

Deliver Check Unit

In Exhibit 6.1, the Deliver Check unit (3.0) revolves around one department (field office disbursements) and one primary function—getting the checks to the appropriate individual. However, in Exhibit 6.4, rather than just show the one department in the map, the customers to the process—payees and requesters—are also shown in this map. In that manner, the actions directly related to these individuals can be emphasized if necessary.

In Exhibit 6.4, the Deliver Check task map again starts with the source of input by listing the previous unit and where the input came from. Notice that in constructing this map we have put the initial department in the center rather than on the left-hand side.

Exhibit 6.4 Payment by Check Request
Deliver Check (3.0)—Task Level

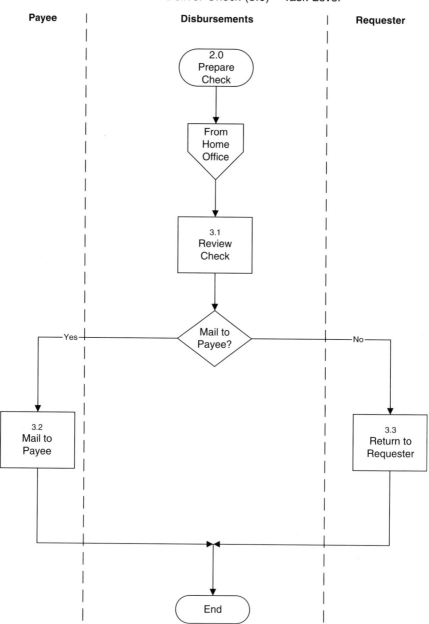

This was done to emphasize its importance in the unit and to better show how work is passed from this department.

The first task in Exhibit 6.4 is Review Check and is listed under the Disbursements heading. The next operation is a decision. If the check goes to the payee, there is one distinct set of actions. If the check is returned to the requester, there is another set of actions. Therefore, they are set up as individual tasks. Notice that no number is assigned to this item. It is not really a task, but a split-off point that sends the process in one of two directions, depending on the answer to the question. As such, no real actions are assigned to it. In general, if there are no actions associated with a decision, it does not need a reference number. However, some decisions include numerous tasks. In those instances, a number should be assigned.

Once the decision has been made, one of two tasks is performed. These are listed under the appropriate headings—Mail to Payee under the Payee heading and Return to Requester under the Requester heading. At this point, the entire process is complete, and the termination is illustrated on the map.

ACTION LEVEL

Prepare Request: Complete Request Task

After all this preliminary discussion, it is time to build the actual detailed map of a specific action. The map in Exhibit 6.5 is of the Complete Request action. This is a "drill down" map starting from Exhibit 6.1, the Prepare Request (1.0) unit, to Exhibit 6.2 and the Complete Request Task (1.1). Let us start at the very beginning. Each mapping level (unit, task, and action) begins with the identified input and trigger. Therefore, this map in Exhibit 6.5 also starts with the requester receiving a bill. Once it is received, the first

Exhibit 6.5 Payment by Check Request
Complete Request (1.1)—Action Level

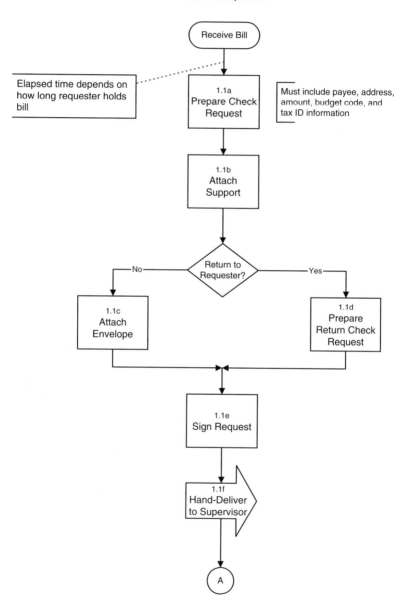

Check Requester

Receive Bill

Elapsed time depends on how long requester holds bill

1.1a
Prepare Check Request

Must include payee, address, amount, budget code, and tax ID information

1.1b
Attach Support

Return to Requester?

—No—

—Yes—

1.1c
Attach Envelope

1.1d
Prepare Return Check Request

1.1e
Sign Request

1.1f
Hand-Deliver to Supervisor

A

action is preparation of the check request (1.1a). Before even getting to the first action, there is a note regarding cycle times. There are any number of types of bills and any number of requesters. Therefore, it is almost impossible to determine the elapsed time between receiving bills and preparing requests. This must be noted for analysis. Also, because there is quite a bit of information required in completing the request, this has been included as a note to the side of the action.

Another requirement, noted in Exhibit 6.5, is to attach the support to the request. Because of the importance of this action as a control, it is included as a separate item. After this, one of two actions occurs, depending on the eventual disposition of the check. If the check is to be mailed to the payee, the requester must prepare an envelope and include it with the request. If the check is to be returned to the requester, a Return to Requester form must be completed. This is illustrated with a decision and two separate processes. These then converge on the next action—the requester signing the request. Note that actions b through e may actually occur in any order. However, the description shows them this way, which indicates that the majority of interviewees stated that they complete them in this order. In completing a map, the most common order should be used.

The final step is hand-walking the request to the supervisor. The specific mode of transfer is included because we already know that there are a number of different methods of delivering documents in this process. Therefore, we want to keep track of each type. This is one reason having a general feel for the process before you start is beneficial.

At the end of the map is a connector to the next actions. The letter "A" is used as a reference to the next page. Depending on the circumstances, you may want to reference the next task, Approve Request, much like we did between tasks.

Prepare Request: Approve Request Task

Exhibit 6.6 is another "drill down" map of the Prepare Request task-level map shown in Exhibit 6.2. This set of actions begins where the last set left off in Exhibit 6.5. This is indicated by the connector marked "A." Since the last map ended with the documents being given to the supervisor for review, we begin Exhibit 6.6 with the supervisor. In an effort to keep the order of personnel consistent between maps, the supervisor is listed in the middle. It may be easiest to think of the whole set of maps being one big map. In that case, the first name to the left would be the requester. This is maintained on the next maps.

The first action in Exhibit 6.6 is the supervisor's review of the documents. This situation is similar to that faced when trying to determine how long bills remain on requesters' desks. Because of the number of supervisors, we cannot determine how long items remain on the desk before review and approval. The note regarding this situation is referenced to a point in the process just after corrected requests are returned. This may indicate that delays exist every time a request is returned for correction. There are no further references to cycle times in this particular map because the time to handle an individual item is very short.

If something is wrong with the request, it is returned to the requester for correction. This is illustrated with a decision, an action that is the responsibility of the requester, and a return to the beginning of the task. If the check is being returned to the requester, the supervisor must sign another part of the request, as well as the Return to Requester form. This is represented by an additional decision. Notice that, to keep time flowing down the page, the next action listed is the one that requires additional steps—in this instance, the signing of the forms. This is followed by the next action required by both choices—approving the request. Also notice that at least two actions are combined in the

164

Exhibit 6.6   Payment by Check Request
Approve Request (1.2)—Action Level

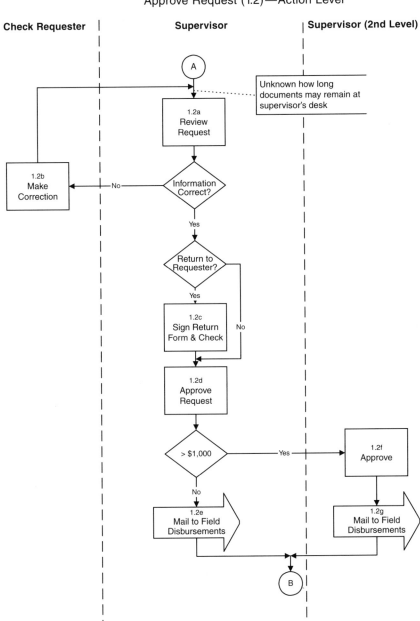

box representing what happens if the check is returned to the requester. Sign Return Form & Check combines signing the form and signing the check. However, because these are very similar actions, the decision was made not to "drill down" any further.

Finally, the supervisor determines whether an additional signature is required. If not, the request is mailed to disbursements. If so, the request is sent to the next-level supervisor, who approves the document and mails it to disbursements. Notice that although the actions are fundamentally the same, they are done by different people with different priorities. Therefore, different index numbers are used for each action.

The task ends after requests are mailed to disbursements. Although separate actions are used for the supervisor and the second-level supervisor, the same connector leads to the next page. This is intended to show that, once out of these individuals' hands, there is no significant difference in the way they are handled.

Prepare Request: Verify Request Task

Exhibit 6.7 again "drills down" from the Verify Request (1.3) task in the Prepare Request map (see Exhibit 6.2). This map continues from the Approve Request (1.2) map in Exhibit 6.6. A connector is used to show the input into the system. All requests wind up in the disbursements clerk's in-bin, so the task begins there. Because batch processing is an indication of a delay, the "D" symbol is used. This includes the amount of time the paperwork may sit, as indicated by the times the batch is processed. Notice that even though there is nothing really happening to the paperwork, it is still assigned an index number.

Exhibit 6.7 shows that when the clerk begins working through the batch, the first thing reviewed is to see if the request is correct. If not, it is sent back to the requester. The decision on the map shows the requester correcting the problem and then sending

Exhibit 6.7 Payment by Check Request
Verify Request (1.3)—Action Level

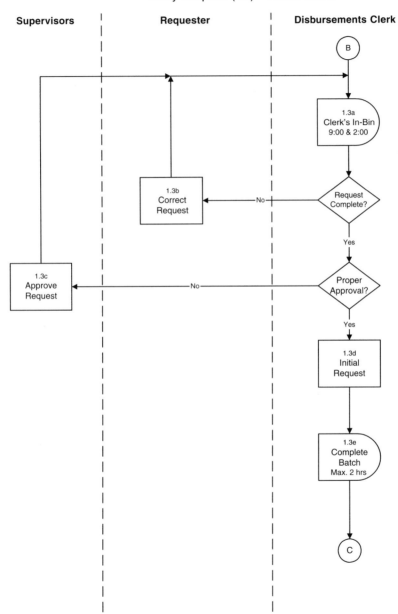

it back to wait for the next batch. Likewise, if the approval is not correct, the request is sent back to the appropriate supervisor. This decision also leads back to the supervisor, who signs the request and then returns it to sit in the in-bin.

If everything is okay, the clerk initials the form. Because this is an important control detail, it is included on the map. Once these three actions have been completed, the request is set aside until all have been reviewed. The delay here shows the reason for the delay and an indication of the maximum amount of time the requests may be held waiting for the batch to be completed.

Because this task is too large for a single sheet of paper, another connector is used at the end of this sheet and the beginning of the next. The next map takes up after the batch is completed.

Exhibit 6.8 combines the end of the Verify Request (1.3) task, continued from Exhibit 6.7, with the "drill down" of the Mail Request (1.4) task from Exhibit 6.2. Continuing from Exhibit 6.7, the next step is to photocopy all the requests. This can take up to 30 minutes. The originals are put in a 5-day hold-file. Notice that the document flowchart symbol was used. This highlights how the documents are handled. In addition, the hold-file is represented by the manual file symbol. It is not necessary to use these— process boxes will work just as well—but a few different symbols can help highlight certain situations.

Exhibit 6.8 shows that the photocopies are batched to be mailed at 3:00 P.M. The "D" (for delay) is used again because of the batch processing. At 3:00 P.M., the documents are prepared for overnight shipment to the home office. A process box representing this action is included. Then a copy of the shipping receipt is made and included in the hold-file. (Again, note the use of the document flowcharting symbol.) The photocopies are sent to the home office, and a connector representing the next unit ends the task. As was mentioned while discussing the task-level flowcharts, there

Exhibit 6.8 Payment by Check Request
Verify Request (1.3 continued) and
Mail Request (1.4)—Action Level

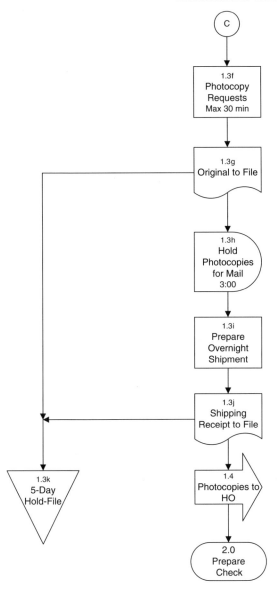

Disbursements Clerk

C

1.3f
Photocopy
Requests
Max 30 min

1.3g
Original to File

1.3h
Hold
Photocopies
for Mail
3:00

1.3i
Prepare
Overnight
Shipment

1.3j
Shipping
Receipt to File

1.3k
5-Day
Hold-File

1.4
Photocopies to
HO

2.0
Prepare
Check

is not a lot of detail regarding mailing the requests. However, it is important enough to be considered a separate task. On this map, it is indexed as Action 1.4. Exhibit 6.8 completes the "drill down" maps of the Prepare Request (1.0) tasks shown in Exhibit 6.2. Exhibit 6.5 showed the "drill down" of the Complete Requests (1.1) task, Exhibit 6.6 showed the "drill down" of the Approve Request (1.2) task, Exhibit 6.7 showed the "drill down" of the Verify Request (1.3) task, and Exhibit 6.8 showed the "drill down" of the completion of the Verify Request (1.3) task and the Mail Request (1.4) task.

Prepare Check: Prepare to Issue Task

The next series of maps will "drill down," starting again with Exhibit 6.1 and moving to the next unit level, Prepare Check (2.0). The task-level map in Exhibit 6.9 "drills down" from Exhibit 6.3 and the task Prepare to Issue (2.1). Overall, this is a relatively simple map. Although there are a number of actions, most are straightforward. Since we have started a new unit, the map begins with a reference to the source of the input—the first unit from Exhibit 6.1, Prepare Request (1.0). Exhibit 6.9 shows that the requests are put in a bin until 1:00 P.M., so the "D" symbol is used and the appropriate information is input.

After this, the steps go in a logical order. One of the clerks notifies the supervisor (2.1b), the supervisor turns on the printer (2.1c), the supervisor relocks the cabinet (2.1d), the clerks sign on to the system (2.1e), and then they open the mail (2.1f). Once the mail is open, the clerks are reviewing to see if they are appropriately initialed. This is shown as a decision on the map. Because the clerical staff does different things in this situation toward the same end, they are both represented in a single box.

The task ends with a connector to the next page. We have used the next letter in sequence from the one used in the prior unit (see

Exhibit 6.9 Payment by Check Request
Prepare to Issue (2.1)—Action Level

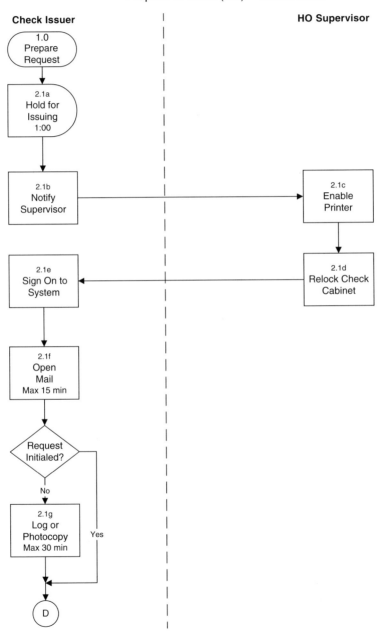

Exhibit 6.8). This is done to help reduce confusion regarding which sheet goes with which process. The more unique the connectors, the less likely it is that there will be any confusion.

Prepare Check: Issue Check Task

Exhibit 6.10 continues the "drill down" from the Prepare Check tasks in Exhibit 6.3 with the Issue Check (2.2) task. Again, this is a relatively simple process. Only one section within a department is involved (the check issuers) and, other than one batch process and one handoff of the documents, everything is a simple action.

After using a connector from the prior task in Exhibit 6.9, there are two straightforward actions—entering the check information and initialing the photocopies. The completed requests are batched until all are completed. The maximum amount of time these are held is included. There are two more actions—actually issuing the checks and signing off from the system. The final step is to hand-walk the forms to the check retriever. The arrow helps emphasize this transfer. Another connector leads to the next task.

Prepare Check: Retrieve Check Task

Exhibit 6.11 shows action taken on the Retrieve Check (2.3) task. After another connector from Exhibit 6.10, we have another task that starts with a delay caused by batching work. The maximum amount of time the batch may wait is listed as one hour. The next series of actions goes back and forth between the check retriever and the supervisor. The retriever notifies the supervisor, the supervisor unlocks the cabinet, the retriever collects the checks, and the supervisor relocks the cabinet. This ends the retrieval process.

Exhibit 6.10   Payment by Check Request
Issue Check (2.2)—Action Level

Exhibit 6.11 Payment by Check Request
Retrieve Check (2.3)—Action Level

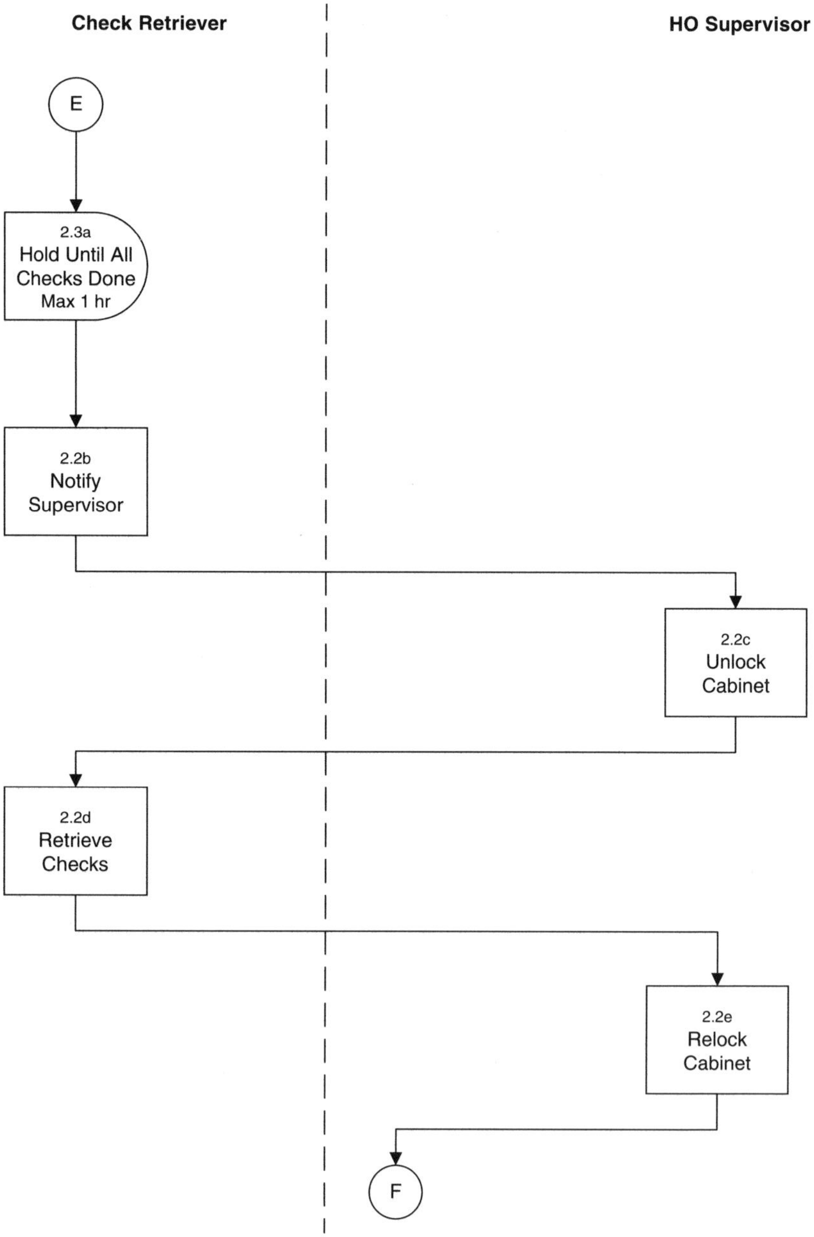

Check Retriever   **HO Supervisor**

```
      ( E )

     2.3a
  Hold Until All
  Checks Done
   Max 1 hr

     2.2b
    Notify
   Supervisor

                              2.2c
                             Unlock
                             Cabinet

     2.2d
   Retrieve
    Checks

                              2.2e
                             Relock
                             Cabinet

      ( F )
```

Prepare Check: Verify Check Task

Exhibit 6.12 combines the final two tasks, Verify Check (2.4) and Return Check (2.5), from Exhibit 6.3. These tasks are handled entirely by the check retriever. The first action is to match the checks and requests to ensure that everything has been completed properly. If they do not match, they are held until all checks are matched and mailed if possible. This is represented by the delay symbol after the decision. However, the process for rectifying nonmatching items is fairly complicated and requires additional "drilling down." Therefore, a reference is made to the detailed map that will be constructed.

If everything is in order, the retriever enters the check number on the copy of the request and initials it. These are held in a bin until each office is done. However, some items may still remain in waiting for up to four hours. Once an office is completed, the checks and photocopies are overnighted to the field office. Once again, the overnighting of the checks, although the only action within the task, is important enough to isolate. Also, since this is the end of this unit, Prepare Check (2.0) (see Exhibit 6.3), the connector shows the output going to the next unit, Deliver Check (3.0) (see Exhibit 6.4).

"Drilling Down": HO—No Corresponding Check or Request Action

Exhibit 6.13 is a "drill down" from action 2.4b in Exhibit 6.12. In the previous map, we mentioned that the process involved when checks and requests do not match was too intricate to explore at that time. Instead, a connector was used to reference another map (see Exhibit 6.12). "Drilling down" into this process in Exhibit 6.13 is important because it is a key control point and, as mentioned before, it is a little more complicated.

Exhibit 6.12 Payment by Check Request
Verify Check (2.4) and Return Check (2.5)—Action Level

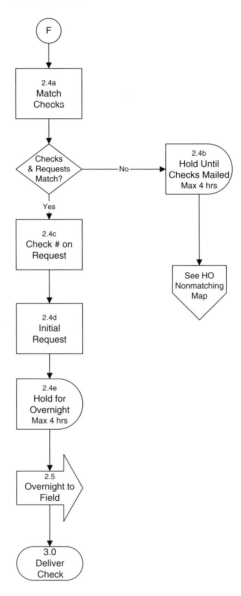

Check Retriever

F

2.4a
Match
Checks

Checks
& Requests
Match?

No → 2.4b
Hold Until
Checks Mailed
Max 4 hrs

Yes

2.4c
Check # on
Request

See HO
Nonmatching
Map

2.4d
Initial
Request

2.4e
Hold for
Overnight
Max 4 hrs

2.5
Overnight to
Field

3.0
Deliver
Check

Exhibit 6.13   Payment by Check Request
HO—No Corresponding Check or Request (2.4b)—"Drill Down"

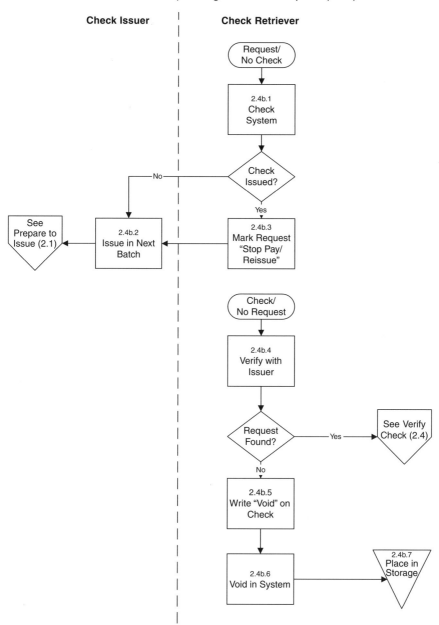

There are really two alternatives here. The first is that there is a request but no check. We start by showing that situation as the beginning of the map. From there, the retriever checks in the system to determine whether a check was actually entered. If not, the decision shows that the request is returned and the check is issued in the normal issue process (as shown by the connector.) If a check was issued, it is stopped in the system. The requester marks the check "Stop Pay/Reissue" and, again, the normal issuing procedures are followed.

Notice that the numbering system used relates to task and actions that lead to this process. The entire activity results from task 2.4—Verify Checks—and from action 2.4b—Hold Until Checks Mailed (referring to holding the unmatched items until the matched checks are mailed.) Therefore, a numbering system relating to those activities is used—2.4b.1, 2.4b.2, and so on.

In the second set of actions, we are looking at a situation in which there is a check but no request. Again, we show this situation to start the map. The retriever will verify with the issuer that the request cannot be found. If the request is found, a connector splits from the decision and shows a return to the Verify Checks map. If the request is not found, a series of actions follows— writing "Void" on the check, voiding the check in the system, and storing the void check. The storage point represents the end of the process.

The numbering system is continued in these processes. Note that the numbers continue the series started with the previous actions.

Deliver Check: Review Check Task

Exhibit 6.14 starts the "drill down" into the Deliver Check (3.0) unit shown in Exhibit 6.4. As with the previous tasks, this task begins by showing the unit that preceded it, Prepare Check (2.0).

Exhibit 6.14   Payment by Check Request
Review Check (3.1)—Action Level

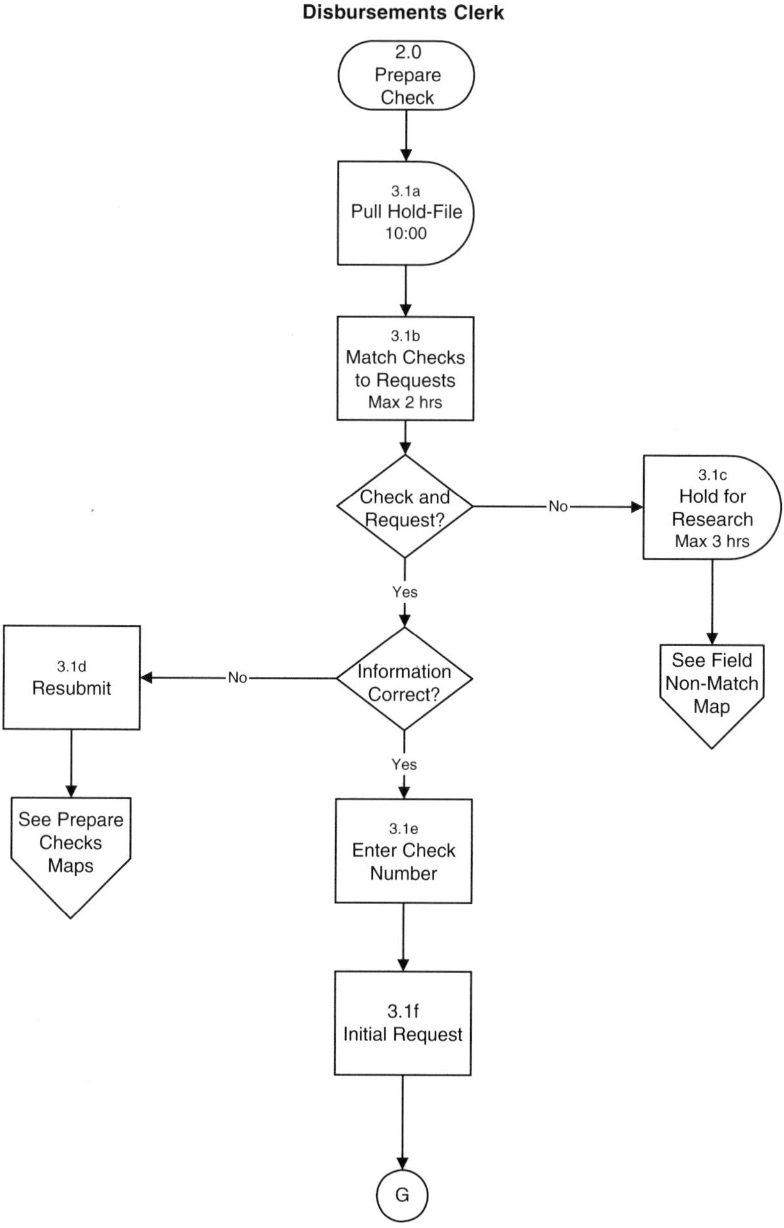

Disbursements Clerk

```
                    ╭─────────────╮
                    │     2.0     │
                    │   Prepare   │
                    │    Check    │
                    ╰─────────────╯
                           │
                    ╭──────────────╮
                    │    3.1a      │
                    │ Pull Hold-File│
                    │    10:00     │
                    ╰──────────────╯
                           │
                    ┌──────────────┐
                    │    3.1b      │
                    │ Match Checks │
                    │ to Requests  │
                    │  Max 2 hrs   │
                    └──────────────┘
                           │
                     ◇ Check and ◇        3.1c
                     ◇ Request?  ◇──No──► Hold for
                                          Research
                           │              Max 3 hrs
                          Yes                │
                           │                 │
    ┌──────────┐     ◇Information◇      See Field
    │  3.1d    │◄─No─◇ Correct?  ◇      Non-Match
    │ Resubmit │                        Map
    └──────────┘           │
         │                Yes
    See Prepare            │
    Checks            ┌──────────────┐
    Maps              │    3.1e      │
                      │ Enter Check  │
                      │   Number     │
                      └──────────────┘
                             │
                      ┌──────────────┐
                      │    3.1f      │
                      │Initial Request│
                      └──────────────┘
                             │
                           ( G )
```

Since all items are held until 10:00 A.M. for processing, a delay symbol is used. The hold-file is pulled, and all requests are matched to checks. If the checks and requests do not correspond, they are held to process later. Again, there is a fairly complicated system used to clear these items, so there is a reference to a "drill down" map. In this instance, the reference is to a field map to differentiate it from the home office "drill down" map completed as part of the Prepare Check unit.

If there are matching checks and requests, the clerk verifies that the amounts and the payees match. If they do not, the request must be resubmitted. The map refers the reader to the Prepare Checks maps. If everything matches, the clerk enters the check number and initials the request. A connector is used to refer to the next set of maps. Again, the letter used for this connector continues from those tasks completed previously.

"Drilling Down": Field—No Corresponding Check or Request Action

Exhibit 6.15 is the first map in this series of "drill downs," from Exhibit 6.14, action 3.1c. This map relates to the situation in which the disbursements clerk has a check but no request. The check is marked "Void" and a "Void Check" form is completed. Although there is a requirement that this be approved, the approval is not included in the map because this level of detail is not necessary. An arrow is used to indicate overnighting the documents to the home office. The check issuer voids the check in the system and places the supporting documentation in storage.

Exhibit 6.16 is the next map in the "drill down" series from Exhibit 6.14, action 3.1c. It represents the beginning of the "drilled down" process when the disbursements clerk has a request but no check. The request is put back into the hold-file. This may

Exhibit 6.15   Payment by Check Request
Field—Check No Request (3.1c)—"Drill Down"

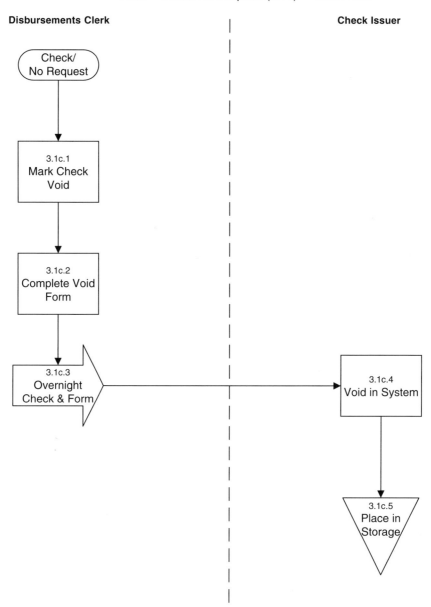

Exhibit 6.16   Payment by Check Request
Field—Request No Check (3.1c)—"Drill Down"

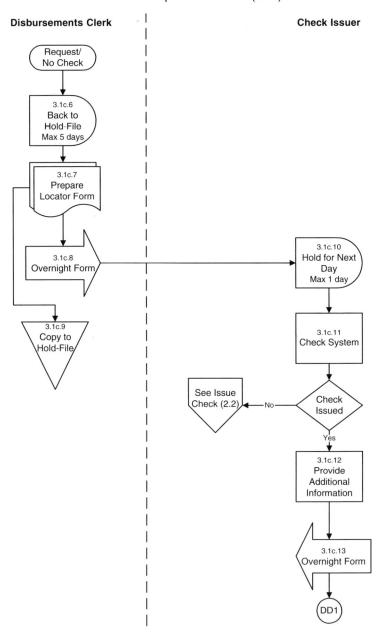

182

delay handling the missing check by up to five days. If the check does not come in, a Check Locator form is completed. Notice that in this instance two copies of the document symbol have been used to represent the original and the copy. The copy is filed in the hold-file. The original is overnighted to the check issuer. The original is held for processing the following day.

The next action is to determine whether the check has been issued. If it has not been issued, the check is issued using the process shown in the Issue Check map. If it has been issued, additional information is added to the form that is overnighted back to the field office. The connector to the next map is slightly different. Because this is a "drill down" rather than a continuation of the existing maps, use of the existing lettering system might become confusing. Instead, "DD1" is used (this stands for "drill down" one).

Exhibit 6.17 is the last half of the "drilled down" process from Exhibit 6.14, action 3.1c, when the disbursements clerk has a request but not a check. The "DD1" connector starts the map. The clerk will verify that the check has not yet been received. If the check has been received, it is implied that the process stops. Therefore, there is no decision and resulting end of the process. At this point a "Stop Pay Form" is completed and overnighted to the home office. Again, there is a requirement that the supervisor approve the stop pay form, but this is not considered significant enough to map.

When the check issuer receives the form, the system is checked to see whether the check has cleared. If it has not cleared, payment is stopped and a new check is issued. The map references the Issue Check tasks. If the check has cleared, the processes that relate to fraud are implemented. Notice that the termination of the map shows this process with an indication that the process has not been mapped. This often happens as you work through a process; additional processes interact with the one under review. However,

Exhibit 6.17 Payment by Check Request
Field—Request No Check (3.1c)—
"Drill Down" (Continued)

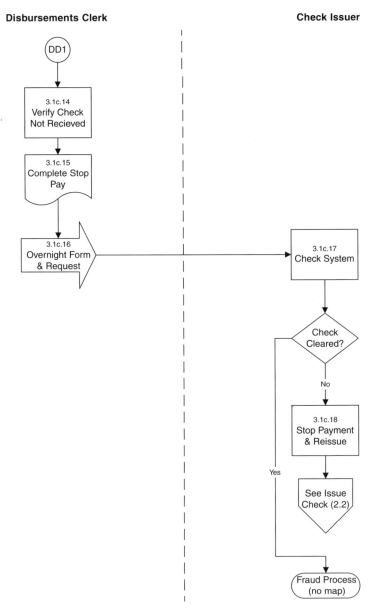

Disbursements Clerk

DD1

3.1c.14
Verify Check
Not Recieved

3.1c.15
Complete Stop
Pay

3.1c.16
Overnight Form
& Request

Check Issuer

3.1c.17
Check System

Check
Cleared?

No

3.1c.18
Stop Payment
& Reissue

Yes

See Issue
Check (2.2)

Fraud Process
(no map)

there is never enough time to look at all of them. Therefore, the map can reference these situations with an indication that it is outside the scope of the review.

Because of the complexity of the process for unmatched items, it is a good idea to raise the map a level. Exhibit 6.18 represents this bird's-eye view of what is occurring. This is also an example of how you may wind up working from the details to the overview rather than the other way around.

The process starts by determining whether the situation is a check with no request or a request with no check. If there is no request, the request to void is prepared in the field office, and the actual voiding of the check takes place in home office. If the check is missing, there are four higher-level steps that occur between the two offices. The field office prepares forms to have the home office locate the check. The home office then verifies that the check was issued. The field office then processes a stop pay. Finally, the home office begins lost check procedures—either issuing a new one or handling as a fraud. This high-level view helps document how the process jumps from one location to another.

Deliver Check: Return to Requester Task

Exhibit 6.19 is the last of the "drill down" maps for the task Deliver Check (3.0) shown in Exhibit 6.4. Notice that this map combines two tasks, Mail to Payee (3.2) and Return to Requester (3.3). This is done because they are closely related and relatively straightforward. The final map starts with the connector "G," which ended the prior map. There are two routes that can be followed, depending on how the payment is to be handled. These correspond to the two tasks.

If the check is to be mailed to the payee (3.2), the envelope is stuffed with the check and any necessary correspondence. The

Exhibit 6.18   Payment by Check Request
Field—No Corresponding Check
or Request (3.1c)—Task Level

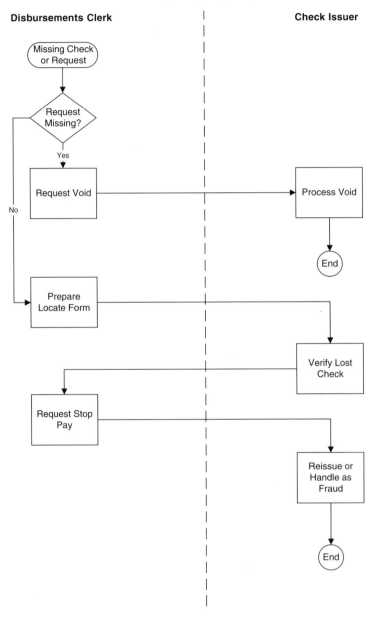

Exhibit 6.19   Payment by Check Request
Mail to Payee (3.2) and Return
to Requester (3.3)—Action Level

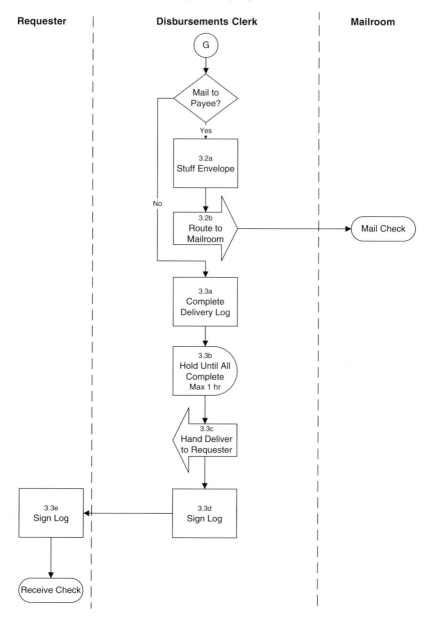

documents are then routed to the mailroom. The end of the process is shown by the mailroom mailing the check.

If the check is to be returned to the payee (3.3), the information is recorded on the delivery log. All items are held until check processing is complete. This is shown as a delay in the system. This is an excellent example of a delay that may be necessary. If the clerk were to deliver each check as it was processed, the entire system would slow down. However, even if this appears to be the best system, it is still better to use the "D" symbol to identify all batch processing systems.

Once all checks are processed, the clerk hand-delivers checks to the requesters. When the check is delivered, both the clerk and the requester sign the log to show transfer of the document. The process ends once the check is delivered.

RECAP

In general, the best way to learn Process Mapping is to do it. This example should have provided you with just that chance. If you completed your own maps before looking through our examples, you probably found that yours are very different. That is to be expected. No one person will build the same map as another.

If you did not try your own hand at Process Mapping with this example, you probably should go back and try anyway. The chances are you are looking at the maps now and thinking that, although there are a lot of them, there does not seem to be anything tough about them. That is the great part about Process Mapping—the final product looks deceptively simple. Almost anyone can understand it, and people who are involved in the process recognize it instantly. Process maps are not easy to produce, and it is only by working on your own that you will learn how to make it look easy, too.

KEY ANALYSIS POINTS

Know the Process

While it is true that one of the purposes of Process Mapping is to learn about the process, that does not mean that you should go in completely clueless. By knowing the basics of how the process works, you will have an insight into what should be documented. In the expense example, knowing that there were a number of transfers between departments meant there should be extra emphasis on this part of the process. Accordingly, these transfers were highlighted by using large arrows.

Begin Visualizing Controls

A corollary to knowing the process is having a rudimentary understanding of the controls that exist in the process. By understanding these controls, you will have a better chance of accurately showing them in the map. This emphasis will help you isolate breakdowns during the analysis phase. In the expense example, one instance of this is specifically breaking out the check issuer and check retriever duties into separate columns. This separation highlights their roles in two-party controls.

Use the Levels to Understand the Process

Units, tasks, and actions are intended to give varying depths of understanding to a process. They should be used accordingly. Starting from the high level gives the broad overview that helps define the purpose of actions. However, starting with the actions makes it easier for the reviewer to build an initial map. Then the understanding of the broad units can be built from there. Ultimately, the approach that provides the best understanding should be used.

CHAPTER 7

Analysis

There is a natural hootchy-kootchy motion to a goldfish.

—Walt Disney on the fish ballet in *Fantasia*

INTO THE EDITING ROOM

By now you should be acutely aware that true analysis for a Process Mapping project occurs from the moment the project is taken on to that final moment when you walk out the door for the last time. If you have been waiting until this point to begin analysis, it is far too late. To show this, we have been including analysis tips and techniques that should be going on from the project's initiation. However, once the maps are close to completion and the interviews have been done, it is time to try to tie all the pieces together.

When the shooting is complete, the actors go home, and the extras get their little checks, the miles and miles of film go into the editing room. While the editing of a film really starts when the writer has that first glimmer of an idea, the real nuts and bolts of developing the finished product—of analyzing the acts, scenes, and shots to develop a coherent product—occurs in the editing room.

So it is with a process map. In some instances, you may have a room that is wallpapered with white sheets and yellow sticky-notes. In that case, you have the Herculean task of translating these notes into a graphic picture that everyone can understand. Other times you may have dutifully recorded the map information at the conclusion of each interview, changing information as you needed to and maintaining a pristine picture of processes as you went along.

But even if you are able to faithfully duplicate the images you have captured with your sticky-notes and arrows, there is still an important task ahead of you. You must take those units, tasks, and actions, and transform them into a coherent product that shows not only how the process is done, but also how it should be done right—determining what is right and what is wrong. There are clues in the maps themselves that will help you determine what is right and what is wrong, but before you dig into the maps, it is a good idea to take a step backward.

Go back to the Process Profile Work Sheet. Whether these have been prepared at the process level or the unit level, look back to see if what you were told matches what really happens. In developing these work sheets, you have been given someone's perception of what starts that process, what ends that process, who owns parts of the process, what the business objectives are, what the business risks are, what the key controls are, and what the measures of success are. Look to see if that initial under-standing is true.

TRIGGERS AND FALSE TRIGGERS

In the beginning, you identified the triggers that initiate each part of the process. If you discussed this in depth with the owner, you probably made sure that the trigger was truly initiated from customer needs. Now, make sure that the *right* trigger has been found. In some instances, you may see that the true trigger for the process occurs earlier or later than first thought. If that is the case, there are a number of things you must review.

First, make sure that you have covered everything you need to. If the trigger actually occurs sooner than was first thought, you must take a look at more of the process. In the expense example, it would be very easy for a reviewer and an owner to come to agreement that preparing the check request is the trigger for the process. It is easy to see this as a precise point in time, and it is the first document created. However, this would result in an important part of the process being missed—the time between receipt of the bill and paying it. If there were significant delays in the payment of bills (a measure of success) that came about because of a delay in the mailroom getting bills to the requester, that part of the process might be missed. Because of timeliness issues, the proper trigger should be receipt of the bill *by the company.*

However, setting the trigger too early can cause just as many problems. Primary among these is that too much information may be gathered and the important analysis missed because of the morass of information. Again using the expense example, a reviewer and an owner may come to agreement that the payment process cannot begin without some action being taken that causes the expense—the janitorial service cleans the office, electrical expenses are incurred during a month, the CEO orders a new magazine, or making a profit results in taxes being owed. In that case, it might be thought that the trigger is incurring the expense. However, setting the trigger too early has resulted in a process that is too broad and complex. The reviewer cannot be expected to look all the way back to how electrical expenses are generated. While this is a problem for the analyst, it is also a problem for the company being reviewed. If the company thinks of its expense process in this manner, it may have unreasonable expectations about timeliness and what it expects of its accounts payable group.

Second, make sure that a company's misconceptions regarding the trigger do not cause problems with interrelated processes. The more a process needs to be completed in a "just in time" manner, the more important this is. An example of misidentifying the trigger—developing a "false trigger"—can be shown from our earlier example of making breakfast. We talked about the trigger for all the tasks for cooking ingredients (cook bacon, cook eggs, heat toast, fry potatoes) being the same—prepare ingredients. However, if this is the actual trigger used for all four areas, part of the breakfast is going to be cold. If the bacon takes longer to cook, the trigger for it may actually occur during the ingredient preparation unit. If the toast gets done fairly quickly, the optimal trigger may be somewhere in the egg cooking task. Therefore, if the cook uses "pan hot" as the trigger for bacon (even though all other ingredients are not used) and "egg cooked for one minute" as the trigger for heating the toast, the final result may be a complete breakfast with all items served at the same time, piping hot.

INPUTS AND OUTPUTS

Inputs

Closely related to the trigger is the concept of inputs to the process. Make sure that people involved in the process recognize all inputs and their sources. If people do not recognize the source of an input, they will not know where to go to rectify problems when they occur.

When evaluating outputs, it probably is more important for you as the reviewer to approach outputs differently than the company does. In the classic definition of output, it usually is easy to understand the resulting product. That information should be recorded on the Process Profile Work Sheet. At the same time, you have identified the customers receiving that output. You have also tried to determine if value has been provided to that customer—whether it is the final customer or the "customer" that is the next step in the process chain.

But to really analyze what a process is producing, it is important to take a broader look. In his book *The Competitive Power of Constant Creativity*,[1] Clay Carr dissects outputs and allows us to take a better look at what really comes from a process.

Outputs

Begin by thinking of each process creating results rather than output. There is an input to the system, a transformation occurs to that input, and there is some result to the company. Carr defines four different types of result. The first is the most obvious and the concept that is normally used—output. This is the result the company anticipates and wants—it is what the company expects to make.

Waste

The next result is waste. The classic definition of waste is product that is thrown away as useless. However, for our purposes it needs to be broader. For example, it should include scrap. Many companies think of scrap as an achievement—waste for which value is found. But it is waste nonetheless. It is a result that does not provide the value expected. Anything produced that does not result in full potential is waste, and a good analysis focuses on how these wastes occur and what is done with them.

One area that often comes under scrutiny during a Process Mapping project is the system in place to correct errors. Very often you will see maps that spend a lot of time focusing on error rates and rework items. However, it is always less expensive for a company to get things done right the first time than to have to go back and fix them. Therefore, it is better for the analyst to understand why errors occur rather than how to fix them more efficiently. Although streamlining the correction process is fine, it is just as important to look upstream in the process to see where the errors occur.

It is also important to point out that you cannot understand what waste is until you actually know what it is you are trying to produce. Even something as easily defined as a cog needs a prototype to ensure that the correct items are produced. Without knowing what is required up front, the entire production may be nothing but waste.

Surprises

Now we move into less obvious results. As stated a number of times, processes are designed to do something (ideally, to provide value to some customer). However, it is a rare process that always does what it is expected to do. These unexpected results are surprises.

New processes are the most susceptible to surprises. When a process is established, everyone has a good idea what they think it will accomplish. But there are too many variables and there will always be surprises. And it does not take a new process to produce surprises. All it requires is a small change to the input or process itself—maybe even something as simple as an employee going on vacation. One company had a process for accepting payments from independent contractors. Cash collections were deposited to a local bank. The independent contractor would write a check from the account and send it in to the servicing office along with any checks received. For one independent contractor, the process was going fine until the bank clerk he normally worked with went on vacation. Because they were good friends, she would always call when his account was about to be overdrawn. However, when she went on vacation, the temporary clerk did not warn him and his check bounced. This was a surprise for the independent contractor. It was also a surprise for the servicing office because it was the first indication of a $20,000 embezzlement.

It is evident that surprises can be either pleasant or unpleasant. This was a pleasant surprise for the company—it discovered and stopped embezzlement. However, this was an unpleasant surprise for the independent contractor.

Another example of surprises can be seen with the expense payment example. In this case, there are a number of unpleasant surprises. The most obvious may be increased costs because of missed discount dates or fines from missed payments. A less obvious surprise might be an increased workload because the designers misunderstood the volume of work that would be experienced. Another surprise might be increased costs because of increased mailings—both the initial mailing and the numerous mailings for error correction.

Invisible Consequences

The final result is invisible consequences. These represent the forest most companies can't see for the trees. The difference between surprises and invisible consequences is that surprises are quickly seen, whereas invisible consequences lie in the dark waiting to strike. Surprises cannot be ignored. Eventually, invisible consequences cannot be ignored either, but it is that "eventually" that is the killer.

There is a joke that a consultant is someone you pay to tell you the time off your own watch. There is some truth to this because the consultant comes in with fresh eyes. A good reviewer (even if working from within the company) has the ability to be naïve in the ways of the department and ask the questions that everyone already thinks they know the answers to. Therefore, the good reviewer should be able to come in and see the invisible consequences that other people are not naïve enough to ask about.

In the expense payment scenario, there could be any number of invisible consequences. These might include the company's loss of reputation within the community because of delayed payments, employees looking to work for a company that respects its employees enough to ensure that their word to suppliers is honored, and the eventual destruction of morale as workloads increase.

In a review we recently completed, a major suggestion we made to the executive in charge of the department is an excellent example of an invisible consequence. We were called in shortly after the executive took over. He had been put in as a developmental assignment and knew almost nothing about that line of the business. His prior experience had been in one of the support services. On top of that, the prior two executives in that position had also been on developmental assignments. They both had some marketing experience, so they understood a little more about the department, but not enough to instill any confidence in the workers. In addition, each had left the department for new assignments within two years. It was apparent in our discussions that the employees were tired of the revolving door. Other companies were hiring in the same line and hiring away the department's good employees. Those who were left behind (including some of the top managers) felt disenfranchised and overlooked. The solution we presented could not solve the entire problem, but it would address some of it. We suggested that the executive spend part of a day with each employee and learn what he or she did. Not just a gratuitous "I'm part of the team" type meeting, but a meeting to actually learn what the nuts and bolts of these jobs were. In this way, the executive could show that he cared about his team while he also showed that he cared what was really occurring. At the same time, by admitting that he did not know as much as anyone else, he was able to show them some of the leadership skills the CEO had seen when he gave him this appointment.

PROCESS OWNERSHIP

Once the maps are complete, it is also a good time to review who thinks they own each process. At the outset, you tried to determine these owners, and in some instances, this was relatively easy. However, there may have been portions that remained unclear—in some instances you may have even walked into turf wars.

This is the point when you can determine who the owners are and possibly make your own decision about who would be the best owner. This can be a tough recommendation to make, but if your map shows that the process is best handled by someone else, then by all means make that recommendation. In one situation, a collection center was overseen (owned) by the accounting department. This seemed to make sense because the collection of cash is normally an accounting function. However, it became apparent that, while the majority of the work was counting and depositing collections, there was also a lot of coordination required with the billing department. This billing department was part of a larger administration department and could not be separated. The result was that the collection department changed its reporting to the administration department. With the new "ownership," the processes between billing and collection became more transparent and customer service was improved.

Beyond determining if the right owners are in charge, you should make sure that everyone understands who the owners really are. And maybe more important, make sure there is an owner who will really take responsibility. In an amusement park, responsibility for various areas was defined by what the people did. Food servers were responsible for preparing and serving food; ride personnel were responsible for getting people on and off rides safely; janitors were responsible for seeing that the walkways, chairs, and tables were clean; and gardeners were responsible for the plants and shrubs and other outdoor accoutrements.

In the middle of one large building was a fountain. It was becoming the disgrace of the park. The food servers did not think it was their job to keep it clean because, although it was in the food court, it had nothing to do with serving food. The ride personnel did not think it was their job to keep it clean because, even though there were rides on either side of it, it had nothing to do with running the rides. The janitors did not think it was their job to keep it clean because; although it was surrounded by walkways, chairs, and tables; there was a definite planter surrounding the fountain. Gardeners did not think it was part of their job because, although there was a planter surrounding the fountain, the fountain itself was not a plant.

No one wanted to be the owner. The solution was an interesting one. Rather than try to force any one department into being the owner, a new arrangement was established. Instead of there being a manager of food service and a manager of ride personnel and so on, one person was put in charge of each area of the amusement park. Suddenly, everyone who worked in that particular building not only had responsibility for the fountain but also had responsibility for everything that went on in the building. The ride operators were responsible for the food court, the food servers were responsible for the walkways, and everyone was responsible for the fountain. By redefining the owner of the process, fewer processes slipped through the cracks.

BUSINESS OBJECTIVE

There is no one single thing that can be lost in the hustle and bustle of getting things done more than remembering why you are doing them in the first place. The same is true of a process. By the time you have mapped and talked and analyzed, you may have forgotten what the process was trying to do in the first place. And many of the employees (if they knew in the first place) have forgotten also.

So this is the point when you look back and reevaluate whether that process is still hitting its mark. Look at the overall process and make sure that it is addressing the primary objective. Take a look at parts of the process and see if they are also supporting those objectives. If not, determine if they are supporting some other objective. This may mean that part of the process must be realigned or even moved to another process. It may also mean that a potentially big objective is being missed and more emphasis should be placed on it.

In a check issuance process we reviewed, there were two major objectives—to issue checks for the correct amount and to ensure that no fraudulent checks were issued. One of the key controls relating to fraudulent check issuance was a systematic managerial review of payments. A listing was printed showing all checks numbers for the selected time period. Managers selected 10 per week for review.

However, the manager did not understand the objective of the process. He delegated the review to a supervisor (one who had check issuance authority and would be reviewing his own checks), and he allowed the supervisor to replace checks for the sample when he could not find support for one in the original selection. The result was that the control was totally ineffective. Once the objective of the process was explained, the manager took control of the operation and completed the reviews (with no substitutions) himself.

201

BUSINESS RISKS

A set of risks were identified at the outset of the project. These were discussed with everyone involved in the project, and agreement was reached on the major risks. There is a chance you have already helped them recognize risks they did not see themselves. Now you have seen the full process, how it fits together, and what it is truly accomplishing. It is an excellent opportunity to see if new risks have been identified. Usually, this does not focus on changing broad risks, but on the portions of those broad risks that may be a concern.

The first situation is that in which an employee has made you aware of a condition no one recognized. Just as we have talked before about employees giving us the best ideas, they have also warned us of some of the largest problems. While reviewing a claims process, one supervisor informed us that original documentation was not always available when the claim was being settled. This would result in portions of losses being covered that were never intended to be covered. Obviously, there was a resulting increase in claims costs. In some cases the documentation was lost, but in most cases it was never prepared or submitted. We told the supervisor we were a little surprised about this because over the last year we had tested this very item and found that everyone currently understood the requirements. Our testing showed that everyone was doing a very good job of following these requirements. The supervisor agreed, but then mentioned that the problem was happening in policies that were more than three years old.

We had the right risk (the exposure of incorrectly paying claims because of improper documentation), but we were focusing on the wrong part. We had focused on the current understanding of procedures and the resulting requirements. Everything was fine in this area—recent training had brought everyone up to speed and our tests showed a good track record. However, we had forgotten the full risk. Complete documentation means more than getting it right from now on—it also means getting things right in the past or making them right. We realized that we had to let our customers know that there was an additional unidentified risk—past documentation was incomplete.

Some new risks may become apparent from the structure or content of the maps themselves. This is really based on the input of employees also (what in Process Mapping is not?). This situation usually occurs when there is a part of the map going in a direction no one anticipated. It usually comes from one employee who handles the miscellaneous operations where so much hides.

One company we worked with was thinking of making changes to its purchasing processes—primarily streamlining approval processes and the resulting paperwork. Purchasing is one of those areas that no one seems to want to change because it is very susceptible to fraud and contains many sacred cows. Everyone had recognized risks regarding fraud, overpayment, and even misstatement of assets. In talking with various employees, it looked like the new process would work well, everyone's concerns could be addressed, and the process would be significantly streamlined. Then we spoke with one of the accountants, who mentioned that the information from the furniture and fixtures listing went into a certain report. As we dug deeper into the report, we found that it was the basis for part of the company's state taxes. We immediately had a new risk—compliance with tax regulations. And it was a very important risk to identify because the new process had not addressed the situation at all. We raised concerns about the new risk, and there was instant agreement to make changes necessary to comply. The process was still streamlined (with a few extra steps), the company had a fuller understanding of the risks it was facing, and the company had fuller assurance that risk was being properly mitigated.

KEY CONTROLS

This is sometimes the easiest issue to identify while reviewing (and even while completing) process maps. The initial discussion with owners has usually identified the primary controls. If the controls do not exist, that is usually discovered before the actual mapping begins. In those cases in which the owners are not sure whether a key control exists, the mapping can prove if it does or does not.

However, the most likely scenario is that the process owner, senior management, or even local management states that there is a good control in place. Procedure may back this up. However, when you speak with the people performing the work, they either never heard of the control or do not bother completing it.

A perfect example is the one discussed previously where the accounting section supervisors were not completing file reviews for payment support. Everyone knew what the procedure was, but they did not think they had the time to do it. The process owners knew there was a procedure and thought it was being completed, and even senior management knew there was a procedure and thought it was being completed, but they all were wrong.

In some instances, everyone may understand the control and be doing their best to comply, but miscommunication results in a breakdown of the control. During the review of processes for a significant unit of a company, we began looking at accounts processing. The accounts clerks handled many transactions, and we completed a number of maps that headed in many directions. We then had to track down those different directions. One account (a collections account) included a task where the monthly numbers were sent to an individual in the company's home office. The clerical staff indicated that there was no further work needed—balancing and adjustments were not their concern. Speaking with the person who received the reports, we found that he was a

204

programmer who had originally written a software program to store and report on the information. He had requested the information four years ago to test the new program. He had been receiving the reports ever since. He threw out any reports he received and, in spite of often asking them to no longer send the reports, still received them.

It is vitally important to follow up and verify all paths in a process map. As is discussed in a little bit, it is the dangling ends that may indicate problems. In this case, it showed that a key control did not exist.

MEASURES OF SUCCESS

Measures of success, too, are relatively easy to see when maps are completed. Primary measures are often a function of elapsed time—issuing checks within 48 hours or returning phone calls within 20 minutes—and the cycle times on the maps can instantly provide evidence that a measure is unreachable. In those instances, a determination must to made—change the process or change the measure.

While reviewing a call center, we learned that the measurement was answering 80 percent of phone calls within 20 seconds. In developing the maps, we learned that every call was logged in a call management system. Because of system utilization, the time between entering the information and going to the next screen could often take up to a minute. Based on the volume of calls and the time spent working within the system, it was impossible to meet the goal. There were two choices available to the process owners. The first choice was to change the goal. A more realizable goal was to answer 50 percent of the calls.

This was unacceptable to the client because it thought that the objective of customer service could only be met by answering more calls in less time. The second alternative was to change the procedure. That is the choice management accepted. Rather than logging all calls, procedures were established regarding which calls to record. By not logging all calls, the objective of completely documenting calls was not going to be met. However, this streamlined the process enough so that the more important goal of customer satisfaction was accomplished.

ANALYZING THE ACTUAL MAPS

So now we return to the actual process maps. There are basic actions you can look for in every map that are indicators of problems—either inefficiencies or control breakdowns. These should be isolated and examined in depth because they represent golden opportunities for improvement.

Remove Approvals

Business has passed through the golden age of empowerment. It was one of the buzzwords of the 1990s, and it seemed that everyone wanted to give everyone more authority. Despite that, companies still find themselves mired in layers and layers of approvals. For every authorization requirement that was removed, 10 or 20 must still exist.

Do not misunderstand. We are not advocating the removal of every level of approval that exists. But in most companies, authority levels are usually a sacred cow that deserves to be slain.

In *At America's Service,*[2] Karl Albrecht repeats a story told to him by Dick Scott, CEO of Longs Drugs stores. Scott was standing at one of his stores when he noticed the store manager approving customers' checks. The cashier would stop the line, walk over to the manager, and obtain the approval. In general, the manager would be talking to someone else, and Scott noticed that the manager was not even looking at the check. Instead, he would initial it and just hand it back to the clerk.

Later, Scott talked with the manager. He suggested that the cashiers just approve the checks so the customers would receive better service. The manager was horrified and thought there would be a significant rise in bad checks. Scott asked him, "When she brought you the check for your approval, what thought process went through your mind as you approved it?" The manager answered, "Well, no thought process, really. I didn't give it much thought to tell the truth." Scott replied, "If you didn't have any thought process going on in *your* head, don't you think we could teach her not to have any thought process going on in *her* head?"

Approvals are extremely time-consuming, and they take up the time of people whose time is most valuable. Look at the example of an approval process in Exhibit 7.1. First, the paperwork can wind up going through many hands. If it is over $1,000, it is touched by two employees, a supervisor and a manager. And that is only if it is all done correctly. If there are constant errors, one piece might go through that same loop a number of times. Also notice that the phrase Journal Correct? is used three different times. That means three different people are required to ensure the correctness of this journal.

It may well be that this is a perfectly legitimate need. It all depends on what the journal is for or what the process surrounding it is. However, these are the kinds of tasks that must be identified to determine if they are necessary, and the need for the control must be weighed against the additional time this takes. What is not included on this particular map are the cycle times and the holding times. Usually, the higher the individual's position, the longer a request for authority will sit in an in-bin. Once again, elimination of the approvals or setting higher authorities for low-level employees may make for quicker customer service.

Exhibit 7.1   Journal Approval

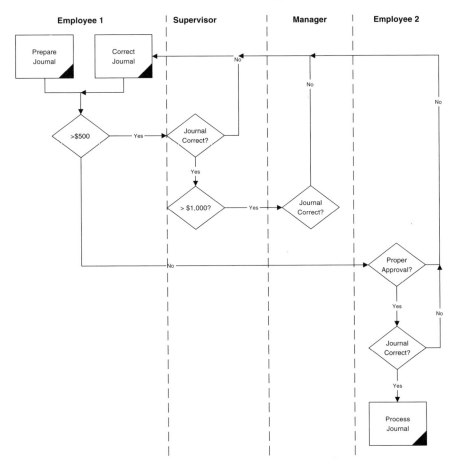

Looping Errors

In computer programming this is known as an infinite loop—a situation in which the programmer has inadvertently set up criteria that force the computer to process the same commands over and over. This results in the program fatally crashing. Likewise, looping errors can make a process fatally crash, even if the loop is not infinite. Exhibit 7.1 is also an example of this.

As mentioned in the previous section, constant errors could cause the document to go through the same loop a number of times. When these types of loops are encountered, there are two things that must be determined. Are all these decisions really necessary and, if so, does everything have to feed back to the beginning? The need for the decisions we discussed in the previous section. But sometimes a better question is whether the information needs to go back to the top of the process map. In our example, the journal is going back to the person who first wrote it. Then it falls back through the same filters to either pass muster or be returned again.

In general, these type of loops stem from a "do the crime, do the time" mentality. In other words, because the employee did it incorrectly, it is up to the employee to fix it. However, this sometimes arises because the company is attempting to help employees learn how to process information correctly by showing them when something is wrong. No matter what the situation, it is always important to also determine if there is an appropriate feedback loop to help ensure that people learn how to complete processes correctly. If not, the same errors will occur and the process will never be streamlined.

Isolate Delays, Rework, and Handoffs

If you have been using the symbols suggested in Chapter 5, this should be very easy—look for the "D" or "R" symbols. If you have not been keeping up on this, there will be a little more work.

Delays exist for various reasons, but some are more apparent and more easily eliminated. One of the main delays to look for is when documents sit in an in-basket. Although not identified as such, there may be significant delays in Exhibit 7.1 at both the supervisor's desk and the manager's desk. There is a good chance journals are set aside until "I can get to them." Or they may be held until there are "enough worth doing." While doing reviews of small businesses—usually two- to four-person operations—we have found situations in which the days' collections are held in a desk drawer because the owner "does not have time to make the deposit."

For these types of situations, you must determine two different aspects of the problem—is it something that should be corrected and what is causing the delay? It is important to think of them in this order because the answer to the first question may eliminate the second—if it is not worth correcting, no one cares why the delay exists. In the case of depositing collections, it is obviously a problem that must be corrected. Collections sitting around are collections that can be stolen, and a key control over a significant business risk is not operating as intended. That means the reviewer would need to determine whether the delays are the result of misunderstanding (or not caring about) procedure or if there is a problem in the process. For the situation in which journals are delayed, it is less obvious if this needs correction. In previous sections we talked about eliminating delay by eliminating approvals. However, if the approvals are needed, it may be an education issue with management. Ultimately, though, it may well be that, although the approval is necessary, it does not need to occur for a couple of days. In that case, there may be no need to improve the process.

Rework is a little more insidious than delay. Not only does rework delay the process (including any associated costs), but also additional resources are expended correcting the problem. Exhibit 7.1 is also good as an example of rework. Every time something goes wrong, the work must be handled a second time. To determine if this is a significant problem in the process, the error rates should be entered. Much like the analysis done for delay, determine if the rework should be eliminated and what is causing it. If an error rate is very low, there may be no need (or it may not be cost-effective) to eliminate the errors. However, it is always worth determining if the errors are based on a lack of education. A little training can solve many problems.

Handoffs occur whenever a product or paperwork (or even a computer file or e-mail) is going from person to person and sometimes back again. Exhibit 7.1 is also one example of a problem with handoffs. The approval process requires that paperwork go from the employee to a supervisor to a manager to a second employee. Four people handle a piece of paper that may only require being handled by two. Since employee #2 is performing a verification, there may be no need for the handoffs to the supervisor and the manager. In fact, if the proper computer systems are put to work, employee #1 may be able to handle the journal without any assistance.

There may be an opportunity to streamline the process anytime a physical transfer exists. This may mean something as simple as replacing memos with E-mail. It may also mean getting people to handle their part of the process at one time rather than spreading it over time. Exhibit 7.2 is loosely based on a process we reviewed a few years ago and is constructed at a fairly high (sometimes task) level. Two departments were involved in accepting or rejecting input received from the field. Department 1 was primarily a clerical function, whereas Department 2 was a professional-level function. The information could be received by computer or on paper. In talking with the people, it seemed a fairly straightforward process. If the field input the information into the system, it went directly to Department 2. If not, Department 1 input part of the information and, barring immediate rejection, input the entire form. Department 2 then reviewed the information, determined what other data were needed, reviewed the data, and then made a final decision.

However, as the map shows, information was being passed back and forth at an alarming rate. These handoffs were hidden in the process and only became apparent when the map was

Exhibit 7.2 Accept/Reject Process

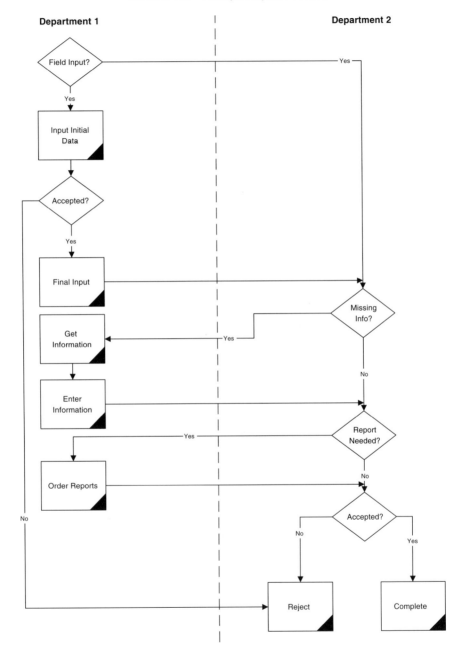

completed. When the process owner was shown these maps, he instantly realized the heart of his problem. The number of times actions cross from department to department becomes painfully obvious. And it was not until it was shown this graphically that the people involved in the process understood how they could combine tasks to gain more efficiencies in the system.

This is also an example of how decisions sometimes hide a problem with handoffs. Most people we spoke with in Department 2 thought their process was very streamlined. They spoke of how they would receive the work and handle it to conclusion. They believed they had a "one and done" process (handle it once and be done.) The people in Department 1 also thought they were handling things efficiently. When they got the work, they completed the task they were supposed to and passed it on. They had never seen the connection that some of the work was being handled two, three, or four times.

People tend to think of decisions as an important step in a process. So when they complete a decision, they often think they have reached a milestone that marks the end of a process. This causes an artificial termination in their minds. Therefore, they may not see the connection with the full process. That was the situation in this example. Because the decision was completed and a resulting process was started, employees thought they had an efficient process. By graphically representing these decisions in the overall process, they could see that each decision was only one step of many.

Follow the Forms

In completing process maps, be sure you are keeping track of the actual forms that are being used, including knowing exactly where they go. Although it was not mentioned specifically in Chapter 5, another useful symbol is the document symbol. You do not necessarily want to go into a lot of detail about individual forms in your process map, but it may be useful in some situations to create a document flowchart. These are usually constructed with the departments across the top. It is not a bad idea when creating this type of flowchart to follow the Process Mapping rule of having events move chronologically down the page. Each form should be represented, along with how many copies there are. Each copy should then be tracked through the various departments it visits. Exhibit 7.3 is a very simple example of a document flowchart for the beginning of a purchasing process.

In some situations, document flowcharts can be analyzed much like process maps. The most obvious situation is when forms are moving back and forth between departments. The situation is much like that described in the previous section. If you see forms flying between departments, there may be a serious problem.

Exhibit 7.3   Document Flowchart—Purchase Order

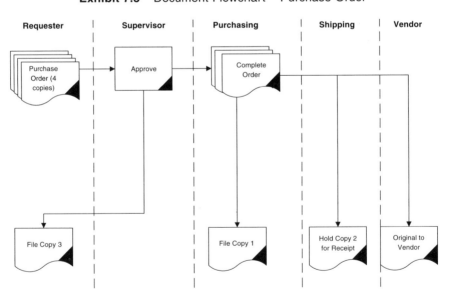

Whether you keep track of the forms through a document flowchart or by some other method, once the maps are completed it is time to take a close look at what happens to the form. Elimination of forms is a quick and easy way to reduce costs—through reduction of time spent handling the forms and elimination of costs resulting from producing the forms in the first place. Make sure the form is actually needed. Look for situations in which forms are filed, but no further action is taken. Often, these may show up as dead ends on the maps. Also look for situations in which multiple forms are going from one person to another. This may represent a situation in which forms can be combined. If the information on the form is needed, see if there is a way the same information could be transferred electronically. Finally, even if you cannot eliminate a form, see if you can get rid of some of the copies. That is one of the primary reasons for ensuring that you track all copies of the form through the system in the document flowchart.

Although reports are not strictly forms, the same approach can be used for reports. We have spent quite a bit of time talking about making sure information is available to measure success. Well, the other side of the story is just as important. Track where reports are going and see if they are actually used. Often, a report has been generated for as long as anyone can remember, but no one remembers why. However, because it has always been generated, everyone assumes that it is necessary and someone must be using it. The process maps should show the same indicators for unused reports that it does for unnecessary forms. And your review of reports should be much like that done for forms—make sure the reports are used; if used, see if they can be distributed electronically; and make sure all copies are needed. If necessary, you can prepare a document flowchart that follows how reports are used.

Incomplete Maps: Dangling Actions and Unanswered Decisions

Somewhat related to the idea of unnecessary forms and reports is the concept of "dangling actions." In a complete map, every action should lead to another action, a connector, or a process termination. If there is any part of the map that shows an action that leads nowhere (or contains the dreaded words "to file"), it should be explored further. It may be that the reviewer has not asked enough questions to fill in this area. In that case, the reviewer must decide whether to look deeper or just drop it. If you are far into the project and time is running out, going back and asking the questions may not be an option. However, it is often these unimportant loose ends that show a backwater that needs attention.

We previously cited the example of reviewing purchasing procedures to determine if they could be streamlined. It was only by following up on a dangling action that we learned of the tax ramification of the change. The original map had shown that information was provided to the tax accountant, but there was no indication of any further action. We went back and spoke with the individual and found out that a serious violation could have occurred if we had continued as planned.

Another aspect of this type of problem is the unanswered decision. Every decision should have two arrows leading from it—one for yes and one for no. If not, additional information is needed. As with the dangling action, this may lead to the discovery of a new area that needs to be included. However, it may also mean that a review is either unnecessary or unused. When we have seen this happen, it usually means that someone is completing a review, but the results are not used. For example, we have spoken with clerks who tell us that they check for correct information (coding, signatures, matching documents) and then complete the process. When we ask more, we learn that they do nothing with the information—they do not correct the information, they do not refer it to anyone, and they do not create a log of errors. This can either mean that they are completing the process without understanding why or that they have decided to do the review on their own. Surprisingly, we have come across this type of situation a few times.

Question Hold-Files

Apparently the world would come to an end if there were no hold-files. Every process you review will seem to thrive on them. That is not to say that hold-files are a bad thing. However, it does mean that people may be relying on them too heavily. Look closely at each hold-file established in the process. Determine what goes in it, how it is used, and why it exists.

Verify that the time frames established for the hold-files are correct. If an individual sets a short hold-file but then just refiles the information for the future, time may be wasted pulling this information unnecessarily. In addition, if the information is pulled too late, it is useless. Determine what situation caused the need for the hold-file. It may be that another portion of the process is not running efficiently and the hold-file had to be established to ensure that work was received on time. Also look at the success rate of the hold-file—how often is there a problem with receiving the information on time? While this can help establish the reason the hold-file was established, it can also be an indication that time-liness requirements for some departments are not effective.

CYCLE TIMES

We have often mentioned keeping track of the cycle times for all events. Implied in this is the understanding that the reviewer would be watching for events that seem to take too long. It may seem obvious, but take a good look at those actions that take the longest. Reducing these times can have the greatest effect on the overall process.

Besides focusing on the individual actions, attention should be paid to the overall process and the associated cycle times. In particular, the critical paths should be determined for the overall process. Once established, the timing for the critical paths can be used for a number of approaches.

The first is to determine where delayed actions are also causing delays in associated actions. As shown in the breakfast example, it is not necessary to wait for every part of some tasks to finish before other tasks can be started. As mentioned before, if we wait for all the ingredients to be ready and cook them at the same time, we will wind up with some cold food. In that situation, a critical path chart would show that the cooking task that took the longest time (e.g., cooking bacon) was holding up all other tasks. It is then necessary to determine if the processes can be streamlined, if new triggers should be established, or if no change is necessary.

The second approach is to determine the length of time related to the entire process and verify that the measures of success based on time can actually be achieved. This approach can also be used for units or tasks that represent measurements. As mentioned before, analysis of the time taken to issue checks in the expense payment example shows that the 48-hour turnaround cannot be met—it is physically impossible.

Another approach is to determine the minimum and maximum cycle times for each action. From this you can determine the minimum and maximum cycle times for the critical path. This is important to understand because standards are often set based on the minimum critical path time. However, reality is that the maximum time will be experienced more often. The claims experience discussed in Chapter 3 is a good example of this. If everything happens perfectly, the claims representative will speak with the claimant within the required one day. However, it is highly likely that the experience will have a few glitches and result in a time frame closer to the maximum. When reviewing this area, determine how often the minimum times and the maximum times are reached. If the maximum time is more prevalent, the area should be reviewed and the criteria should be reexamined.

Ultimately, time is one of the major resources a company is trying to conserve. In doing any assessment of risk, a major component is financial volume. The idea is that the larger the financial volume, the higher the risk that there will be a financial loss. Including and analyzing cycle times will show where it is being used the most and where the greatest risk of wasting time exists. Accordingly, it shows where the most effort should be spent finding solutions.

FINALIZING THE PROJECT

After all the discussions and all the interviews and all the maps and all the frustration, it is time to finalize the project. While not actually an analysis process, it is what the analysis has led to. Plus, every time you talk about the maps, you will be learning a little more. Each discussion may lead to another discovery. Analysis is never finished.

Finalizing the project entails a number of reviews of the maps. As you have talked with people, you should have been reviewing the final maps with the employees to ensure that your understanding is correct. There are a number of miscommunications that may occur, and you want to have these cleared up before you go farther in the project. An interesting point about these reviews is that it may be the first time the employees really recognize that what they have said was taken seriously. Most employees will be glad about this, but you may have a few who suddenly panic about the information they may have shared. There is no good answer for these individuals, but it is a good idea to be prepared for them.

Once the whole project is done, it is time to review the maps with the owners. They may well have seen bits and pieces before the meeting, but it probably will be the first time they have seen the entire package. Give it to them ahead of time. No one should be expected to absorb the information contained in all these maps in just a few minutes. This will often be the point when they first discover that their understanding of the process is incorrect.

Once they have reviewed the map, get their input regarding correctness. Ask for their questions and concerns first. They will not be interested in your comments until their issues are addressed. Also, it may give you additional insight or issues you want to include. Remember that this is still a part of the analysis process. Go over any questions that remain open. There should be very few, but there will also be issues that only the owner can answer. Finally, begin talking about the findings. The intent of this part of the meeting is to prepare the owner for the content of the final report. It is usually a good practice to keep the owner up-to-date regarding issues as the project continues, but this is the point where all those issues should be summarized. It is also an opportunity for the owner to start thinking about solutions to the issues that are raised. Even if you have worked with the staff to come up with viable solutions, the owner will want time to take ownership of them.

In some instances, the maps may have pointed out areas where additional research is needed. Depending on the circumstances, you may want to do additional testing. Even if you do not have the time, it is a good time to suggest that the owner initiate a similar project. In a recent review, we recognized that the processes over account controls were faulty. We talked with the owner, who requested that we determine how big the problem was. This resulted in our looking at a large number of files to support our understanding of the problem. Because we had the time available, we were able to expand the Process Mapping project and provide additional value.

The actual report will vary widely, depending on your individual needs and circumstances. However, there should be a final report that spells out what was reviewed, what was found, and, if possible, how things have been improved. The report should also contain copies of all maps. Make sure the owner gives copies of the maps to all employees involved in the project. Managers and supervisors should get all maps; employees should get copies of the processes they are involved in. This is one final opportunity for the reviewer and the process owner to show employees that they were part of this project and that their participation was appreciated.

RECAP AND KEY ANALYSIS POINTS

We have been providing key analysis points at the end of each chapter. However, since this entire chapter is about analysis, the recap provides the same information.

Once maps are completed, it is time to get into the real analysis. There are two separate approaches that should be completed—revisiting the Process Profile Work Sheets and searching through the maps

The primary approach to revisiting the Process Profile Work Sheets is to ensure that your initial understanding is still correct and to make sure that the final analysis ties in with the major categories of the work sheet. These include triggers, inputs, outputs, process ownership, business objectives, business risks, key controls, and measures of success.

Most of these reviews are based on the same information contained in the work sheets when they were originally established. However, outputs should be viewed in a different light. It is important to think of outputs as results and to recognize that there are four different types of results: outputs (what you expect the process to produce); wastes (items produced that do not meet the expectations of outputs); surprises (offshoots from the process that can be favorable or unfavorable but were unexpected); and invisible consequences (long-term effects that are not recognized until after the process has been in place for a while). Recognizing and analyzing these results will help identify areas that may warrant additional attention.

While analyzing the actual maps, the reviewer should be aware of indicators that represent areas that warrant further review. Removing approvals helps empower the workers to complete their actions in a more timely manner. Looping errors are situations in which the process tends to go back through the same loop a number of times until restrictive conditions are met. Delays, rework, and handoffs should be eliminated or streamlined. Forms and reports should be reviewed closely to see if they can be eliminated or reduced. Situations in which maps are incomplete, (e.g., dangling actions and unanswered decisions) should be identified to ensure that all avenues have been properly reviewed. Hold-files should also be reviewed to see if they are necessary and, if so, that they have been established correctly.

Also look closely at cycle times. For the individual actions, identifying those that take the longest will show where streamlining may have the greatest effect. The overall cycle time for the processes, units, and tasks should also be reviewed to determine if measures of success based on time can actually be met. Finally, the critical paths based on cycle times should be reviewed to determine where restrictions on timeliness might occur.

Before meeting with the owners to finalize the project, individuals interviewed for the maps should have a final look at the maps to ensure that they are correct. The same should be done with any supervisors and managers involved. Finally, the process owner's buy-in should be obtained. This discussion should help identify any problems with the map and prepare the owner for the final report. The structure of the report will depend on the needs and constraints of the situation. At a minimum, it should include what was reviewed, what was found, any known solutions, and copies of the map.

NOTES

1. Clay Carr, *The Competitive Power of Constant Creativity* (New York: Amacom, 1994), pp.23–25.
2. Karl Albrecht, *At America's Service* (New York: Warner Books, 1992), p.126.

CHAPTER 8

Map Analysis:
An Example

When you make the finding yourself—even if you're the last person on Earth to see the light—you'll never forget it.

—Carl Sandberg

THIS IS ONLY AN ATTEMPT

We have seen the basic process of expense payment and have developed the majority of the maps. In addition, we have developed the fundamental Process Profile Work Sheet. With this information it is time to do some preliminary analysis on the process.

Much of the analysis can be completed by reviewing only the work sheets and maps, but that is only part of the job. As mentioned earlier, it is the entire Process Mapping approach that leads to the best results. By looking at the bits and pieces, a true holistic approach cannot be taken. However, there is enough information available at this point to show many of the fundamental aspects of analysis.

PROCESS PROFILE WORK SHEET

The first step is to revisit the Process Profile Work Sheet. Exhibit 8.1 (a repeat of Exhibit 4.5) is an example of a Process Profile Work Sheet for the Expense Payment Process, and it provides the basic information we need. However, to complete some of this analysis, we must make assumptions about what was discussed or learned during other phases of the project. Despite this, the basic approach to analyzing the work sheet should become evident.

Triggers

Some of the concerns about triggers for the Expense Payment Process were discussed in Chapter 7. By defining the trigger as "Receive bill," the process owners have shown a good understanding of what starts the process. As already mentioned, setting the trigger later could allow an integral part of the process to be missed. In this case, the time from receipt of the bill to the time the request is prepared might not be properly reviewed. This trigger might show a fundamental misunderstanding of one of the major objectives of the process—timely payment of expenses.

A review of the "Other events" as defined in the work sheet shows a fairly good understanding of these items. However, there could be a disconnect between the events listed and those used to define units. Although it is not necessary for these to match, it is important to ensure that everyone is in agreement. Discrepancies between these two areas may indicate the need for additional discussion. However, there is evidence that agreement has already been reached based on the list of process units listed in that section of the work sheet. These same units closely match the final unit-level map.

Finally, the event ending process is defined as "Distribute check to employee or mail to payee." This may be an incomplete

Exhibit 8.1 Process Profile Work Sheet

Process Name and Number	Process Owner
Expense Payment Process—EP	J. Doe—Treasurer M. Bucks—Mgr HO Disbursements P. Change—Mgr Field Accounting

Description
The process of paying for incurred business expenses other than travel and purchase order

Triggers
Event beginning: Receive bill Other events: Complete check request, obtain approval, submit request, issue check Event ending process: Distribute check to employee or mail to payee

Input—Items and Sources
Bill/Invoice, or other support—employee

Output—Items and Customers
Reimbursement check—vendor

Process Units	Process Unit Supervisors
Check request	Field Disbursement Supervisor
Check issuance	Home Office Disbursement Supervisor
Check retrieval	Home Office Disbursement Supervisor
Check distribution	Field Disbursement Supervisor

Business Objective(s)	Business Risks
Prompt and accurate payment of valid, properly approved business expenses.	Fraudulent payments Delayed payments—missed discounts Customer dissatisfaction

Key Controls	Measure of Success
Segregation of duties—requester and approver—requester, issuer—issuer, retriever	All checks issued within 48 hours Utilization of early pay discounts Complaints about delays Absence of duplicate payments

definition. In general, the review has focused on the company's receipt and payment of the bills. But if we look at the ultimate customer (the payee), we cannot ensure satisfaction until that check is received. There are two basic situations that end this process. The first is distribution of the check to the employee, and this correctly represents final completion of the process (the customer has received payment.) However, the second situation—mailing the check to the vendor—does not perfectly complete the transaction. The timely payment of expenses objective is not met unless the customer actually has the check. It may be better to define the event ending process as "Vendor receives check." If this is the true termination point, the maps are incomplete. While it is impossible to take into account all aspects of delivery of checks to vendors, the maps could at the very least take into account the company's mail service (whether it is an internal process or an external process.) If the termination point is redefined, there is more work to do.

Inputs and Outputs

The input items (bill or invoice) are properly identified. The reviewer might want to ask a few questions to determine if there are any other documents that can generate expenses, but the major documents seem to have been identified. The stated source of the input (employee) shows there may be some confusion internally. We already discussed how identifying "Receive bill" as a trigger shows a good understanding of the customer involved in the process. However, that customer is also the true source of the document and identifying the employee as the source may be inadequate. A more accurate source is the vendor. If the focus of the review is to stay within the company, the employee can be the correct source. However, if a broad focus (a truly customer-focused approach) is used, the person supplying the bill actually generates it. Since we ultimately want to focus on customer satisfaction, the external approach is necessary to include the customer in the process. In our example, this redefinition only means that additional discussions may need to be held with the process owner to ensure a complete understanding of the customers, the triggers, and the inputs.

The basic output is the check, and the ultimate customer is the vendor. However, there are deeper concerns with the outputs. Remember that the actual output is only one of the four types of results that may occur from a process. The second result is "waste." Looking at the maps, there are a number of situations in which inaccurate or incomplete output can result. One obvious example is the "Verify Request" map that is repeated in Exhibit 8.2. There are two separate reviews done by the disbursements clerk. The first review is to ensure that the request is complete, and the second review is to ensure that the approval is proper. If there are problems, both actions will end up causing waste, a result that does not provide the value expected. Another good example are the two "Field—Request No Check" "drill down" maps and the "Field—No Corresponding Check or Request." These are shown again as Exhibits 8.3 through 8.5. Each of these represents a specific process intended to identify and correct errors. Any time spent on these processes represents waste, both in the loss of time and in the production of a useless product. We look at this more closely when we begin to analyze the maps.

The next result is surprises. Three basic surprises were discussed for the Expense Payment Process in Chapter 7:

1. Missed due dates,
2. Increased workload, and
3. Increased mailing costs.

The final result is invisible consequences. This also was discussed in Chapter 7 and includes loss of reputation and decreased morale.

Exhibit 8.2   Payment by Check Request
Verify Request (1.3) — Action Level

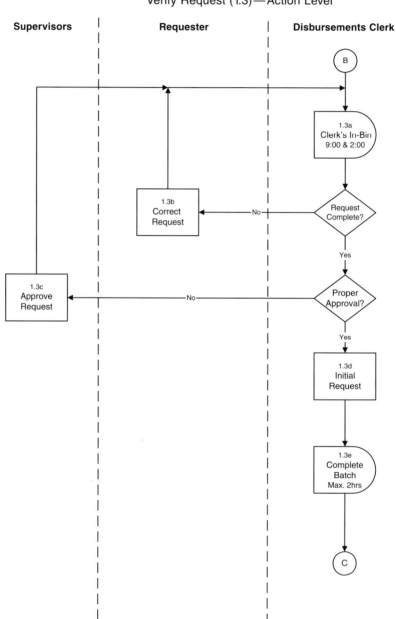

Exhibit 8.3   Payment by Check Request
              Field—Request No Check (3.1c)—"Drill Down"

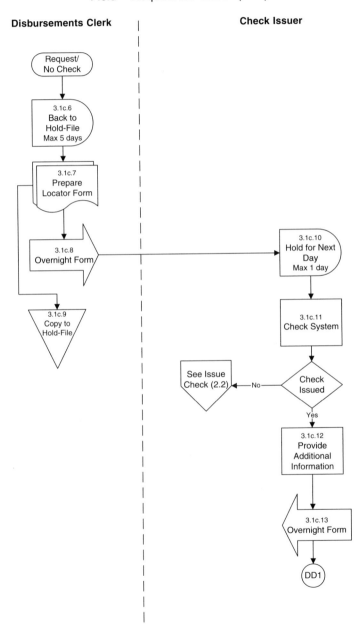

Exhibit 8.4 Payment by Check Request
Field—Request No Check (3.1c)—
"Drill Down" (Continued)

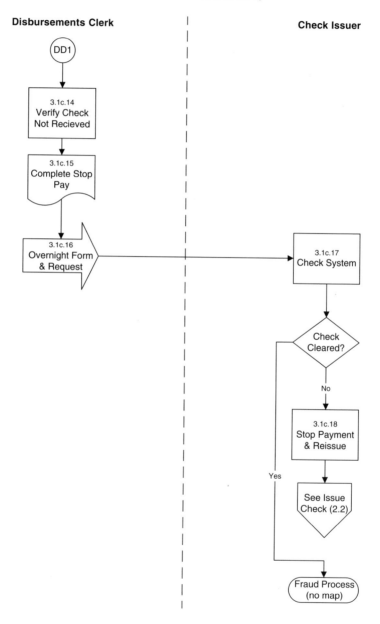

Exhibit 8.5   Payment by Check Request
Field—No Corresponding Check or Request (3.1c)—Task Level

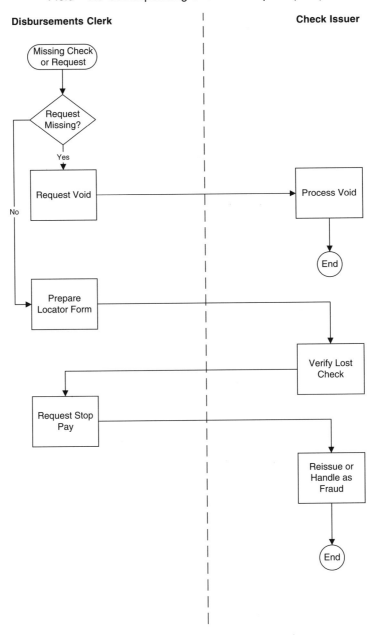

Each of these results becomes apparent as a part of the map analysis. But identifying it early in the analysis phase makes the information available at the earliest possible time. Ultimately, the value in identifying these outputs is in helping sell results to the process owner. At first blush, they may not be concerned about numerous approvals or needless loops. However, when the types of results listed above are shown to occur because of how the process functions, the process owner becomes much more concerned about those situations.

Process Owners

We can only assume that the process owners are properly identified. Ultimately, the treasurer appears to be the primary owner. The identification of the two managers—home office and field office—is also important because of how the process works between these two departments. This becomes evident as final decisions are made about changes to the process. The manager level will be used to get actions implemented. The treasurer level will be used to resolve arguments.

Business Objective

The business objective has been identified as "prompt and accurate payment of valid, properly approved business expenses." The objective itsef seems well defined—including timeliness, accuracy, and propriety. It is important to verify that all steps in the process help support these objectives.

As an example, it is already apparent that the timeliness objective is not being met. We previously discussed how the delays in processing (the numerous holding bins, transfers, and batch processing) make it impossible to meet the promise of a 48-hour turnaround. A deeper look reveals that the emphasis on the other two aspects—accuracy and propriety—may contribute to the inability to ensure the first—timeliness. The number of approvals and reviews are indicative of this problem. We look at these further when we discuss the actual maps, but it is always important to keep the objective of the process in mind during the analysis. In the final assessment, it may be that the company's approach to centralizing the payment process is the ultimate culprit in its inability to meet the timeliness requirements. We cover that at the end of this chapter.

Business Risk

The original business risks identified—fraudulent payments, delayed payments, missed discounts, and customer dissatisfaction—seem to still be applicable. They tie in with the objectives and explain the need for certain steps in the process. In addition, there have been no new high-level risks identified that might have been missed.

Key Controls

Everything we have learned about this process's problems leads us to suspect that key control identification is incomplete. Currently, only one control has been identified—segregation of duties. This is followed by a list of some of the segregations—requester/approver, requester/issuer, and issuer/retriever. It is becoming apparent that the accuracy and propriety objectives are the only ones the process owner cares about. Despite the owner's protestations that all are of equal importance, key control identification shows that this is not correct. If timeliness were truly important, the process owner would have quickly advised the reviewers of any key controls over that area. Since there are none, the owner is sending a message that this is not important.

There are measurements in place (as discussed in the next section), but no way to ensure that these benchmarks are met. In fact, some of the actions in the process show a decided lack of interest in achieving timeliness. In the description of the check matching process, the point is made that all checks are held until all checks for that office are completed. There is no evaluation to determine rush items. There is no accommodation to send partial groups of checks if the overnight deadline is approaching. In general, completing the tasks is more important than timely delivery of checks. Implementation of either one of these suggestions would show that the owner had some concern for timeliness issues.

Ultimately, there must be a key control that deals with the timeliness objective. None is apparent from the existing maps, and that provides evidence of the problem we are seeing. Discussions must be held with the process owner to develop these key controls and might include a rush payment process, an on-line tracking system, or a daily report on timeliness. However, the best solution will be one developed within the department. It is possible that the process owner might disagree and believe that such controls are unnecessary. In that situation, the final report may need to indicate the disconnect between the objectives of the process and the reality, allowing the reader to reach the necessary conclusions.

Measures of Success

Analysis of the measures of success continues to reveal some of the disconnects between objectives, controls, and measurements. Three of the measurements relate to timeliness—issuance within 48 hours, utilization of early pay discounts, and complaints about delays. However, there is no control to ensure that these occur. Likewise, the measurements of success relating to the other two objectives (accuracy and propriety) are effectively nonexistent. The other measure—absence of duplicate payments—relates to only a small part of these objectives. Furthermore, one major business risk was identified as fraudulent payments, yet there is no measurement relating to that situation.

The lack of measurements over accuracy and propriety begins to provide some understanding as to why there is a preponderance of controls over them. Because there is no way to measure success, there is no assurance that controls are effective. In response, management has developed more and more controls. In its quest to completely mitigate risks associated with these objectives, the objective of timeliness has taken a backseat.

There must be extensive discussions with the process owner on this area. The first task is development of a measurement system. Something as simple as keeping track of the error ratios might provide sufficient information. The second task is to see if some of the approvals and reviews can be eliminated. We discuss this in more detail when reviewing the maps, but it is important to note that until we know how successful certain tasks and action in the process are, we cannot determine which to eliminate without compromising controls.

ANALYZING THE MAPS

Now it is time to dig into the actual maps. Rather than explore each map individually, the basic approaches listed in Chapter 7 are used. As frequently stated earlier, the true value comes from looking at the process as a whole, but some benefits can be found in these individual reviews.

Remove Approvals

It is apparent from the previous discussion that the high reliance on segregation of duties (including approvals) in this process is the result of the disconnect between objectives, controls, and measures of success. Approvals are an important part of that segregation. Obviously, not every approval can be eliminated, but removing or reducing some approvals is one step that might be taken to help alleviate the bottlenecks we are seeing.

In going through the maps, the primary approval process we see is the one related to approving the request itself (see Exhibit 8.6, a repeat of Exhibit 6.6). (There are additional approval-like actions, but these are dealt with in other sections.) This is a basic control and a sacred cow to many people, but it warrants immediate analysis. One place to start is by asking how the budget process is used in expense control. A well-designed budget is a control in itself. If that type of budget exists, approvals may not be needed. In that situation, the ultimate control is how well the department meets its budget.

Even if such a budget does not exist, verify that the approval levels are accurate. Why do all expenses have to be approved? Can this be changed to require approval only on those items under $250? Why do expenses greater than $1,000 need a second approval? There may be legitimate answers to these questions, but they must be asked to see if the approvals can be removed.

In reviewing the need for approvals in this process, there are two important issues that should be addressed. The first issue relates to one of the basic reasons approvals exist—assurance that requests are completed correctly. If this is a major problem in the company, the approval process is not the answer, training is. In addition, a backup process exists to ensure correct completion—the disbursements clerk's review (Exhibit 8.2).

The second issue also deals with the disbursements clerk's review. In this instance, it is the second review—the review for approvals. If the approvals are not on the form, the request must be returned. Elimination of the approval cuts down on the time

Exhibit 8.6 Payment by Check Request
Approve Request (1.2) — Action Level

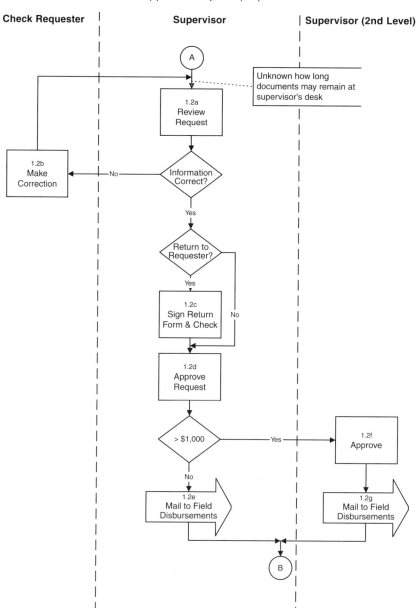

spent by the requester, the approver, and the clerk, and it reduces the amount of product that might be considered waste. It is interesting to note here that by redefining our parameters (what a properly approved document is), we have redefined waste. In the current situation, waste is created whenever a request is not approved. If approvals are removed or reduced, the opportunity for waste is correspondingly reduced.

Although they are not included in the maps, there are also approvals related to stop pays, voids, and checks returned to requester. In each of these situations, a similar analysis should be made. What is the objective of the approval, is there a compensating control, and is the risk associated with that control high enough to warrant delays in processing?

Looping Errors

There are a number of major loops in the Expense Payment Process. Some of these relate to the way the "drilled down" processes work within the Expense Payment Process and are discussed later in this chapter. However, two of the biggest loops are in Exhibit 8.2. The first is one just discussed — reviewing for proper approvals. Under these circumstances, the result is returning the document to the supervisor for the approval. As long as the approval is required, there is no alternative to this loop. It must go back to the approver to get that approval.

However, in the same exhibit there is a loop that can be eliminated immediately to reduce processing time. That is the requirement that the request must be returned to the requester to correct errors of completeness. In some instances, this may be necessary. However, there are at least as many times when the disbursements clerk already knows what the correct information is. By allowing the clerk to make those changes, the elapsed time could be reduced by days.

As discussed in Chapter 7, there is a tendency to want to force the individual who made the mistake to also correct that mistake. In addition, there is a concern that, if the individual does not understand that he did anything wrong, he cannot correct it. Rather than delay the process by forcing instruction or punishment, it is much better to facilitate processing and provide instruction at a later date. This is one loop that can be eliminated.

Isolate Delays

The Expense Payment Process is rife with these types of situations (as well as rework and handoffs). There are 13 different instances in which the "D" symbol is used to indicate a delay. (Note how easy it is to identify these when the symbol is used.)

While it is true that the first instances of delay might occur when the request is waiting for approval, the first two instances on our maps are in Exhibit 8.2. These, like most of the delays in these maps, are the result of batch processing. There are always good reasons for batch processing (as we will see in a little bit), but batches are often just as big a sacred cow as approvals. In the first instance here, the clerk is waiting to process received requests. This makes some sense in that batching these items probably allows the clerk to work on other projects at other times. If the clerk were required to handle each request as it came in, the interruptions might result in a decline in quality for other processes. However, this delay also means it takes even longer to get incorrect requests back to either the requester or the approver. Let us make another assumption and say that the clerk mails incorrect requests back to the requester, and the mail comes only at 9:00 A.M. and 2:00 P.M. By delaying the review, the correction could take as much as an additional day.

The second delay occurs when the clerk batches the initialed requests, preparing to photocopy and file them. It is obviously a good idea to collect a number of items before making the trip to the photocopy machine. But this raises the question, why do they need to be photocopied? The answer (because the originals cannot be mailed to the home office) is not completely satisfying. We are starting to see the problems inherent in centralized processing as practiced in this example. In this situation, the batch itself is not a problem, but it points to the broader problem in the process.

The next delay is in Exhibit 8.7 (a repeat of Exhibit 6.8). All photocopies are held for overnight mailing, which occurs at 3:00 P.M. The initial evaluation of this seems to show it is a necessary delay. This will occur very often during analysis—problem steps cannot be eliminated and are necessary. It is important to remember that the purpose here is just to take a second look, not to eliminate everything. There are similar such delays in Exhibit 8.8 (a repeat of Exhibit 6.10).

A delay warranting additional analysis exists in Exhibit 8.9 (a repeat of Exhibit 6.9). The check issuance actions begin at 1:00 P.M. However, the information about the process indicates that the requests are received as early as 10:00 A.M. There may be extenuating circumstances that result in this delay, but with the information we have, this delay may be unnecessary. This is particularly important because overnight mail is picked up at 3:00 P.M. Depending on the volume of requests, it may be unreasonable to expect this entire unit to be completed in less than two hours. Yet that is exactly what must happen to achieve the 48-hour turnaround. Beginning the action closer to 10:00 A.M. would allow an additional 3 hours.

These same types of analyses should be done on all 13 delayed actions. It is also a good idea to complete another review of the maps to see if delays exist that were not identified the first time through. Again, all delays cannot be eliminated, but they should all be reviewed. And when completing that analysis, begin to look at the broader issues, just as we did with the first delay.

Exhibit 8.7 Payment by Check Request
Verify Request (1.3 continued) and
Mail Request (1.4)—Action Level

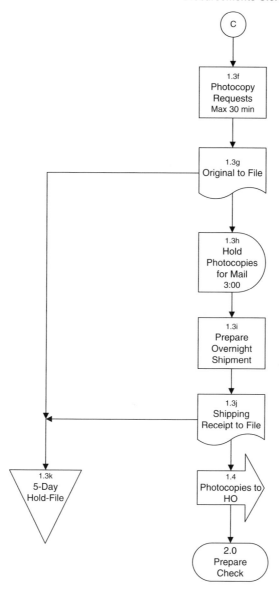

Disbursements Clerk

C

1.3f
Photocopy
Requests
Max 30 min

1.3g
Original to File

1.3h
Hold
Photocopies
for Mail
3:00

1.3i
Prepare
Overnight
Shipment

1.3j
Shipping
Receipt to File

1.3k
5-Day
Hold-File

1.4
Photocopies to
HO

2.0
Prepare
Check

Exhibit 8.8 Payment by Check Request
Issue Check (2.2)—Action Level

Check Issuer

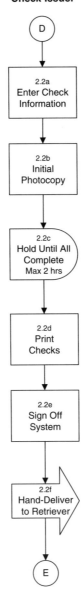

Exhibit 8.9   Payment by Check Request
Prepare to Issue (2.1)—Action Level

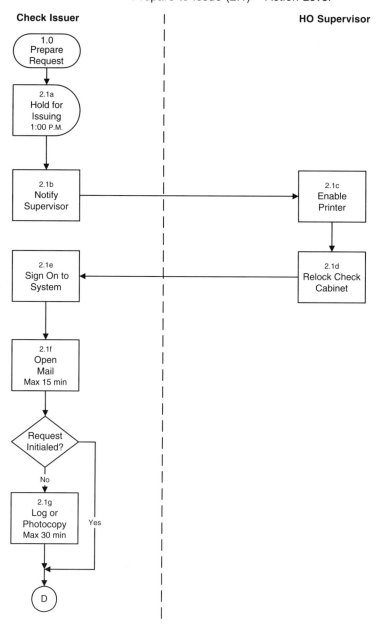

Isolate Rework

Identifying these situations in the process maps is a little more difficult than identifying the delays. While the "D" symbol was used for delays, the "R" symbol was not used for rework. Just trying to isolate these instances shows how important the symbols can be. However, there are some other obvious signs to look for. One example is the upstream movement of arrows. This usually means items are going back to their source for additional work. The example we have already looked at a number of times is Exhibit 8.2. We have also discussed many solutions to this situation.

Another telltale sign of rework is connectors to maps that are not part of the normal process flow. In the expense report system, these are usually represented by "drill down" maps. Prime examples are Exhibits 8.3, which we looked at before, and Exhibit 8.10 (a repeat of Exhibit 6.13). In Exhibit 8.10, the situation Request/ No Check shows an example of rework. If the system shows the check was already issued, the check is stopped and reissued. This requires inputting the same information a second time and is a good example of rework. It is obvious that, in the given situation, rework is required—the check must be reentered. But in analyzing this rework, we are not focused on elimination of the step, only on its occurrence. Rework is an indicator of problems in the system. In this instance, the reviewer should determine the error rate (something that could have been included on the maps) and then determine why these situations occur. Again, the intent is to determine what flaws in the process require this rework.

Exhibit 8.3 shows a similar situation—a request but not a check. However, this time the check cannot be located in the field office. As is evidenced by the map, this is a much more complicated process. Ultimately, the rework is also the same—inputting data for a new check. But, again, the purpose of identifying the rework is not so much to evaluate the rework task itself as to

Exhibit 8.10   Payment by Check Request
HO—No Corresponding Check or Request (2.4b)—"Drill Down"

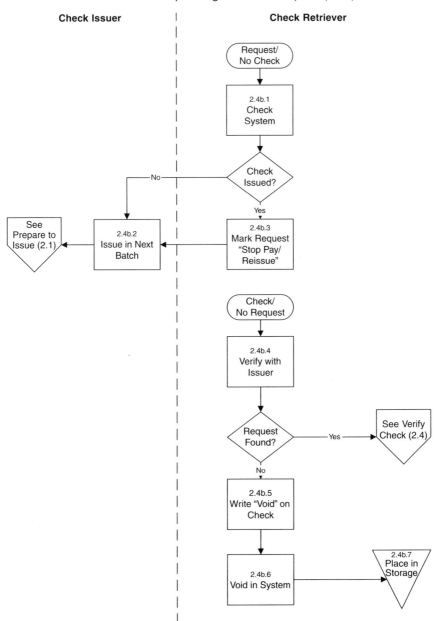

analyze the associated processes. The same steps should be performed, including determining error rates and the causes of these errors. However, in this instance, reducing that error rate will result in much more significant savings to the company. The more complicated the process that is eliminated, the greater the benefits.

Isolate Handoffs

The purpose of isolating handoffs is a hybrid between isolating delays and rework. In some instances, the handoffs can be eliminated just as delays are. In other instances, they are akin to rework, an indicator of other problems. Because the expense payment process has been centralized, there are a lot of handoffs. The number is increased because of the focus on segregation of duties. Throughout these maps, the majority of these handoffs are shown with larger arrows. This was done to highlight those situations. However, in general, any time the map moves from one individual to the next there is a handoff.

The use of handoffs is shown in Exhibit 8.11, the unit-level map (previously shown as Exhibit 6.1). The unit-level map shows the first unit occurring in the field office, the second in the home office, and the final one back in the field office. The following task-level maps (Exhibits 8.12 through 8.14, repeats Exhibits 6.2 through 6.4) then show the handoffs between departments within each of these offices. This high-level cursory review does not reveal any particular problems. There is no real evidence that handoffs are going back and forth between offices or departments. It is important to point out here that no single handoff is necessarily bad. Problems begin to occur in the way handoffs combine.

The first time large arrows are used to show handoffs is when the requests are approved. In these situations, the request is mailed to disbursements. These have been highlighted because the reviewer understood that mailing the requests creates a delay.

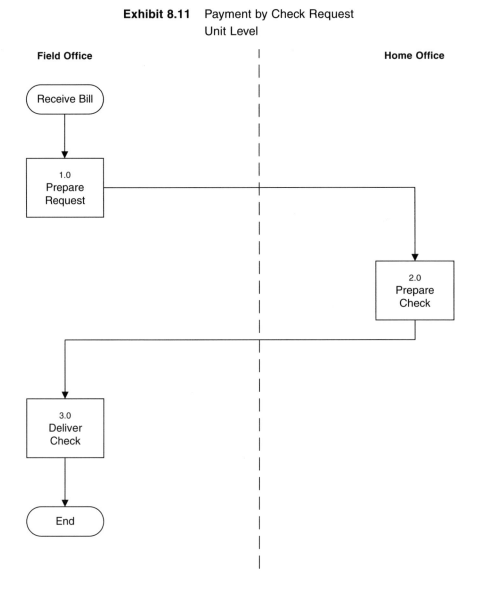

Exhibit 8.11   Payment by Check Request
Unit Level

Field Office   **Home Office**

Receive Bill

1.0
Prepare
Request

2.0
Prepare
Check

3.0
Deliver
Check

End

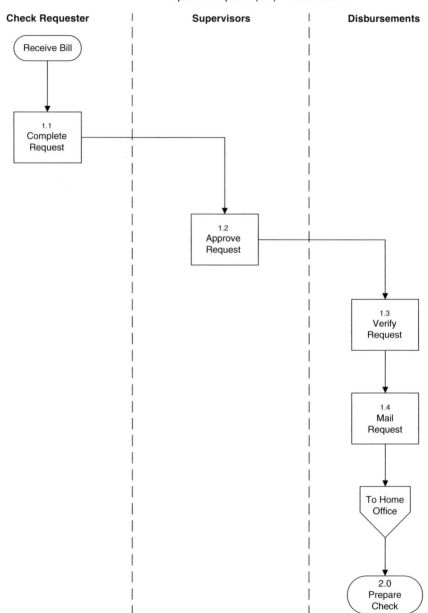

Exhibit 8.12 Payment by Check Request
Prepare Request (1.0)—Task Level

Check Requester | **Supervisors** | **Disbursements**

Receive Bill

1.1
Complete
Request

1.2
Approve
Request

1.3
Verify
Request

1.4
Mail
Request

To Home
Office

2.0
Prepare
Check

Exhibit 8.13 Payment by Check Request
Prepare Check (2.0)—Task Level

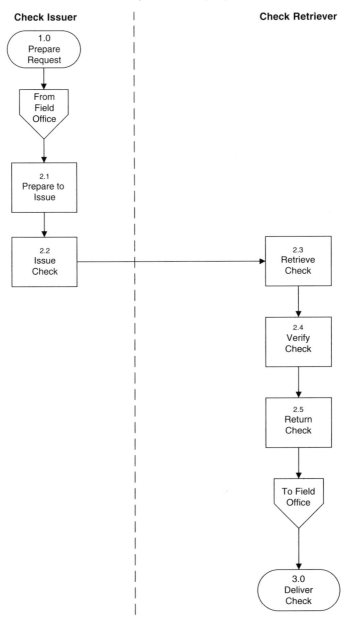

Exhibit 8.14   Payment by Check Request
Deliver Check (3.0)—Task Level

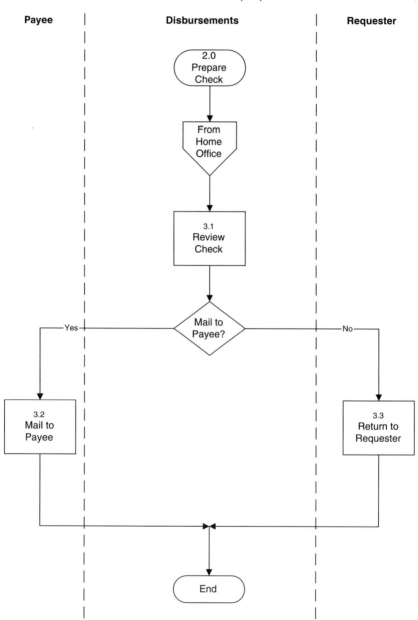

A "D" could have also been used, but the arrow helps accentuate the handoff's attributes. This is an instance in which the problem may relate to the method of handoff. Let us make the assumption that mail is picked up twice a day, routed to the mailroom, and then distributed during that twice-a-day run. In some instances, there may be no delay. In others, this could result in as many as two extra days being added to the process. There may not be an easy solution, but this must be evaluated to understand the impact.

The first major handoff occurs in Exhibit 8.7 when the photocopies are mailed to the home office. This is another handoff that in and of itself is not bad. The photocopies must go to the home office, and overnight mailing is the quickest way to get it done. However, when this is evaluated in conjunction with the other overnight mailings and the processes that surround them, problems begin to crop up. A perfect example of this has already been discussed. Overnighting the requests means that they are available at 10:00 A.M., yet they are not worked on until 1:00 P.M. The speed of overnighting does not match the practice of holding the items an additional three hours.

Analyzing this handoff may also lead you to one of the surprises discussed in the output section. There probably will be a lot of items that require overnight shipping. The cost may not have been factored into the initial development of the process. If not, this surprise might be identified by the reviewer at this point.

Another handoff worth looking at is not represented by large arrows. In fact, at first blush it might not be thought of as a handoff. This is shown in Exhibits 8.9, 8.10, and 8.15. (This last is a repeat of Exhibit 6.15). Technically, nothing is handed off. However, the flow of the process goes back and forth, first between the issuer and the supervisor and next between the retriever and the supervisor. In some respects, the flow is handed off. Whenever this type of back-and-forth situation is encountered, the reviewer should

Exhibit 8.15   Payment by Check Request
Field—Check No Request (3.1c)—"Drill Down"

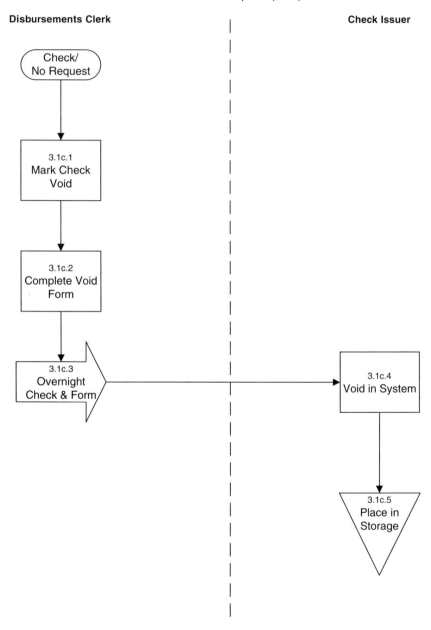

take a look to see how much of it is really necessary. In this instance, there is an obvious concern for control over the check printer. The supervisory control over the check printer in these situations actually represents a kind of approval process (the type mentioned before that is not obvious.) It may be that this causes no real delay and is not important. However, it interrupts the supervisor's day and may cause delays for that individual. The need for this control should be evaluated and weighed against the benefits of eliminating it.

The two most convoluted handoffs in the overall process are shown in Exhibits 8.3, 8.4, and 8.5. In both instances, documents are going from the field office to the home office numerous times. In both situations, there normally are three transfers between the offices, and these transfers take time (and money). Because these transfers relate to incorrectly processed items, the same analysis done for rework should be completed here. (What is the error rate and why does it occur?) But the analysis should also include ways to streamline the process. In Exhibit 8.5, for example, why does the disbursements clerk have to prepare the request for stop pay? If the check issuer completed the request, there would be two fewer handoffs. Keep in mind that there may be control issues requiring this, but, as has been mentioned before, it is something that should be reviewed to make sure it is the best process available.

Follow the Forms

No document flowcharts have been developed for this process because the number of documents is not overwhelming. In addition, it is not hard to follow what happens with them. But there are a couple of points about the documents that become obvious as the maps are reviewed.

The first relates to the request itself (or the photocopy of the request.) It is the primary document, and it is at the heart of most of the process. It is used as a control in the field office when the photocopy is mailed, and the photocopy is used as a control in the home office when the check is issued. This is as it should be, and the maps show that there is a good understanding of the document's impact.

The second point relates to the Return to Requester form. Much is made about this form at the beginning of the process. There is an emphasis on its being prepared and approved. However, it completely disappears after the first action-level map. There may be a number of reasons for this. One reason might be that the maps did not go into additional detail on this area with the assumption that any process the request went through included the return form. Another reason might be that the form is not reviewed after that initial request because completing it serves the fundamental purpose of ensuring that the check must be returned to the requester. However, this is a form that should be closely analyzed. It may be that there is no need for it and it can be eliminated (along with the elimination of any associated processes.)

Incomplete Maps: Dangling Actions and Unanswered Decisions

Looking at the maps, there are three instances in which the maps are not complete. The first occurs in Exhibit 8.9 and is not overtly obvious. At the end of this map, the issuer verifies whether the request is initialed. Depending on the issuer, the information is entered on a log or photocopies are made. However, there is no indication of what happens to the log or photocopies. As with any of these situations, it is possible that the reviewer purposely did not include that information on the map. However, there should be a reference to an unmapped process (as was done with the fraud process in Exhibit 8.4.)

The more likely scenario is that there is no follow-up by the department on these items. This means that one of two things should happen. The first is to develop a system that allows adequate follow-up. In this situation, it might be gathering statistics to determine which office has the highest error rate (noninitialed items) or referring the items back to the servicing office to see if these are potentially fraudulent requests. The second solution is to eliminate the review entirely. In this instance, that could also mean eliminating the need for the disbursements clerk to sign the form in the first place. As in all other situations, the need for a control must be weighed against the cost of that control.

The next two occurrences of incomplete maps are on Exhibits 8.10 and 8.16. This is the situation in which the map is incomplete because information goes into a file and never comes out. In this instance, it is most likely because the time period for retention of voided checks is based on statutory requirements. The map could include this destruction date, but there is not a lot of evaluation required for these items.

Question Hold-Files

There is really only one hold-file evident in the process maps. (This ignores any hold-files individual requesters may establish to ensure that the check is issued.) This hold-file appears in Exhibit 8.7 and reappears in Exhibit 8.3. The hold-file itself seems to be a necessity. It is the only way to ensure that checks are received. It also seems to be developed in a very logical fashion. What may need analysis is the time frame established. The company is promising a 48-hour turnaround. Yet the hold-file is set for five days. This represents a very pessimistic attitude toward the objective. It may be a good indicator of just how long the process actually takes. However, our analysis of this process shows that it may be very slow. The five-day hold-file may be overly optimistic and

Exhibit 8.16   Payment by Check Request
Field—Check No Request (3.1c)—"Drill Down"

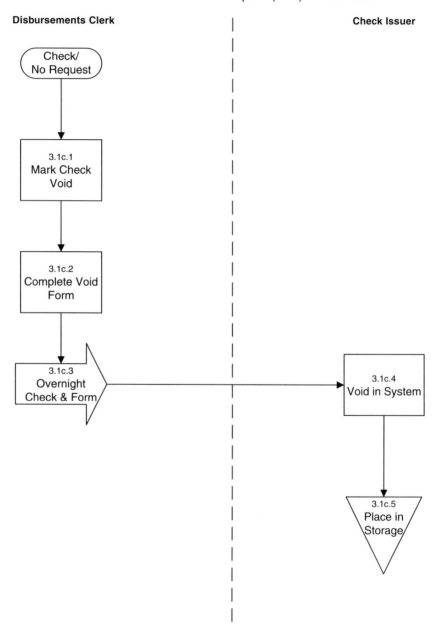

may result in the clerk pulling numerous items just to rediary them. The analysis should include a recommendation on the adequacy of the length of the hold-file.

Another aspect of the use of hold-files may relate to how few of them there are. While it is true that the analysis is trying to determine which hold-files might be eliminated, it may be that the hold-file is the perfect control (as described previously) and its absence is as much a problem as anything. For example, there are a few situations in which the field office requests that a check be voided or a stop payment be placed on the check. There is no indication that they verify that these actions actually occur. The quickest and easiest solution is the establishment of a hold-file an appropriate number of days after the request is submitted. When the hold-file comes up, the system can be reviewed to ensure that the appropriate action took place.

Miscellaneous

The prior discussion has focused on the basic reviews that can be done to find problems in the process map. However, there may be many situations you face that do not fall into these categories. For example, it is interesting to note that the check request must be typed. (This is not specifically on the map, but it is included in the information on the process.) This becomes particularly curious because the Return Check to Requester form does not have this requirement. The reviewer may want to take the time to analyze why this is required and how much additional time this takes the requester. It may relate to inputting errors or it may be an arbitrary decision made by a clerk at some time. (We have seen such things happen.) If a typed form is required, it might also be a good idea to see if a standardized form is available on computer. This seems obvious, but it often is not thought of by individuals creating new processes.

Another example exists in Exhibit 8.7. The map reflects that copies of the shipping receipt are kept with the hold-file. This is slightly unusual and may call for additional review. There are a number of legitimate reasons this occurs, but one reason might be that the home office constantly insisted that the photocopies were not sent. By keeping the shipping receipt with the requests, the field office was able to show that the home office, not the field office, lost the requests. Such turf wars are common, and looking for hints of them can help identify larger problems in the process.

A final example exists in Exhibit 8.9. We discussed the handling of noninitialed requests but glossed over an important point. Some issuers are photocopying exceptions, while others are logging them. There should be one standard approach. While the analysis may show that either is unnecessary, if value is found in the action, everyone should do it the same way. The solution to this depends on what the process owner wants to accomplish. Logging items helps show trends that can be provided to the field offices. Photocopies can be used to determine the legitimacy of the request.

There are probably more flaws and problems with the system that you have identified, but this is intended to give just a few ideas on how analysis can be completed. In fact, if you have seen additional problems, you are starting to get the hang of how to use maps for analysis.

THE BIGGER PICTURE

Looking at this entire process, there appears to be one fundamental flaw. The centralization of the expense payment process is not providing customer value. Because there has not been a full commitment to this approach, the overall result is bad. As with so many other aspects, the solutions depend on what the process owner ultimately wants to achieve. But the analysis completed through process mapping should help in the decision. Overall, these solutions fall into two different categories—full centralization or full regional operation.

The first solution is to take the middleman (field accounting) out of the process. This would require submission of requests directly to the home office. This cannot work if the layers of approvals and reviews are maintained. The process maps show the delays that are already occurring because of these hierarchies. If these are maintained, the problems will only be exacerbated. This solution only works if the requesters are empowered to spend as they see necessary and the home office is allowed to make corrections with as little help from the field office as possible.

The second solution is to move check issuance to the field office. This would require access to on-line systems and an increase in the number of issuance facilities. This would allow the maintenance of tight controls over accuracy and propriety while increasing the timeliness of issuance. The associated costs would have to be weighed against these benefits.

In general, the review has helped establish not only the smaller problems that are causing this process to fail, but also the large overriding problem. Implementing any of these solutions helps lead to the ultimate success of the process. But just addressing the large one still requires an understanding of the way the smaller parts work together.

RECAP AND KEY ANALYSIS POINTS

This chapter provided some practical application of the analysis techniques described in Chapter 7. As such, it covers much of the same territory but in a less theoretical way.

While analysis of the process should be done holistically, just as all other aspects of Process Mapping, following some simple rules may help. Start with the Process Profile Work Sheets and then look through all aspects of the maps. Never forget that the focus of the process must be on the customer. Evaluating the work sheets and maps with this in mind will help ensure that the process adds value.

When analyzing maps, take a close look at the standards that have been established. Output is the normal result of a process, but waste is another. However, waste is defined by the user. Changing the standards (e.g., eliminating the need for an approval) may result in a reduction in the number of items considered waste.

Also remember that it is not necessarily identifying individual items in the maps (e.g., rework, delays, and handoffs) that leads to solutions; it is determining what causes them to happen. In general, Process Mapping is not about the *what*, but about the *why*.

Ultimately, Process Mapping should help lead to the big picture of what is wrong. Despite that, it is the details from Process Mapping that provide the best results.

CHAPTER 9

Pitfalls and Traps

We're drowning in information and starving for knowledge.
—Rutherford D. Rogers, Librarian, Yale University

CHALLENGES

We were first introduced to Process Mapping almost eight years ago, and since that time we have had incredible successes, humiliating defeats, and everything in between. In this chapter, we share some of the things we have learned through those years of experience. Every project brings new challenges and every project is different. While the basic techniques remain the same, this approach requires constant refocusing on what is important. Your first project will be radically different from the one you will do in a year or two. And you will make mistakes—it takes a while to perfect your technique. Do not get discouraged, do not skip steps, and do learn from your mistakes.

MAPPING FOR MAPPING'S SAKE

Mapping projects are undertaken with some broader issue in mind. It may be to examine efficiencies, review controls, ensure that the efforts of employees support strategic goals, or isolate the root cause of a particular problem. But whatever that issue, mapping is a tool used to help answer those broader questions. The map is the means, not the end.

Reviewers sometimes forget this. They focus on the mapping effort—on the drawings on the wall and the details of the process. They forget to look at what they are mapping and why. They are compelled to map every piece of information given to them and to produce more and more maps. By focusing on the map, they lose sight of the true purpose of the project. Instead of achieving results such as efficiencies and goal-oriented processes, the reviewer has . . . well, the reviewer has a lot of maps. Despite tons of information, the project has failed.

We were involved in a project in which every employee in a very large department was interviewed. Detailed maps were created of each person's job activities. Many of the maps listed only a single employee and all the steps that employee went through in a day to complete the job tasks. The reviewers were busy for several months and created a multitude of maps. But in the whole time they spent developing maps, they never analyzed them. At the end of the project, all they had were maps of individual tasks. They had transcribed information, but they had not made any effort to interpret it. They had not matched the process to the business objectives to ensure that the objectives were being accomplished. They had not summarized the details into an overview. It was as if they had created a bunch of single shots but had not put them together into a scene, much less organize them into the overall theme of the movie. They were mapping for mapping's sake. When we first started using the mapping approach in our audits of claim offices, we performed quality assurance reviews on a large number of the maps completed by other offices. We looked at all the maps and the reports for these audits and provided feedback to the auditors on the mapping process. We often saw reports that indicated there were no control issues, although there were glaring control breakdowns obvious in the maps. The auditors had completed the assignment—creating the maps—but they never looked at them. They never stepped back and took a good look at what they created. They thought the maps were the end product.

Merely creating maps is not what Process Mapping is all about. The reviewer must step away from the details (and you *will* be buried in details) and take a good look at the processes under review. The reviewer must examine the maps to see what the information is revealing about the process. Does the process work as everyone expects it to? Does the process accomplish its objective? Are sound controls in place to ensure that the business objectives are accomplished and risks are minimized? Are there bottlenecks and inefficiencies? Does this process hang up another process due to excessive delays? Are moments of truth revealed in the maps? How does the process look from the customer's perspective?

You cannot create only the border and call the puzzle done. You must fill in all the pieces and see how they relate to the whole. The goal of Process Mapping is a holistic view of the function under review. It is visualizing the process as it relates to the whole. It is seeing how the function or process affects the strategic efforts of the company. Do not forget the analysis phase.

LOST IN THE DETAILS

Getting "lost in the details" can be fostered by a "mapping for mapping's sake" approach. However, this problem is often due to the inability of the reviewer to put the details into an appropriate context. When you interview people, they will tell you literally *everything* about their job. It is the interviewer's job to decide whether the information is pertinent and how much detail needs to be documented.

Assume that someone tells you, "First thing in the morning I open the mail, I unfold each piece, I stack the mail in a pile, I look to see whose name is on the mail, I start stacks for each person who has mail, then I put the mail in everyone's incoming mail bin." What is critical in this process?

To answer this question, it is helpful to think in the verb–noun format. If you mapped every detail of this person's morning, you would have boxes for "open mail," "unfold mail," "stack mail," "identify recipient," "sort by recipient," and "file in mail bin." Six boxes detailing how to open the mail. You could even "drill down" farther regarding what happens if the recipient cannot be immediately identified. This would lead down an entirely different path with even more details. However, unless there is a major concern about this area, we probably could document the process with two entries: "sort mail" and "distribute mail."

Making sense of the details is one of the hardest things to do when you start mapping. You must synthesize information very quickly. Someone may talk to you for five minutes, and you summarize it with one box. Another person may give you more important details in five minutes than you got from anyone else in one hour. Using the team approach to mapping is helpful. As described before, one person is taking notes and another person is interviewing while they create the process map in real time with sticky-notes.

The note taker should be taking detailed notes summarizing the critical issues that are being discussed. The note taker is not merely a transcriber—taking notes verbatim—but someone who is charged with summarizing the critical events in the process. Reviewing the notes should show a synopsis that provides all the details necessary to complete the map. That means it must have just the right amount of detail without bogging down completely.

The mapper should also be synthesizing information as the conversation is progressing. The mapper must listen to what is being said and summarize the information concisely in a verb–noun format on the sticky-note. The mapper need not create a box for every detail. Instead, the details of the map should reflect the necessities of the project. If additional information is needed after the interviewee is gone, the team can always refer back to the notes.

The mapper also must decide where the information fits. The people being interviewed are usually involved in only a small portion of a process. The interviewer must be able to take the details provided and determine whether they are important only to this small part of the process or to the process as a whole. Tasks must be related to processes, and the appropriate "bucket" for this information must be found. If you have done a good job in the preliminary information-gathering phase of the project, you should already have a good idea of what tasks are involved in each process. Inputs and outputs as well as critical trigger events should have been identified. These should help you determine where the random pieces of information you receive should be ordered. Go back to the Process Evaluation Work Sheets if you are getting lost in the details. Review the objectives, risks, trigger events, inputs, outputs, and measures of success.

As a side note to getting lost in the details, it is also important to maintain a positive relationship with the interviewee. Although you want to avoid unnecessary details, you must find a tactful way to bring them back to the core of the discussion. Sometimes, even if you are not particularly interested in the information they are providing, you must make sure you are actively listening and acknowledging the contribution. We sometimes write sticky-notes with more detail than we ever intend to put into a final map just to let the interviewees know that we heard what was being said and that we realize it is important information to them. Just because it is on a sticky-note does not mean it has to be in the final map. When you translate from the sticky-note medium to a mapping software program, you again have an opportunity to synthesize information. Know your path, synthesize, synthesize, synthesize, and do not get lost in the details.

ROUND AND ROUND—UP AND DOWN

Process maps should represent a flow of tasks over time. Some people, especially those trained in traditional flowcharting techniques, tend to make process maps look like traditional flowcharts. Numerous symbols may be used to depict different types of operations or documents. Lines and arrows are going up, down, and all around the page. A related mistake that is commonly made results from people being obsessed with keeping the map on one page. They violate the time rule and place sequential tasks at the top of the page with appropriate lines and arrows directing the reader back to the top of the page.

Remember that time is running down the page just like water over a waterfall. Water running over the waterfall drops straight to the bottom and then proceeds on its journey down a river or stream. The water may split as it falls, veering off on slightly different paths, but it all eventually gathers in the pond at the waterfall's end. There will be eddies and spray where water, for the moment, leaps up, but gravity and time always win and the flow continues down.

Just as water cannot run up the waterfall, sequential tasks should not be forced back up to the top of the page. Adhering to the sequential linear flow helps simplify the maps. When the process is laid out showing the appropriate time progression, delays in the process can be visualized and quickly identified.

Process maps should adhere to the KISS (Keep It Simple, Stupid) principle. When done correctly, process maps can summarize both high-level information on multiple processes and very detailed information on units or individual tasks. Use "drill down" techniques and create additional maps as necessary. Avoid the temptation to cram everything onto one page. If it doesn't fit, it doesn't fit, and you will need to use a connector that allows the map to spread over multiple pages.

Flowcharts generally are confusing to people who have not been trained in flowcharting techniques. A map may perfectly represent a process, but if it appears overwhelming, no one will use it. If symbols go up, down, and around and arrows and nodes go every which way, only the creator will use the map. Process maps should provide value to the customer after the reviewers leave. Maps can be used to assist in reengineering efforts, to help train employees, and to help educate employees on where their piece of the puzzle fits into the whole. However, if they are so complicated that they require an interpreter; the customer will never look at them. The goal is to produce maps simple enough so that someone who does not know anything about the process could look at the maps and follow the basic flow of events. The lay user should be able to easily identify who is involved in the process, the major tasks performed in the process, and possibly the duration of the process and various associated tasks.

A good process map is like a work of art. The lines should be aesthetically pleasing, flowing naturally from task to task. A map should be clear and concise, pleasing to the eye and mind. It should not be cluttered with too much detail or too many symbols.

FAILURE TO FINALIZE

We generally try to finalize maps as we go rather than waiting until the end of the project to do so. We already discussed our initial Process Mapping engagement, where we left the mapping until the end and were totally overwhelmed. Now, as soon as a sticky-note map is complete and has been verified with the interviewees, we try to transfer that map to a flowcharting package the same day.

Maps should be finalized while the details are still fresh in your mind and while you still have access to the people who were interviewed. Loose ends may become apparent as you start finalizing the map. You may have decision diamonds that do not lead to a conclusion, or something that made perfect sense when the interviewee was speaking may now appear to be Greek. Finalizing the map as soon as possible results in less confusion and allows you the opportunity for a quick discussion with the person you interviewed to clear up any hanging issues.

Finalizing the maps means more than just completing them. It also includes reviewing them with the unit owner. The maps that have been created reflect how individuals involved in the process perceive, or want you to perceive, the process works. This may be very different from how the unit owner perceives the process, or it might be different from how the process is actually working. (As discussed later in this chapter, testing may be necessary to validate the accuracy of the maps.)

We once were in an office reviewing the procedure for paying rental car bills. The procedure stated that the bills should be paid as soon as they were received. The unit owner indicated that the procedure was being followed. Discussions with clerical personnel revealed a different story. There had been some turnover in the office, and the clerical staff was spread very thin. The staff told us that the bills were being placed in a pending file until they could get to them. They did not know how long it was taking to pay the bills, but they knew they were behind. They just kept filing them in alphabetical order to detect any instances of duplicate bills. If a vendor called, they would pull the bill and request payment the same day. If a vendor did not call, the bills stayed in the pending file for an undetermined time.

We reviewed the map with the clerical personnel, who agreed that we had properly documented the process. However, when we were reviewing the map with the unit owner, we got to the area where the bills were placed in a pending bin awaiting payment and the unit owner disagreed with us. He believed there was no way the process could have broken down this way. We then asked the clerk to pull the pending folder. There were over 300 bills in the folder, with initial billing dates up to 6 months old. Needless to say, the unit owner was extremely surprised and had no idea the bills were being pigeonholed. By reviewing this map with the unit owner and verifying what was actually taking place, we were able to get corrective action immediately. Overtime was authorized to alleviate the problem, and the process was changed so that batch payments could be made to the vendor on a weekly basis, eliminating the need to issue a check for each individual rental car bill.

When problem issues are identified in the mapping process, it is a good idea to get the input from all parties on potential solutions to the problem. Ultimately, either the unit owner or the process owner is responsible for resolving the problem, but people doing the work may come up with some excellent ideas. Side notes can be included on the map indicating where improvements could be made. You can use these side notes as a discussion point with the unit owners and process owners.

We think it is more effective to review the final maps face-to-face with the parties involved—whether that be the interviewees or the owners. While you may want to leave the map so the client has time to review it and develop questions, we find it beneficial for the reviewer to walk the person through the map, one step at a time during the verification process. This should only take a minute or two per map and provides much better results than leaving a copy of the map with the person and asking to be advised if anything is wrong. Sometimes you do not have the luxury of being able to review the maps face-to-face, and you may have to leave them for comments. If they must be left before they are finalized, you should follow up with a phone call to discuss any outstanding issues.

LETTING THE CUSTOMER DEFINE THE PROCESS

The ultimate success of a Process Mapping project means total buy-in by all customers involved. It also means getting input from the people who know the process. Many times you will become involved in a process where you may have a good feel for the overall process, but underlying details are yet to be understood.

Despite this, you must facilitate discussions and help develop an end product that will give real value to all parties involved. The customer may be the expert on the process, but you are the expert on Process Mapping. We have spent a lot of time going over the terms and ideas that are fundamental to completing a Process Mapping project. These terms are common enough that everyone thinks they understand what they mean, but in a Process Mapping situation (as we have learned) there are subtleties involved in those definitions. That means that as you lead the group through discussions, you must tactfully lead them away from their own preconceptions.

This is true for almost any of the definitions—trigger, input, output, even customer. However, one of the biggest pitfalls usually involves a misunderstanding of what a process is. We were involved in a mapping project that the department head planned on using for developing objectives for the following year. Accordingly, it was a more high-level review than those we have discussed. To begin the project, we actually spoke with the heads of each section about risk structures and how controls affect final objectives.

Eventually, we began discussing what processes they thought were involved in their department.

Many of the processes were basic and fell in line with the types you would expect to see in any company. But as we continued, the participants began identifying areas that were not true processes. Examples included areas such as decision making, customer service, and management. Now, each one of these might be thought of as a process, but they are not business processes of a type that can actually be analyzed. For example, decision making is actually a part of every function. Every input must go through a transformation, and there is usually a decision made regarding that input. So it is often impossible to separate decision making from the actual processes themselves. Customer service (although, as we mention later, we both have an ongoing argument regarding its legitimacy as a process) is usually only a process if you specifically have a customer service department. And in those instances, the processes are usually better defined as complaint handling or order processing. However, these processes were apparently a concern to the department and they wanted to bring that point forward.

Unfortunately, we did not help direct the customer to the correct processes. While it did not significantly sabotage the project (again, this was not an in-depth "drill down"), it did cause many subsequent discussions to become bogged down. As new concepts regarding Process Mapping were introduced to the customers, the nonconforming processes did not match the model being described. This ultimately resulted in wasted time for the customers and for us.

At the end, the final product was still good, but there were areas where arguments and discussions were not as strong. Those were the areas where nonprocesses were forced into the process model. Always remember that you are the one who knows where the project is going, and it is important to help the customer get there based on your knowledge.

LEADING THE WITNESS

In a court of law, attorneys are prohibited from asking leading questions or putting words in the witness's mouth. When you are interviewing someone and you know the process very well, it is sometimes tempting to direct people to the right answer. The minute you start "leading the witness," you start getting responses that tell you what you want to hear rather than responses that tell you what is actually going on.

In the auditing world, every auditor eventually uses an internal control questionnaire at some point in his or her career. These questionnaires are designed to ensure that the auditor covers the important aspects of the control structure in a given function. Good internal control questionnaires use open-ended statements such as "Explain how the process is performed." The less effective questionnaires ask yes or no questions such as "Are you reconciling the account?" People can figure out what the proper answer is to a yes or no canned question. Auditors are often surprised when someone answers "yes," and test work reveals the answer is really "no." A good auditor, even when faced with a set of yes or no questions will use open-ended questions, encouraging an interactive response on the part of the auditee. The auditor will then determine if the question deserves a "yes" or a "no" based on the discussion with the auditee.

The reviewer in a Process Mapping engagement must capture the process as it actually occurs. Yes or no questions do not lend themselves to the give-and-take necessary to effectively achieve this. Let us say the procedure states that all check requests over $500 must be approved by the supervisor. When you are interviewing the accounts payable clerk, she states that she inputs all of her own check requests. The interviewer could lead this person to the correct answer if she asks, "You do get your supervisor's approval on all check requests over $500, don't you?" The better question would be, "Under what set of circumstances do you have to get approval before issuing a check?" In the second question the person could answer, "There has never been a situation where I had to get my supervisor's approval" and still think she is answering the question correctly. Another response might be "Whenever a request is greater than $1,000, I get my supervisor's approval." Had the leading question that included the $500 amount been used, the interviewee might have seen the mistake and answered differently.

It is also important to remember that if the person does answer incorrectly, it is not appropriate to tell them that they are not following the proper procedure. As mentioned before, it is also inappropriate to give a reaction that might make the interviewee think a horrible mistake has been made. Reaffirm the answer and go on. The issue should be addressed with the unit owner along with any proposed corrective action. The unit owner would then be responsible for educating and monitoring the employee's performance to ensure that proper approvals are being obtained.

Ultimately, the best question is always, "What is the next action you take?" or "Could you explain what you do?" This allows the interviewee the opportunity to expound on the work being done without the restraints of yes or no questions. Ask open-ended questions whenever possible and try not to "lead the witness."

VERIFYING THE FACTS

Even if you are careful to ask open-ended questions and you create a great interactive environment, people may still misrepresent the facts—intentionally or unintentionally. If reliance is being placed on certain key controls, it is prudent to perform some limited testing to verify that the control is working as represented. For example, if you are relying on approval controls, pull a quick sample of transactions that should have evidence of the proper approval and verify that the actions are being taken. If a receptionist tells you all calls are answered in three rings, phone the office a few times and see if the statement proves to be true.

A prime area for testing is the measures of success for the process. Is there hard evidence that shows the measures of success are being met? If not, you may need to review a sample of transactions to determine why the process is not accomplishing the intended goal. The maps you have prepared can help guide you through the process of reviewing transactions. You may find that some people told you what they know should be done, not what is actually being done.

Verifying the facts can often be done through simple observation. When we review a check disbursement operation, we want to make sure issued checks are properly safeguarded and promptly mailed. In one office we visited, interviews with employees indicated that checks were put in envelopes and mailed out immediately after they were issued. However, when we walked through the office, we saw two desks piled with issued checks, some with dates from five days earlier. No one had mentioned this obvious bottleneck. Further discussions revealed that the person normally responsible for mailing the checks had been assigned phone duty in the afternoon and was not able to keep up with her check distribution duties. Sometimes observation and additional testing are just intended to see what else to ask.

Determining what transactions to verify and how many transactions to review is always a tough decision. Critical transactions that pose a high risk to meeting key objectives are the transactions that should be verified first. Targeted samples of just those transactions can then be examined quickly to determine if the process is working as intended. Sample sizes will often depend on the resources you have available. Volumes have been written on sampling methods and techniques, and we do not explore those issues here.

Another area that should usually be reviewed relates to any self-audits conducted over the area. It is best to select a small sample of those items to validate the results of the self-audits. First, this will tell you the quality of the self-audits. Second, reviewing sample items will often bring out other areas of concern that may not have been covered in the initial mapping effort. Even a small sample of 5 to 10 transactions or a casual observation of the process can provide the reviewer with some assurance that the maps reflect reality.

DO NOT FORGET THE CUSTOMERS

When you are heavily involved in analyzing processes, it is very easy to lose the customer's perspective. You can become so focused on the internal processes that you forget to look at how they are affecting external customers. Do not forget that the maps should help show where the moments of truth are occurring. Take a look at all of the areas where the business has some interaction with the customer. At each one ask the questions, "Is it easy to do business with this company? Why? Why not?"

The authors have had a standing disagreement on whether customer service orientation is a process. It may or may not be a process, but it is an attitude that permeates a department, a function, and the entire business. When you process map a function, you will get a strong indication of whether the entity has a positive customer service orientation.

In one of our first Process Mapping engagements, literally everyone we spoke with in the office mentioned that their first responsibility was to see that the customer was taken care of. This was from the highest level of management to the transcription clerk. The transcription clerk went into great detail explaining how important her work was because the letters she produced were seen by every customer. The office exemplified a positive customer service orientation. Conversely, in another office, it was clear from our discussions with employees that many had an adversarial relationship with customers. It was a classic "us against them" mentality from the top down.

Both offices operate under the same strategic guidelines and the same procedures. However, it is clear that management in one office fostered the positive attitude, whereas management in the other office did not. While these may be soft issues, difficult to quantify, they are critical to the success of the business. Whenever possible, we try to include these types of problems in our final report. It is not always well received by the process owners, but we feel a responsibility to give them the complete picture. It is the reviewer's duty to look at the business through the customer's eyes and report any adverse findings back to upper management.

RECAP

The fundamentals of Process Mapping are simple, but its application is as complicated as the processes you review. You will make mistakes, and it is important to learn from them. These are the mistakes we have made that we hope you learn from.

Mapping for Mapping's Sake

You are not being asked to make maps—you are being asked to assist in the analysis of a process. However, it is very easy to get so wrapped up in the actual development of the maps that the purpose of the project is lost. Every time you finish talking with someone, take a look at the map and start analyzing. Get in the habit of making analysis the objective of the project rather than allowing the maps to exist on their own.

Lost in the Details

As an offshoot to the prior pitfall, it is just as easy to become so wrapped up in the minutiae you are receiving that you lose sight of the big picture. As you are getting the details from interviewees, always try to keep the overall objectives of the process in mind. If the details are unimportant to either the process being mapped or the objectives of the Process Mapping project, they are not necessary. One excellent way to help maintain this focus is by using two people—a recorder and a mapper—to complete each interview.

Round and Round—Up and Down

Maps are a very effective tool—for the reviewer and for the process owner or unit owner. However, convoluted maps that only the reviewer can understand are useless. To help maintain the simplicity of process maps, remember that they should be constructed so that they flow chronologically down the sheet of paper. There are rare instances in which a map references an earlier step and will momentarily flow upstream, but this approach should be used sparingly. An additional point related to this is that the reviewer should use as many sheets of paper as necessary. There is no requirement that a map be completed on one page.

Failure to Finalize

There are two important steps in bringing the mapping project to a close—transferring the sticky-note maps to a charting software and talking with the process owners. Maps should be transferred to software as soon as possible. It should be done while the information is still fresh in the team's minds and the individuals interviewed are still available. Once maps are done, it is just as important to make sure that they are discussed with all levels responsible. This helps ensure that the information is correct and helps bring the process owners into the completed project.

Letting the Customer Define the Process

While the language of Process Mapping is not based on unfamiliar vernacular, it does have nuances that may not be understood by the customers. Accordingly, it is up to you to help facilitate discussions in such a way that accurate information is obtained. That means helping lead the customers to the correct conclusions without leading them to what you think the conclusions should be. Ultimately, do not let the customers allow the project to get off track. You have been brought in as the expert on Process Mapping—use that responsibility to lead the project to a successful conclusion.

Leading the Witness

If you want a true picture of how a process works, you must allow the people involved in the process the chance to tell you how it is done. Questions should be expressed in a way that prompts dialogue—an exchange of information from the interviewee to the interviewer. Closed-ended and leading questions only serve to stifle discussions or, even worse, promote incorrect responses. Using open-ended questions may increase the length of interviews, but it will also increase the information obtained.

Verifying the Facts

You will be given a lot of information. Some of it will be correct and some of it will be less than correct. In some instances, you will be able to verify this information through additional interviews. However, depending on the time available and the criticality of the information, actual testing may be necessary. Key areas for testing include measures of success, high risk objectives, and self-audits conducted within the department.

Do Not Forget the Customer

As you dig deeper and deeper into a process, it is important to take a breath and remember the ultimate purpose of the process — satisfying some customer. These customers were identified at the beginning, and they should be considered throughout the project. As each map is constructed, look for the moments of truth and ask if these are being used to their fullest example. In addition, look to the employees and determine if they understand the importance of the customers to the process.

KEY ANALYSIS POINTS

While they are not true analysis points, keeping the following issues in mind while completing the Process Mapping will result in a better analysis of the process,

Why Am I Here?

Why was the project initiated, and what is the reviewer's purpose? Do not lose sight of what the project is all about. Do not get lost in the details.

Where Are We Going?

Is the process meeting some business objective? If the process is not accomplishing a business objective, does it even need to exist? Does everyone involved in the process understand what he or she is trying to accomplish?

Who Cares?

Ultimately, everyone's job depends on how the customer experiences each interaction with the company. Where are the moments of truth? Are they fostering a positive, caring customer relationship, or is anyone even paying attention to the customer's perspective? Walk through the business processes in the customer's shoes.

Who Is in Charge Anyway?

The only person who truly cares about what goes on in a process is the individual who owns or has some responsibility for the process. The owner generally must authorize changes in the process. Know who the owner is and make sure he understands how the process is really working.

No Tool Is an Island

Process Mapping is more than just producing maps. It is a holistic approach to reviewing a business or a segment of a business. The maps are not the end product; the analysis of the operation is.

Information Is Power

Do not forget to gather data on the various measures of success. Gathering the data may lead you to areas where the process is breaking down or help you identify areas where it is working very well.

Keep It Simple

Chart the highest level possible, and if more detail is necessary, prepare a separate "drill down" map.

CHAPTER 10

Where Do We Go from Here?

Somewhere, something incredible is waiting to be known.

—Carl Sagan

ADDITIONAL APPLICATIONS

The Process Mapping approach is more than just a method for making extensive flowcharts. It is a holistic approach to analyzing a business, an entity, or a function. As such, many of the techniques described can be used in whole or in part in other disciplines. Process Mapping can be a valuable tool in risk assessment, control self-assessment, reengineering, and training.

RISK ASSESSMENT

Risk assessment philosophies abound in the business world. Models have been proposed to systematically classify risks a business faces. Risks are classified, quantified, and ranked using a variety of criteria. One methodology classifies risk one way, and another classifies risk in a slightly different way. All are striving for a better understanding of the challenges a business faces.

How can Process Mapping assist in the risk assessment process? To assess the risks a business faces, the business processes must be understood. In the first phases of mapping, the reviewers are defining the processes that make up the business. This is first done at a high level with the process owners. Later the high-level processes may be broken down into individual units and tasks with more detailed definitions. The identification and definition of business processes can be the starting point for any risk assessment.

As discussed in Chapter 3, examining business processes gives the company an opportunity to look at the business differently, outside its normal organizational structure. This facilitates a more complete and comprehensive risk assessment. When Process Mapping is done with a holistic approach, the identification of business objectives and business risks is included in the preliminary information-gathering phase of the process review. These are documented in the Process Evaluation Work Sheet. As maps are generated, the process can be analyzed to determine if risks are being appropriately controlled. In addition, the maps may be able to assist in determining the magnitude of a particular risk exposure.

As mentioned in the previous chapter, we were involved in a project with one department where the specific objective was to help identify processes and the associated risks with the intent of helping develop the following year's objectives. Initial meetings were held with team leaders and managers to help identify these basic processes as well as the overall strategic objectives. A second meeting was then held to help identify the risks inherent in meeting those strategic objectives. After these were identified, all 100+ plus employees were then involved in meetings to discuss what specific objectives were needed the following year to help achieve the strategic objectives. As mentioned before, the customers had too much control over the process identification portion of the project, but this did not detract from the overall success of the project. While not a complete Process Mapping project, the initial stages were identical. This also laid the foundation for a Process Mapping project that was completed in the same department two years later.

Many businesses keep the risk assessment process at a very high level and never really perform a risk assessment at the process level. As auditors, we have found it very beneficial to be able to perform a risk assessment at the process level as well. When we conduct an audit, we must deal with limited resources. We cannot examine every process in the function under review, so we must have a methodology for determining which processes pose the highest risk. Those are the processes we want to target. One method we use is to perform a process-level risk assessment.

In our reviews of claims processes, we identify all the critical processes involved. These are defined along with critical trigger events. While these may be generic, an office in one particular area may face different business and operational risks that directly affect the process. Next, we identify the critical business and operational risks inherent in the process. Finally, we quantify the business and operational risks of each process for an individual office. A raw risk score for each process is calculated and audit areas are selected based on the risk score.

We have also found it beneficial to obtain the input of claims management in the risk assessment process. We ask them to review the process definition work sheets and to perform a process risk assessment. Our final assessment may then be adjusted based on the information provided by claims management.

The real beauty of this methodology is the ability to perform a risk assessment at either a very high, strategic level or at an individual process level. The methodology remains the same. Only the individual process names and definitions change.

CONTROL SELF-ASSESSMENT

Control self-assessment is a tool developed just over 10 years ago that is intended to get all necessary parties together to determine the obstacles and strengths affecting achievement of key business objectives. It has been defined as "a formal, documented process in which management and/or work teams directly involved in a business function judge the effectiveness of the processes in place and decide if the chance of reaching some or all business objectives are reasonably assured." Much of this is the result of the Committee of Sponsoring Organizations of the Treadway Commission (COSO) report that was issued in 1992. Ultimately, this report (along with similar reports issued by similar commissions in England and Canada) helped redefine the meaning of control structures.

According to the COSO report, "internal control is defined as a process, effected [sic] by an entity's people, designed to accomplish specific objectives."[1] The five internal control components include the control environment, risk assessment, control activities, information and communication, and monitoring. This represents a focus that is changing from traditional "hard" controls (e.g., policies, procedures, approvals, and two-party controls) to less traditional "soft" controls (e.g., trust, leadership, openness, and high ethical standards.) Accordingly, new approaches had to be found to analyze these controls. Control self-assessment has been one of the most popular of these tools.

While every control self-assessment practitioner uses his or own methods, there are some steps that are basic to all. Generally, teams are brought together from similar functions to discuss the control framework. A facilitator introduces the purpose of the project and helps ensure that the discussions stay on track. The focus of the discussions from this point on usually includes identifying the business objectives, the risks, and the controls, and determining if the control framework is sufficient to ensure achievement of the objectives. One of the primary benefits of this method is that the members of the department are determining the answers themselves. Because it is their evaluation, they have buy-in to the project.

This description helps point out how Process Mapping can be used to facilitate or enhance the control self-assessment project. The most obvious point is that many of the introductory steps in completing the Process Mapping project are similar to those used in control self-assessment. The forms and skills learned from Process Mapping can be easily translated into the control self-assessment situation. The reviewer can facilitate this by using the Process Profile Work Sheet to capture the objectives, risks, controls, and monitoring systems. Looking at inputs and outputs as well as process beginning and ending points can help control self-assessment participants assess the information and communication aspects of the process. This is a perfect opportunity to show process owners how controls can help them accomplish business objectives. It can also help establish ownership of both the controls and the measures of success. The systematic completion of profile work sheets for all critical business processes can be the starting point for determining if the processes in place provide management reasonable assurance that business objectives will be reached.

A second, less obvious use of Process Mapping is in those situations in which process owners or upper management are leery of the control self-assessment approach. Many people have trouble believing that team members can be counted on to successfully participate in these types of projects, and some team members are afraid to become true participants because of disconnects between management and employees. As mentioned previously, the Process Mapping approach lays the groundwork for control self-assessment. This allows people to begin thinking in terms of business objectives, associated risks, and the other trappings of process assessment. In addition, as the project continues and the maps are developed, it gets everyone used to the collaborative process in which everyone's ideas are respected. In this way, Process Mapping can be used to obtain an initial analysis while laying the groundwork for future control self-assessment projects.

REENGINEERING

Reengineering projects became a mainstay for many companies and consultants beginning in the late 1980s. They are still an important tool in redesigning processes. Most reengineering efforts focus on streamlining processes and eliminating non–value-added activities. They tend to focus on radical changes rather than on incremental changes.

As we have seen in the previous chapters, Process Mapping provides a visual representation of the process that can highlight inefficiencies such as multiple handoffs, areas where rework is required, or areas where delays are occurring. Whether you are starting with an existing process and trying to determine where appropriate changes can be made or starting with a blank piece of paper and reengineering the whole process, you still need a map to see where you have been and where you are going. The complete story still must be captured so everyone can look at it with the same set of eyes.

If the purpose of the reengineering project is to change an existing model, Process Mapping can be used to get that initial snapshot. If the process is being blown up and the company is starting over, Process Mapping can be used to graphically show the new system.

Reengineering often begins with a change agent and an idea. Not unlike Walt Disney's attempt to portray Pinocchio to his animators, the change agent must convey the idea to others so they can conceptualize the new theme. Everyone must understand the overriding theme so changes made to the business remain consistent with the theme. The best way to verify that the theme is remaining consistent is to visually capture the reengineering effort in a process map. It is much easier to make changes on paper, before people are involved, than to fix problems due to a lack of foresight.

The primary pitfall for most reengineering projects is losing focus of how the process fits in with the corporation as a whole. This is often the result of a lack of attention to the details. It may be a failure to recognize how one event affects another. It may be a failure to recognize moments of truth. It may be a focus on minimum cycle times instead of maximum cycle times. It may be a failure to consider all the risks. Or it may be a failure to consider the soft issues—how people interact in the process. However, using the holistic approach to Process Mapping, including creating complete process definitions, identifying business objectives, identifying risks, and identifying measures of success, can help ensure that critical details are not missed. Mapping the actual process and analyzing those maps can help create the road map to a successful reengineering project.

TRAINING

The old saying "a picture is worth a thousand words" is very true, especially when it comes to training people how to perform a specific job. A company may have very detailed procedure manuals with explicit instructions on how to complete the job, but it may find that people just do not read the manuals. Most of us, with the exception of a few auditors, never take the time to read the actual procedure manuals. We may look up things from time to time, but we never review all of the areas that may relate to our job. We are trained how to perform specific tasks, but we often do not know why we are performing them or how they impact the entire operation.

Process Mapping is an excellent tool for developing training materials. Overview maps can be created that will give the employee a sense of how his or her work fits in with the whole. Detailed maps can also be created at the task level to visually show individuals where the work comes from, what they need to do with it when they get it, and where it goes when they complete the task. The "drill down" technique can also be used to link the detailed procedure manual to the actual tasks.

For example, the map may show a task 1.1 as "Verify customer data." A "drill down" map of this task could be created that may have tasks such as "log onto computer," "input customer name," "review address information," and so on. However, if all of these steps are in a particular procedure manual, it may be just as easy to reference task 1.1 to a "drill down" narrative that is the procedure manual, with the various steps involved in the process. At some point, drawing more boxes does not make sense, and you can just go to a narrative that includes the appropriate details for the task.

The development of the maps is also an excellent training tool on a number of other levels. First, the employees involved are beginning to learn how their work interrelates with everyone else's work. At the same time, they may begin understanding what the overall objectives are and how their job helps.

Second, management's involvement may help the managers learn the operations they supervise better. In some instances, just going over the maps helps instruct them on correct procedures. During a recent review, a new supervisor was put in place after we started reviewing a particular area. Rather than reviewing the maps to make sure we understood the process, we reviewed them with him to help teach him what the processes were.

Third, a member of management may become part of the team and learn how processes work directly from the employees. You must be careful with this approach—the involvement of management may mean people feel less secure in talking. However, their involvement will mean they learn a lot about day-to-day operations. In one instance, we brought in a manager from another part of the country. In this way the employees felt secure while management was trained.

At the very least, when you leave a mapping project, the detailed maps are valuable as documentation of the process. It can be a future training tool or a reference for procedures. Ultimately, it is that graphic representation of what everyone is doing.

THAT'S NOT ALL FOLKS

After Walt Disney talked with his animators, they gathered information, mapped the movie with storyboards, and eventually provided the world with another animated gem. Then they went home, flushed with success, never to produce again.

Well, we know that is not true. There was a lot more work to do—more projects, more storyboards, and more international successes. And they did not wait until *Pinocchio* was completed. Animated movies take years to go from idea to movie house. There is no way a company can wait until one project is finished before beginning the next. While *Pinocchio* was in production, additional classics were already being started—*Bambi, Dumbo, Fantasia*. And as each of those was begun, another idea was in the background waiting to take its place. And, while it is never easy, the process was streamlined by the skills the animators learned from each project. Principle among these was storyboarding.

You have been reading about a similar tool—a tool that is the cornerstone of a valuable assessment technique. And its versatility has been shown in many different ways. We have tried to pass on the successes and failures in order for you to gain an appreciation of the power of this tool. And we have tried to provide you the basic information necessary to take this tool and make it your own.

There is nothing fancy in what has been discussed, and there is nothing sacrosanct either. Take these tools and suggestions and bend them to your needs. Take the ideas and build newer and better projects. Learn from your successes and failures. But most of all, take the first step and become involved in a Process Mapping project. After that first success, you will not want to look back. It is really up to you. Just like Walt Disney, you have to sell your ideas. Then you have to count on success — selling the next idea before the last one is finished. Eventually, your string of successes will be your Oscar that opens additional doors.

Ultimately, Process Mapping is just one more analytical technique meant to make businesses run better. But, ultimately, *Pinocchio* was just one more story meant to make people feel better. The final success is up to you.

And they all lived happily ever after.

NOTE

1. *Internal Control—Integrated Framework,* Volume 1—Executive Summary, Committee of Sponsoring Organization of the Treadway Commission (Jersey City, N.J.: American Institute of Certified Public Accountants, 1992) pp. 1–3.

INDEX